MacMillan and Co.

Scotch Sermons

MacMillan and Co.
Scotch Sermons
ISBN/EAN: 9783743343191
Manufactured in Europe, USA, Canada, Australia, Japa
Cover: Foto ©Lupo / pixelio.de

Manufactured and distributed by brebook publishing software (www.brebook.com)

MacMillan and Co.

Scotch Sermons

SCOTCH SERMONS

1880

London
MACMILLAN AND CO.
1880.

Edinburgh University Press:
THOMAS AND ARCHIBALD CONSTABLE, PRINTERS TO HER MAJESTY.

PREFACE.

This volume has originated in the wish to gather together a few specimens of a style of teaching, which increasingly prevails amongst the clergy of the Scottish Church.

It does not claim to represent either the full extent of that teaching, or the range of subjects on which in their public ministrations its authors are in the habit of discoursing. It may, however, serve to indicate a growing tendency, and to show the direction in which thought is moving. It is the work of those whose hope for the future lies, not in alterations of ecclesiastical organisation, but in a profounder apprehension of the essential ideas of Christianity; and especially in the growth, within the Church, of such a method of presenting them, as shall show that they are equally adapted to the needs of humanity, and in harmony with the results of critical and scientific research.

Some of the Sermons were preached exactly as they now appear, and are no more than samples of popular religious teaching. Others have been written expressly for the volume, or have been considerably enlarged after having been delivered from the pulpit. The writers are all clergymen of the Church of Scotland.

Should this volume accomplish its aim, it may be followed by another series.

THE EDITOR.

Christmas 1879.

CONTENTS.

		PAGE
I.	CORPORATE IMMORTALITY,	1

By the Very Rev. JOHN CAIRD, D.D., Principal of the University of Glasgow.

II. UNION WITH GOD, ... 18

By the Very Rev. JOHN CAIRD, D.D., Principal of the University of Glasgow.

III. HOME-SPUN RELIGION, . 36

By the Rev. JOHN CUNNINGHAM, D.D., Crieff.

IV. THE RELIGION OF LOVE, . 50

By the Rev. JOHN CUNNINGHAM, D.D., Crieff.

V. LAW AND MIRACLE, . . 66

By the Rev. D. J. FERGUSON, B.D., Strathblane.

VI. THE VISION OF GOD, 90

By the Rev. D. J. FERGUSON, B.D., Strathblane.

VII. CONSERVATION AND CHANGE, . . 99

By the Rev. WILLIAM KNIGHT, LL.D., Professor of Moral Philosophy in the University of St. Andrews.

VIII. THE CONTINUITY AND DEVELOPMENT OF RELIGION, ... 119

By the Rev. WILLIAM KNIGHT, LL.D., Professor of Moral Philosophy in the University of St. Andrews.

IX. THE LAW OF MORAL CONTINUITY, . 140

By the Rev. WILLIAM MACKINTOSH, D.D., Buchanan.

X. THE RENOVATING POWER OF CHRISTIANITY, 162

By the Rev. WILLIAM MACKINTOSH, D.D., Buchanan.

	PAGE
XI. AUTHORITY,	195

By the Rev. WILLIAM LECKIE M'FARLAN, Lenzie.

XII. THE THINGS WHICH CANNOT BE SHAKEN,	219

By the Rev. WILLIAM LECKIE M'FARLAN, Lenzie.

XIII. THE SUCCESSORS OF THE GREAT PHYSICIAN,	244

By the Rev. ALLAN MENZIES, B.D., Abernyte.

XIV. THE CHRISTIAN PRIESTHOOD,	259

By the Rev. ALLAN MENZIES, B.D., Abernyte.

XV. THE ASSEMBLING OF OURSELVES TOGETHER,	270

By the Rev. JAMES NICOLL, Murroes.

XVI. INDIVIDUALISM AND THE CHURCH,	283

By the Rev. THOMAS RAIN, M.A., Hutton.

XVII. THE PHARISEE AND THE PUBLICAN,	307

By the Rev. THOMAS RAIN, M.A., Hutton.

XVIII. ETERNAL LIFE,	324

By the Rev. ADAM SEMPLE, B.D., Huntly.

XIX. RELIGION—THEOLOGY—ECCLESIASTICISM,	336

By the Rev. JOHN STEVENSON, Glamis.

XX. UNITY,	354

By the Rev. PATRICK STEVENSON, Inverarity.

XXI. ETERNAL LIFE,	365

By the Rev. PATRICK STEVENSON, Inverarity.

XXII. CHRIST'S AUTHORITY,	373

By the Rev. ROBERT HERBERT STORY, D.D., Rosneath.

XXIII. CHRISTIAN RIGHTEOUSNESS,	387

By the Rev. ROBERT HERBERT STORY, D.D., Rosneath.

SCOTCH SERMONS.

I.

CORPORATE IMMORTALITY.

BY THE VERY REV. JOHN CAIRD, D.D., PRINCIPAL OF THE
UNIVERSITY OF GLASGOW.

> These all, having obtained a good report through faith, received not the promise : God having provided some better thing for us, that they without us should not be made perfect.—HEB. XI. 39, 40.

THERE is something at once of exultation and of sadness in the words with which the writer of this book closes his recapitulation of the glorious roll of the saints and martyrs and heroes of ancient times. They were men "of whom the world was not worthy." They were inspired with a noble enthusiasm for great ends, with dauntless fortitude and self-devotion, with an unquenchable faith in things spiritual, with high hopes for the future of humanity. But, judged by the outward eye, their life was a failure : they never attained to the end of their aspirations; one after another, like breaking waves on the strand of time, they were compelled to succumb to the universal limits of human endeavour. In the midst of their noble struggles they were constrained in succession to yield to the inevitable summons, their work unaccomplished, their hopes unfulfilled, the dearest object of their lives nothing better than a far-off goal. "These all died in the faith," it is written, "not having received the promises, but having seen them afar off." And again, "These all, having obtained a good report through faith, received not the promise."

At first sight, therefore, the language of the text is simply a repetition of the old refrain, "Vanity of vanities," with which writers, inspired and uninspired, have summed up their trite moralisings over the evanescence and incompleteness of human life. The saddest aspect of human existence, this writer seems to say, is, not simply that in which it seems to be full of care and sorrow and trouble, but that in which it suggests the impression of frustration, abortiveness, incompleteness. We never receive the promise. We never are the thing we seem designed to be. There are in our nature the beginnings and materials of great things, but they are never realised. The foundation is ever grander than the superstructure, the outline than the picture, the promise than the fulfilment. We can form soaring ideals of individual and social perfection, but they only serve to throw contempt on the poverty and meanness of our actual life. Human nature seems to be a thing of boundless possibilities but of miserable performances, of capacities which are never, or only feebly and partially, developed, of desires, hopes, aspirations, to which, even when the will to realise them is present, the poor results which our brief life permits us to reach are ludicrously disproportionate. Moreover it is precisely in the case of the best and greatest of men that this incompleteness is most marked. If all men were, what so many seem to be, creatures of mere animal and selfish desires, finding all the satisfaction they care for in eating, drinking, money-making, in dress and gossip and foolish display and petty social rivalries and triumphs, there would be no sense of incongruity in the brevity of human life. There would be nothing to startle or surprise us in the fact that an existence of such mean and shallow aims should cease for ever when its brief earthly career has run out. Far less, indeed, than threescore years and ten suffices often to play out that poor plot, to exhaust its whole interest and significance. But it is when we turn to contemplate human life in its nobler representatives that the sense of unfulfilled promise forces itself on our minds. Its minds of rare and piercing intelligence, filled with the ever-growing thirst of knowledge, catching glimpses on all sides of unexplored regions of thought, into which it would be their delight to penetrate, and who seem to themselves, after the labours of a lifetime, to be only standing on the very outskirts of the realm of truth; its great originative intellects, capable of striking out new discoveries, of penetrating into the secrets of nature, of discerning the wants of society, and of framing comprehensive plans for its amelioration and progress; or, finally, its beautiful, heroic, saintly spirits, refined and purified by the discipline of years, exalted above all that is selfish and sensual, and sometimes doing deeds at the mere recountal of which our hearts thrill with involuntary admiration, and which are the silent prophecy of an unrevealed splendour in the spiritual nature of man,—it is in the case of such natures as these that the cruel limits of life strike us most palpably. The whole being of such men seems moulded on a scale that is pure waste and extravagance, measured by the few and rapid years of our individual life. The infinite hunger for truth and goodness, the thoughts that wander through eternity, the feelings of love and adoration which point to an object nothing less than infinite,—it seems strange and monstrous that these inexhaustible capacities have no longer time for satisfaction than the lust or appetite which an hour will cloy. Of what use the vision of infinite perfection, if the same fell stroke is to shatter it alike with the poorest dream of worldly success! What meaning is there in the capacity of conceiving and living for objects the very least of which it would require many lives to accomplish—in a mind filled with great designs, the results of which it needs generations to develop, or fired with enthusiasm for the progress of the race in civilisation and goodness, when soon and for ever it shall cease to have any more a part in all that is done beneath the sun?

Now it is this view of human life which in the latter clause of our text the sacred writer seems to meet. Is our life indeed an incomplete and broken thing? Is human existence but at the best a splendid failure? Is the promise which our nature contains never fulfilled? The common answer, as we all know, to such questions is that which finds in the notion of the "immortality of the soul" the solution of the difficulty. The life that seems so incomplete is only a part of man's duration. It will receive its complement in a future world. But whatever truth there is in the notion of individual immortality, it was obviously not this, but another and different idea, which was before the mind of the writer of our text, as that in which he found consolation for the fragmentariness and imperfection of the life of man. "These all died in the faith," he writes, "not having received the promise." "These all, who obtained a good report through faith, received not the promise." Their life, replete with immortal hopes, instinct with the spirit and promise of a splendid future, was abruptly terminated. But it was not really so. The promise was not left unfulfilled, the continuity was not broken. Their story has not been left without a sequel. The life they lived is one that is never broken, that never dies, that is ever deepening, developing, ever through the ages advancing to its consummation. Every one of these ancient saints and martyrs, he seems to say, has had a share in the advancing life of humanity, and in the Christian Church of his own day he sees only the flower and fruit of the same plant of which they were the seed or germ, the maturity of the same organic life of which the Church of a former day was the childhood or youth. These passed away, he exclaims, and life in them was one of unfulfilled promise. But of that promise *we* are the fulfilment: "God having provided some better thing for us, that they without us should not be made perfect."

Let us for a moment consider what is involved in this view of the spiritual life of man, and try to gather from it the lessons with which it is fraught.

The imperfection which this writer ascribes to the individual lives of a past time arises necessarily from this: that it constitutes the very grandeur and nobleness of human life to be incapable of a purely individual perfection, and that each successive generation can say of the men and the ages that are past, "They without us could not be made perfect."

And to see this you have only to consider how all existences rise in the scale of nobleness just in proportion as they are incapable of individual perfection. The stones which are intended to form part of a building lose their separate unity and any completeness they possessed merely as stones. Taken apart, they might seem unmeaning or even grotesque and unshapely in form and outline. But it would be a foolish and vain thing to try to give them a kind of individual completeness by rounding off a ragged edge here or filling up an unsightly gap there. It is just that which makes them individually imperfect that lends to them the capacity of contributing to a higher perfection. When the stone is built into the shaft or column, or when around and above the unsightly structural fragment rise the other portions which form its complement in the unity of some fair and stately edifice, we perceive how, lacking or losing individual completeness, it has become sharer in a greater and higher completeness, a necessary contribution to and participant in the perfection and beauty of the whole.

That incapacity of individual perfection is the measure of inherent dignity and excellence is still more clearly seen when we take the example of the living organism. Here too, as in the previous illustration, we have a multiplicity of individual parts or members, each of which, taken apart by itself, has no worth or significance. Here too that which would be a mere imperfect fragment, a maimed or mutilated thing, if disunited from the other members, receives, in its union with them, a share in that larger life, that symmetry, order, proportion, that excellence and beauty of diversity in unity, which belongs to the organic whole. It is in the absolute surrender of any isolated existence, in the fulfilment of its function as existing for and contributing to the welfare and growth of the other parts of the organism, that the individual member or organ receives back into itself a participation in a richer and ampler existence. Its own perfection is impossible without them. So long as in the living organism any one part or member is undeveloped, there is something lacking to the perfection and happiness of the rest. They without it cannot be made perfect. Lastly, there is this peculiarity in the final perfection of the organism, that it is reached, not, as in the former example, by accretion, but by the perpetual change and renewal of its elements,—by absorption and development. As it rises through its successive stages, the materials of which it is composed do not remain, like the stones of a building, fixed and permanent, one stone or series of stones superimposed on another, each, from foundation to copestone, remaining to the last what it was at the beginning. On the contrary, wherever there is life, its earliest beginnings are present indeed, but in a far more intimate and subtle way, in the beauty and perfection of its latest and highest form. Seed or germ, rising stem, leaf and blossom, fruit and flower, do not continue side by side; the last is the perfection of the first, but it is a perfection attained by unresting mutation, by the seeming extinction and absorption of all that went before. When you have reached the rich profusion of summer, the tender grace of the vernal woods is a thing that is gone; when you gather the fruit, the gay blossom has passed away. And each successive phase of the living organism, as it passes from the embryo to the full-grown frame of manhood, is the vital result of all that it has been. The past lives in it—it could not be what it now is but for the past,—but nothing of that past remains as it was; it does remain, but it remains as absorbed, transformed, worked up into the very essence of a new and nobler being. The unity of the fully developed life gathers up into it, not by juxtaposition or accumulation, but in a far deeper way, the concentrated results of its whole bygone history. Thus the nobleness of imperfect life lies in its very imperfection. It is greater than even the most complete and finished of material things, because it is full of yet unfulfilled promise, because the possibilities of an ever-advancing progress are concealed in it, because it contains in it the promise and prophecy of a future without which it cannot be made perfect.

Now it is in this idea, rather than in that of a merely individual immortality, that the writer of the passage before us finds the explanation of the seeming incompleteness and evanescence of human life. It is here that he seeks the solution of that contrast of greatness and littleness, of nobleness and meanness, of beginnings so full of promise and results so poor and insignificant, on which moralists in all ages have been fain to dwell. Regarded from the individual point of view, human life *is* the paradoxical thing which such reflections make it to be. Individual happiness, individual perfection, are never attained; but it is, he declares, the very greatness and glory of man's nature to be incapable of it. The key to the riddle of human life, the explanation of the scale on which our nature is constructed, of the boundlessness of its hopes, the inexhaustibleness of its desires, of its eager longing for a larger, fuller, more lasting life, of the splendour of its ideals, and the dissatisfaction with their best attainments which the noblest spirits feel, is this: that he who lives nobly and wisely, who rises above the narrow life of sense, to identify himself with that which is universal and infinite, is sharer in a life of humanity that is never arrested, and shall never die. It needs little reflection to perceive that the whole order of things in which we live is constructed not on the principle that we are sent into this world merely to prepare for another, or that the paramount aim and effort of every man should be to make ready for death and an unknown existence beyond the grave. On the contrary, in our own nature and in the system of things to which we belong, everything seems to be devised on the principle that our interest in the world and human affairs is not to terminate at death. It is not, as false moralists would have us believe, a mere illusion, a proof only of the folly and vanity of man, that we do not and cannot feel and act as if we were to have no concern with this world the moment we quit it.

It is not a mere irrational impulse that moves us when, in the acquisition of knowledge, in the labours of the statesman and legislator, in the houses we build, the trees we plant, the books we write, the works of art we create, the schemes of social amelioration we devise, the educational institutions we organise and improve, we act otherwise than we should do if our interest in all earthly affairs were in a few brief years to come to an end. It is not due to a universal mistake that we work for a thousand ends the accomplishment of which we shall not live to see, that the passions we feel are more intense, the efforts we put forth immeasurably greater, than if we were soon and for ever to have done with it all. Even the desire of posthumous fame, which has been the theme of a thousand sarcasms and satirical moralisings, the passion that impels us to do deeds and create works which men will be thinking of and honouring when we are gone, does not rest on a mere trick of false association which your clever psychologist can explain so deftly, but is the silent ineradicable testimony of our nature to the share we have in the undying life of humanity. So again it is no mere logical abstraction which rises before the mind when we talk of a national life which embraces and transcends that of the individuals who pertain to it, and which, when *they* seem to come and go like shadows, goes on broadening, deepening, developing in knowledge and power and freedom. It is no imaginative fiction, for example, but a sober fact to which we refer, when we speak of the silent, steady growth of that organic unity, that system of ordered freedom, which we designate the

Constitution of England, and when we say that that is the collective result of all that was valuable in the intellectual and moral and religious life of the myriads who, from the first pioneers of England's civilisation downwards, have contributed to her progress; that all that her poets have sung, and philosophers taught, and statesmen, legislators, warriors, patriots, have achieved,—nay, all that has been accomplished by thousands of nameless and unhonoured lives which have been poured out like water in the cause of her civil and religious freedom,—all this, assimilated and transmuted into the very bone and fibre of her social existence, lives still in that great and still growing personality, the national life of our country. And when we take a wider range still, it is no mere figure of speech when we say that there is another and still grander personality which comprehends within it the life of nations as well as of individuals, and which, when the place of nations knows them no more, when their function in the providential order of the world has long been finished, and their glory and splendour is a thing of the past, retains in it the elements of spiritual good which it was their vocation to work out, gathered up and transfused into that undying life of humanity without which they could not be made perfect. The perfection of man is not the perfection of the Jew, nor of the Greek, nor of the Roman; but there is a richer, fuller, more complex life, into which the Hebrew consciousness of holiness and sin, the ideal beauty of the Greek, the sense of law and order which Rome left as her legacy to mankind, flow together and are blended in the unity of the Christian civilisation of the modern world. And that too, in its turn, is still far short of that ideal perfection which our Christian faith reveals, and for the realisation of which it calls us to live and labour. Eighteen centuries ago a vision of human perfection, a revelation of the hidden possibilities of our nature, broke upon the world in the person and life of Jesus Christ; and as we contrast with this the highest attainments which the best of men or communities have yet reached, it seems an ideal towards which as a yet far distant goal, with slow and stumbling steps, humanity is tending. Yet for this at least the belief in it suffices, in the hearts that have become penetrated with the sense of its sublime reality and beauty—to assure them that whatever of greatness or goodness in the long course of ages humanity has attained, is but an augury of that splendid future which is yet in store for it. For no ideal of a perfect state, no dream of a golden age or paradise restored which has ever visited the imagination of genius, or risen before the rapt gaze of inspired seer or prophet, can surpass that future of universal light and love which Christianity encourages us to hope for as the destiny of our race—that time when human society shall be permeated through and through with the spirit of Jesus Christ, and the whole race, and every individual member of it, shall rise to the point of moral and spiritual elevation which that life represents, when "we shall all come into the unity of the faith, and knowledge of the Son of God, unto a perfect man, unto the measure of the stature of the fulness of Christ."

It is then in this idea that we find, as I have

said, the true solution of that contrast between the largeness of human desires and hopes and the brevity of human life, between our far-reaching aims and aspirations and the contempt which death seems to pour on them. Death does *not* pour contempt on them. You can think and desire and work for more than the petty interests of your brief individual life, because you *are* more and greater than the individual, because it is possible for you to share in a universal and undying life, with the future of which your most boundless aspirations are not incompatible. It is little indeed that each of us can accomplish within the narrow limits of our own little day. Small indeed is the contribution which the best of us can make to the advancement of the world in knowledge and goodness. But slight though it be, if the work we do is real and noble work, it is never lost; it is taken up into and becomes an integral moment of that immortal life to which all the good and great of the past, every wise thinker, every true and tender heart, every fair and saintly spirit, have contributed, and which, never hasting, never resting, onward through the ages is advancing to its consummation. Live for your own petty interests and satisfactions, waste the treasure of an immortal nature on the lust of the eye and the lust of the flesh and the pride of life, and death will indeed be the destroyer of all your hopes and ambitions. But live for the good of others, live to make your fellow-men wiser and happier and better, take part with those nobler spirits of all time who have striven for the rectification of human wrongs, the healing of human wretchedness, the redemption of human souls from evil, the advancement of the world in knowledge and wisdom and goodness,—live for these ends, and the whole order and history of the world, and that Gospel of Heaven's grace in which we believe as the revelation of God's purpose and plan for our race, must prove a fable, if your most boundless hopes and aspirations be doomed to disappointment.

But what, after all, avails for me, does any one ask, this idea of a future perfection of humanity, these hopes and endeavours for a world in whose good or ill I shall soon have no place or part? It is not the immortality of the race, but my own, that is the great and all-important question for me—not whether the progress of mankind shall go on in a world I am so soon to quit, but whether there is another world beyond the grave, and whether death shall find me prepared for it. Even if it be true that this dream of a perfect social state is in some far distant day to be realised in this world, what personal interest can I have in a perfection and happiness I shall never know and in which I shall never participate?

I answer, that the idea of the text, far from destroying, only lends new significance and reality to, the hope of a personal immortality. It leaves the arguments for immortality which reason and Christian faith suggest precisely what they were; only it bids us think of that immortality, not as a vague and shadowy state of blessedness in some unknown existence beyond the grave, but as the realisation of those possibilities of perfection which our nature contains, and which are present here and now, ready to be elicited in the common earthly life of man. "These all died in the faith, not having received the promise." That for which these ancient heroes and martyrs lived and laboured, that which would be to them the crown and consummation of their dearest hopes and the reward of their sacrifice and self-devotion, was not a heaven of dreamy isolated happiness, to which at the hour of death they should withdraw, no longer to be affected by the struggles and sorrows of humanity. They toiled and suffered and died for the good of mankind; their dearest, deepest desires were not for selfish happiness here or hereafter, but for the redemption of the world from evil; this was the heaven they longed for, and the bliss of any other heaven would be incomplete without it.

And we too, if we inherit their spirit, shall feel that for the heaven we seek we need not fly away on the wings of imagination to some unknown region of celestial enjoyment where we shall summer high in bliss heedless of mankind—where, lost in seraphic contemplation, steeped in voluptuous spiritual enjoyment, we shall forget or be unaffected by the good or evil of the world we have left. The materials of our heaven, the elements of that glorious future in which we hope one day to share, are present here, within us and around us, in our very hands and in our mouths. The Divine and Eternal are ever near us. God does not dwell in some far-off point of space; He is not more present anywhere else than on this earth of ours, nor could any local transition or physical transformation bring him nearer. God is here, above, beneath, around us; and the only change that is needed to bring us to the beatific vision of his presence is the quickening and clarifying of human souls. Purify and ennoble these, let pure light fill the minds and pure love the hearts of men, and heaven would be here, the common air and skies would become resplendent with a divine glory. The eternal world is not a world beyond time and the grave. It embraces time; it is ready to realise itself under all the forms of temporal things. Its light and power are latent everywhere, waiting for human souls to welcome it, ready to break through the transparent veil of earthly things, and to suffuse with its ineffable radiance the common life of man. And so, the supreme aim of Christian endeavour is not to look away to an inconceivable heaven beyond the skies, and to spend our life in preparing for it, but it is to realise that latent heaven, those possibilities of spiritual good, that undeveloped kingdom of righteousness and love and truth, which human nature and human society contain.

Does any one press on me the thought that, say what you will of the future, death to each of us is near, and no ulterior hope can quell the nearer anxiety as to what is to become of us, and how we are to prepare for that fast approaching, inevitable hour? Then I answer, finally, that to whatever world death introduce you, the best conceivable preparation for it is to labour for the highest good of the world in which you live. Be the change which death brings what it may, he who has spent his life in trying to make this world better can never be unprepared for another. If heaven is for the pure and holy, if that which makes men good is that which best qualifies for heaven, what better discipline in goodness can we conceive for a human spirit, what more calculated to elicit and develop its highest affections and energies, than to live and labour for our brother's welfare? To find our deepest joy, not in the delights of sense, nor in the gratification of personal ambition, nor even in the serene pursuits of culture and science,—nay, not even in seeking the safety of our own souls, but in striving for the highest good of those who are dear to our Father in heaven, and the moral and spiritual redemption of that world for which the Son of God lived and died,—say, can a nobler school of goodness be discovered than this? Where shall love and sympathy and beneficence find ampler training? or patience, courage, dauntless devotion, nobler opportunities of exercise—than in the war with evil? Where shall faith find richer culture, or hope a more entrancing aim, than in that victory over sin and sorrow and death, which, if Christianity be true, is one day to crown the strife of ages? Live for this, find your dearest work here, let love to God and man be the animating principle of your being; and then, let death come when it may, and carry you where it will, you will not be unprepared for it. The rending of the veil which hides the secrets of the unseen world, the summons that calls you into regions unknown, need awaken in your breast no perturbation or dismay, for you cannot in God's universe go where love and truth and self-devotion are things of naught, or where a soul, filled with undying faith in the progress and identifying its own happiness with the final triumph of goodness, shall find itself forsaken.

II.
UNION WITH GOD.

BY THE VERY REV. JOHN CAIRD, D.D., PRINCIPAL OF THE
UNIVERSITY OF GLASGOW.

That they all may be one; as thou, Father, art in me, and I in thee, that they also may be one in us. . . . And the glory which thou gavest me I have given them; that they may be one, even as we are one: I in them, and thou in me, that they may be made perfect in one.—JOHN XVII. 21, 22, 23.

By those who reject the doctrine of the Divinity of Christ great stress is often laid on the argument that whatever tampers with Christ's real and simple humanity deprives Christianity of that which gives it its chief value as a religion for man. The mysterious grandeur which is thrown around the personality of the Author of our religion is dearly bought if it removes him beyond the reach of our human sympathies, or makes it impossible to think of him as in any real sense sharing our sorrows, infirmities, and temptations, and as exhibiting in his life an ideal of excellence to which all human beings may aspire. The most precious ingredient of Christianity is, it is said, the ideal which Christ's character and life present of what humanity essentially is, and of what we may become. It communicates a new inspiration to virtue, a new impulse to moral endeavour, to contemplate in him a revelation of the hidden beauty and greatness of our nature. It ministers strength to us amidst the temptations of life to see how a noble human spirit triumphed over them; and human wretchedness, through a hundred generations, has found its sweetest consolation in the thought of the tender sympathy of one who drank more deeply than all other mortals of the cup of suffering, who was pre-eminently "the man of sorrows and acquainted with grief."

But, it is argued, all this consolation and encouragement are lost the moment you introduce a foreign or superhuman element into the conception of Christ's person. Not only does the mind become confused in the attempt to grasp such a notion as that of a being half-human, half-divine, but the life and history of such a being are deprived of their exemplary value. What we need is a type, not of superhuman, but of human excellence. If it is to afford any stimulus to effort, what is set before me must, however exalted in degree, be an example not of what is possible for an angel or a God, but of what is possible for a man. It gives me no encouragement, in facing the temptations to which flesh is heir, to be told how a being whose human nature was rendered infallible by combination with a Divine nature overcame them. It does not make me more courageous in fighting life's conflicts to witness a being, practically omnipotent, coming scatheless out of them. When I vainly try to conceive of an immutable sufferer, an omnipotent weakness, of a consciousness of pain and doubt and perplexity experienced by a being who is at the same time impassible and omniscient, the sense of sympathy is overawed and repressed. I can no longer feel the magic thrill that responds in the hour of sorrow and darkness to the touch of a tender human hand. Set before me the example of a being of flesh and blood, and however splendid it be, I can at all events feel rebuked by its faultless purity and nobleness; but by the example of what was achieved by a God in human shape I am no more humiliated, than the crawling worm or browsing cattle by the eagle's soaring flight. If Christ was man, and nothing more than man, though I fall miserably short of the perfection and beauty of his life, I can at least try to be like him, and be ennobled by my very failures; but is there not a kind of blasphemy as well as folly in the very thought of a finite being straining after resemblance to infinitude and omnipotence?

Now, whilst there is, no doubt, a way of thinking about the nature of God and man which would render this objection to the Christian doctrine unanswerable, there is another and different conception of them which our Lord's words in this passage bring before us, and which completely meets the difficulty. He makes it possible for all men to sympathise with him, not by levelling down his own nature, but by raising theirs; not by disclaiming his own Divinity, but by declaring that there are Divine elements, Divine possibilities, in the common nature of man. He does not impoverish himself of his own infinitude, but He reveals the possibilities of an infinite wealth in us. "It is true," He seems to tell us, "that I am Divine, that the human consciousness in me is in absolute union with the consciousness of God: 'Thou, Father, art in me, and I in thee.' But in so saying, I do not place an impassable gulf between my nature and yours, so as to remove myself beyond the reach of your human fellowship and sympathy. I do not say that what I am you can never hope to become. In the contemplation of my example and of the ideal of goodness and greatness which I set before you, there is no point at which human sympathy and hope need be arrested. You too may become 'partakers of a Divine nature.' It is no impossible and extravagant aspiration for you also to entertain, that ye 'may be perfect as your Father in heaven is perfect.' 'This is the record that God hath given to you, eternal life,' 'that eternal life which is in the Father and in his Son Jesus Christ.' To enter into such identification with the very nature of Deity that your thoughts, like mine, shall be God's thoughts, your will and actions, like mine, a Divine will, a Divine activity—to become thus one with God as I am, is not to transcend but to realise your true nature as men. For nothing less than this is the height of spiritual attainment, the glorious consummation which I seek for humanity, for all my brethren after the flesh, 'That they all may be one; as thou, Father, art in me, and I in thee. . . . I in them, and thou in me, that they may be made perfect in one.'"

Now, there can be no question that these words have to the ear what, if we met them in an uninspired book, many would be disposed to characterise as a pantheistic sound, and that the oneness or identification with Deity to which they point seems to be open to the same objections which are often urged against pantheistic teaching. What our Lord here speaks of is not a mere outward relationship between God and man, such as subsists between distinct and independent persons, as, for instance, between a master and servant, between a ruler and subject,—between beings, that is, who, though they may enter into such external relations, have yet a distinct and separate individual life of their own; but it is a oneness or union with God, of which his own indivisible personality is the type,—a union therefore which is not that of two beings, a human and Divine, existing side by side or in contiguity with each other, but in which the consciousness—the thought and will—of the one, is absolutely blended and identified with that of the other, in which the human is no longer divisible from the Divine: "As thou, Father, art in me, and I in thee, that they may be one in us." But is not the great objection to pantheism and pantheistic religions and philosophies just this, that they tamper with or swamp the individuality, the moral independence and responsibility of man? Our high prerogative as moral and spiritual beings is, that we have each of us a separate self, a consciousness and will which no other being can invade, and in virtue of which we are each of us responsible for his own acts and architect of his own moral life and destiny. Amidst the myriads of beings who constitute the human race, is there not given to each a moral individuality, a life which belongs to him apart from all around him, a career of duty which no other can fulfil for him, and which in time and eternity he and he alone must accomplish? Is not each human soul, as is often said, alone amidst the crowd? However close the relations into which we enter with others, however intimate the ties of kindred or friendship, or of common inclinations and pursuits, can the closest of these for a moment break down the impassable barrier between each and all other souls? In my sorrows you may pity me, but the tenderest affection cannot make my pain yours. In my guilt and sin you may grieve for me, but my sin can never become yours, the burden of my moral acts can never be rolled over to you, now and for ever my goodness or my guilt is all my own. And is not this gift of spiritual individuality, which in some of its aspects is so awful, just that which raises man above all other finite beings—above the mere unconscious life of nature, above the life of animals in whom the race is all, the individual nothing—and which makes it possible for him to attain a height of spiritual excellence, a perfection gained by free self-development, a wealth of character wrought out by individual effort, which no otherwise could be reached? In this precious gift, this possession of an inalienable self, this right of each man to be himself, and to make and develop himself, have not men recognised the root of all liberty of thought, of all social, political, and religious freedom? Take this away, annul that in the individual in virtue of which he can say, in the face of every human power and authority, You may possess yourself of my property, fetter, imprison, and torture my body, but you cannot master my thoughts or invade the sanctuary of my soul,—take away this, and would you not deprive man of his spiritual birthright, of a treasure for which nothing else could compensate? Nay, may we not say with reverence, that it is the greatness and blessedness of man as a spiritual, responsible being, that herein he possesses a prerogative which even Omnipotence cannot invade? It is because I can offer to God a free obedience and love that He is glorified in my service and devotion. And if you could conceive even a Divine Being suspending or taking away this individuality, breaking down the barrier which divides my will and consciousness from his, taking possession of my thoughts and volitions so that they should no longer be my own but his, making the movements of my mind as much the expression of *his* will as the motions of my limbs are of mine; you might call this the elevation of the human into unity with the Divine, but it would be no real elevation, it would be rather the degradation and destruction of that in virtue of which I am a being made in God's own image, and which distinguishes my nature from that of the beasts that perish.

Now, undoubtedly, this idea of human individuality and of what is involved in it is just and true, and it is impossible to tamper with it without subverting the basis on which morality and religion rest. But whilst it is the fatal objection to all pantheistic theories that they do tamper with it, I think we shall see that our Lord's words in the text are the expression of what may be described as a Christian pantheism which is not only consistent with the individuality of man, but gives to our conception of it new significance and reality. He tells us of a oneness with God so absolute that we may be said to be *in* God and God in us, that our spiritual being shall be no more separate from God's than Christ's own, and yet in which, so far from being infringed or sacrificed, our nature as men shall reach its highest perfection.

Now, in order to see how absolute oneness with God may be consistent with the most perfect individuality of man—in other words, that a state of being is conceivable in which thought, feeling, will, the whole consciousness of man, shall be no longer separate from the Divine; in which God shall be all in all, and yet at the same time the moral individuality, the personality and freedom of man, so far from being suppressed, shall attain to its highest realisation—to see how this may be, I will ask you to reflect for a moment what is the deepest and most real kind of unity you can think of, what is that oneness which is most absolute and indestructible, and whether that is a unity which is attained by the suppression, or not rather by the free play and development, of individual differences. The parts of a stone are all precisely alike, the parts of a piece of mechanism are all different from each other; in which case is the unity deepest?—in that in which all distinction is suppressed, or in that in which each separate part has a distinct character, an individuality of its own? No one portion of a mass of sandstone differs essentially from any other; any one of the same size and shape would supply the place of another, and in the unity which they compose even the poor distinction of size and shape is completely lost. In a watch, a steam-engine, or other elaborate machine, each part has a distinctive character and worth, a place and function of its own; and so far from losing that individuality when brought into the common unity, it is there and only there that that individuality is manifested and realised. Apart from the other pieces of the mechanism, each separate portion sinks into a mere lump of metal. Yet who will hesitate to pronounce in which case the unity is deepest? In the one the parts have no inner essential relation to each other, no deeper connection than that of mere juxtaposition. In the other they are not merely stuck together externally, but they exist and act, each for and by the others; each is necessary to the rest, and no one could be left out without marring or subverting the existence of the whole. The inner bond of a common idea or design, and of order, harmony, proportion, runs through them all and welds them together into a unity far transcending that of arbitrary and outward contiguity. Surely it is here, in this latter example, that the unity is most profound, and yet it is just here that individuality is best preserved.

But there are deeper unities than this. A living organism, such as the body of man or any other animal, is a unity not merely of parts, each of which fulfils a function necessary to the rest, so that the brain, heart, lungs, the various members and organs, have absolutely no separate or separable existence or life, so that each lives in and by the rest, their life its life, its life not its own but theirs; but, more than that, it is a unity which, unlike that of the machine, the parts themselves *feel*, so that each suffers in the injury or suffering, is happy with the happiness and well-being of the rest. But here, again, the closer and more integral oneness is not attained at the cost, but rather by the more intense development, of individual distinctiveness. Each member and organ is itself, attains to the richest development of its individual nature, gains itself, so to speak, only where it surrenders itself, its whole being and activity, to the unity in which it is comprehended. If it begin to act for itself, to seclude itself, to display any independent phenomena, any slightest movement that is not conditioned by the organism to which it belongs, the isolation is a fatal one. And if it is entirely separated from the rest, if it ceases to be permeated by a life that is other than its own, the severed limb or dissected organ loses its whole reality and worth, and becomes mere dead inorganic matter.

And now, to apply this thought. I think we may begin to see that the isolated unity of each individual self, the separate, solitary consciousness which makes each human soul the bearer of its own burden of good or ill, though so far true, is not the last word that is to be said in the account of the spiritual nature and life of man. However important, it is only one side of the truth, and it is possible to exaggerate its significance. There is a sense in which this conception of a solitary, individualistic unity gives place to a deeper and higher thought, the thought, viz., that no man liveth to himself; yea, that the true life of self is never realised till the life of others streams into and becomes a part of our own, and last of all, until our shallow separate life is taken up into the universal and infinite life, and we then begin to live truly when we live in the life of God.

"I in them, and thou in me, that they may be made perfect in one." This is true, in the first place, of our relations to each other, and it is still more profoundly true of our relations to God. It is true of each individual, in his relations to other beings like himself, that his and their perfection is only in their unity. Union with other minds and lives is not the suppression but the evolution and realisation of our own individual nature; and the more nearly that unity approaches to absolute identification, so much the more intense and rich does our own individual life become. Not more true is it that the heart has no separate life from the brain, the nervous system, the other parts and members of the organism, and that each becomes mere dead and worthless matter if severed from the rest, than that a human spirit, asserting and standing by its own independent identity, is dead, being alone.

Nay, some one perhaps will answer me, it is surely the extravagance of rhetoric thus to exaggerate a mere physical analogy. The member of an organism is not the whole, and has no life apart from the rest; but I have in myself all the elements of humanity—intelligence, feeling, will, conscience, irrespective of any other human being, and I should still possess them if all other human beings should cease to exist. The true account of the matter is that, having an individual identity, a nature of my own, self-contained and complete, I *choose* to enter into relations with other and equally independent members of the race. I answer, in the first place, it is not true that you are or can be thus independent. Whether you will or no, there is a sense in which other minds and wills are a part of you. Not merely physically, but intellectually and morally, you are *not* related to others only as you choose to relate yourself. From the very dawn of your existence your spiritual nature is steeped in the life of the past, in the spirit of the age and society into which you are born, and in the unconscious influences that emanate from other minds. Hereditary tendencies live in you and mould your opinions, feelings, beliefs, ways of thinking and acting, as really and involuntarily as ancestral features impress their stamp on your countenance, or the health or disease of bygone generations is transmitted to your bodily frame. Each soul does not make a new start to shape its own independent career. For good or ill, it is part of an organic whole. It can no more shut itself off from the universal life than the most secluded loch or bay can cease, in the rippling and receding of its tiny waters, to respond to the great tidal movements of the ocean. But I answer, in the second place, that if we *could* conceive a thoroughly isolated individual, he would not be truly man, but only a fragment of humanity. Suppose a human being shut up from infancy in isolation from all other human beings, of how much would his nature be mutilated that is necessary to the very idea of humanity! One side of man's spiritual nature would remain practically extinct. All that range of qualities which are possible only in the various social relations, all those thoughts, feelings, emotions, moral tendencies and activities which can exist only in and through the existence of other men,—affection, sympathy, love, admiration, reverence, compassion, self-devotion, patriotism, philanthropy,—would never emerge into existence in us, would remain at best only unrealised possibilities within the spirit. To a human being thus reared in a solitary world, the creation of a brother spirit would be as the creation of a new soul within his breast; in another life a second self would start into being. And once more on this point, I answer, that we grow in elevation and nobleness of nature just in proportion as we merge our individual life and happiness in the life and happiness of others. Love, friendship, philanthropy, self-sacrifice,—what is the true significance of such words as these? What does the lover or friend mean when he says that another's happiness is dearer to him than his own? What does the patriot mean when, far more expressively than by words, in the language of a life of self-devotion to country or cause, giving up all thought of self and of his own particular interests and enjoyments, he sacrifices time, thought, ease, pleasure, ambition, all that most men hold dear, nay even life itself, for the sake of others—what does he declare but this, that the life and being of others has to him taken the place of his own, that the good of others has become to him not merely as his own, but more really his than his own? And yet by all this identification of self with the wider life of mankind, has he suppressed or quelled his own true individuality? Nay, rather, when we think of the widening of thought and deepening of feeling, the expansion of the whole moral nature, the pure unsought joy and blessedness that crown a life devoted to impersonal and unselfish ends, might we not put into the lips of such an one the declaration, "I am dead to self, nevertheless I live"? And if we could only conceive a state of human society, in which such love and devotion should be universally reciprocated, in which each member of it lived no longer to himself, but found his life, his own deepest joy and satisfaction, in the life and joy of others, might not this emphatically be described by such words as these:—" I in them, and they in me, that we may be made perfect in one"?

Lastly, the religious man's life is a life lived not merely in the life of others, but in the life of God.

Does religion mean belief in God as the "Almighty Creator and Moral Governor of the world," and obedience to His commands? Is it a true and exhaustive account of the religious life to say that it is a life governed by a sense of responsibility to that Being who is the Omniscient and Righteous Judge of man, and who will reward and punish us according to our deeds? No doubt this is much; no doubt to believe in any moral authority and submit to it, to lead for any reason a virtuous life, is better than to follow our unrestrained impulses and lead a life of immorality and licentiousness. But something more and deeper than this surely is implied in that relation to God which can be described by such words as these: "I in them, and thou in me." It is indeed a great thing to be a conscientious man. We cannot help respecting the man who methodically and deliberately orders his life in obedience to duty and the will of God. There is even a certain dignity in self-command, in a life of repressed inclinations, restrained passions, and actions uniformly regulated by the dictates of reason and conscience; and our sense of the stern dignity of such a life is, in one point of view, enhanced by the amount of struggle and self-discipline which it costs to maintain it. And yet, dignified and praiseworthy though such a life be, it is still something far short of that ideal of religion, and of the religious man's relation to God, which Christ's words set before us. If this were all, if this were the true ideal of religion, there would be some ground for saying that it represses the spiritual nature, and overbears the freedom and individuality of man. To bow to any external authority, even that of an Almighty Being, to yield up my will to any outward law, even though it be that of the Supreme Ruler and Lord—that may be right; but what it means is, that I am no longer free, that there is a part of my nature, that there are desires, tendencies, inclinations, which are simply suppressed in deference to an external power. It means that Duty has still for me the aspect of a foreign thing, a law or limit which I respect and obey, but that, even in conforming myself to it, there is within me that which is not one with it, another self which is hindered and repressed.

But, my brethren, it is the great idea which Christianity has disclosed to us, that the law and will of God is no more external to our true nature than it is to the nature of God Himself, and that it is possible to reach, and that then only have we attained to the perfection of our being when we have reached, a spiritual state, in which the very mind and will of God is no longer distinguishable from our own,—in which to think God's thoughts shall be to think our own thoughts, and to do God's will shall be only another name for doing our own. When eternal truth discloses itself to any mind, it dissipates and destroys all mere individual opinion, it subjugates thought with an absolute and irresistible authority. Yes, but then only have I attained to the true knowledge of Divine things when the voice that speaks *to* me is at the same time that which speaks *in* me; and it is not two concurrent voices, that of a finite and an infinite mind, that speak, but the one indivisible voice of eternal reason sounding through the spirit of man. When the law of duty and of righteousness utters itself to a human spirit, it is with an imperative authority to which human inclination and passion are constrained to bow. Yes, but then only have I attained to that which deserves the name of goodness, to that moral perfection of which Christ is the type, when law has passed into life, when duty has ceased to be a thing of self-denial, and has become a kind of self-indulgence, the expression of an irresistible inward impulse, the gratification of the deepest passion of the soul; then only have I reached the elevation of nature to which Christ would exalt us, when I not only hearken to the voice of duty, but when, listening to the inmost utterances of my own spiritual nature, it is the very same accents I hear; when the dictates of conscience not merely echo, but blend themselves indistinguishably with, the commands of the living God; and when, as I yield myself up to their sway, it is not two wills, but the one will of infinite goodness that rules and reigns within me. And so, it is just because our deepest nature is in harmony, not with error but with truth, not with evil but with good, not with the lust of the flesh, and the lust of the eye, and the pride of life, but with the things invisible and eternal, with the very spirit of God himself,—it is just because of this, that to become partakers of the Divine nature is to come to the perfect realisation of our own. Absolute identification with God, if we shall ever attain to it, is not a state in which our individuality shall be absorbed or annihilated, but in which our whole conscious being shall leap forth to life and freedom. Even here there are moments, few and far between, when the infinitude of our nature reveals itself, when the gross vesture of carnality and finitude seems to fall aside, and to disclose in higher and nobler natures a latent splendour of spiritual nobleness nothing less than divine. When thought comes with a rush of inspiration on the mind of the man of genius, when the imagination glows with the ecstasy of creative intuition, and burning words flow forth from lips touched with prophetic fire; when in moments congenial to spiritual thought and feeling, infinite hopes and aspirations come upon us, and bear us above the pettiness of life and the littleness of our ordinary motives and ambitions, and every ignoble thought is silenced and every baser passion quelled; when the call for some great sacrifice has arisen, and we feel it in us to respond to it, a great impulse comes upon us, a power mightier than of earth takes possession of us, and the heroic deed is done : in these and such like experiences there are premonitions of a larger, diviner life, momentary outflashes of an element of boundless spiritual power within this poor nature of ours. But here, alas! these are but rare and transient visitations. Here, in the best of us, union with God is only intermittent and imperfect. In the atmosphere of worldly passion, amidst the perturbations of selfishness, there is much to check the flow of that electric current that unites the finite spirit to the infinite, much to arrest the free play of that vital energy that binds the members of the spiritual body to each other and to the Head. But the words of Christ point to a time when every disturbing, dividing element shall pass away, when every mind shall be the pure medium of the infinite intelligence, every heart shall throb in unison with the infinite love, every human consciousness be possessed and suffused by the spirit of the living God. And then shall come at last the fulfilment of that prayer: " That they all may be one; as thou, Father, art in me, and I in thee. . . . I in them, and thou in me, that they may be made perfect in one."

III.

HOME-SPUN RELIGION.

BY THE REV. JOHN CUNNINGHAM, D.D., CRIEFF.

I have glorified thee on the earth : I have finished the work thou gavest me to do. . . . I have manifested thy name to the men which thou gavest me out of the world.—JOHN XVII. 4, 6.

THIS text carries us back to the time when the Son of Man was about to finish his earthly career. He knew that the priests, alarmed by his teaching, were plotting his destruction; and He was already within the shadow of the cross. He had spoken to his faithful followers his parting words; the language of comfort merged in the language of prayer; and from discoursing with his human brethren He rose to communion with his heavenly Father. He had come into the world, Heaven-sent, with a work to do, and He had done it, and now, calmly contemplating his approaching death, He was able to say to his Father, "I have glorified thee on the earth : I have finished the work which thou gavest me to do."

What was this God-given work which Jesus could now say He had finished? I think we have an explanation of this in the context: "I have glorified thee on the earth—I have manifested thy name." These two things are not greatly different. In manifesting God we glorify God: and therefore we may safely say that the manifestation of God was the work which Jesus felt had been given to him to do, and which He had done. And what work more truly grand than to make known God to a people who were yet in great manner ignorant of him! To give the world one new glimpse of God were worthy of the noblest life that was ever lived.

But how manifest God? "The heavens declare the glory of God; and the firmament sheweth his handywork." We have but to look to the illimitable universe for a manifestation—the grandest possible manifestation—of the power and wisdom of God. But it is certain such a manifestation was not enough for the reason of man. Amid all the marvels of creation —at the base of mountains which pierced the sky— on the shores of seas which no plummet could fathom and no vision embrace—men were found worshipping their own impure conceptions embodied in marble and stone, or vainly rearing altars to a God they confessed to be unknown. Nature, thousand-tongued though she be, had not let out the great secret of God.

Did Christ then come into our world to manifest to us God as He is? Such a revelation had been impossible. In one sense God ever must be unknown —unknowable. The finite cannot contain the infinite. Stretch our faculties as we may, we cannot comprehend the incomprehensible. We cannot take within our grasp that which is beyond all grasp, the absolute—the unconditioned—the great Being who inhabits eternity and fills all space with his presence. When we make the endeavour, our feeble intellect, baffled and beat back, is compelled to acknowledge that it cannot "by searching find out God." Even in the future world, where we have reason to believe our faculties will be greatly enlarged, our knowledge of Deity will still be very imperfect—I might almost say infinitely imperfect, as the finite can never bear any relation at all to the infinite. We may, and no doubt shall, know much which we do not know now; we may obtain glimpses of his glory far brighter than any we have upon earth; but still we shall never know him as He is. Just as this fair world at present hangs like a mighty curtain screening its Creator from our view, yet showing his shadow projected upon it; so in eternity shall the God of Heaven be manifested only through the golden glories of heaven, and refuse to be gazed upon with unveiled eye, for He must ever dwell amid light inaccessible and full of glory;—no mortal eye hath seen him, or can see him.

The work of Jesus then was not to manifest God in his essence—in his infinitude; for our nature was incapable of such a manifestation. And while Philosophy may properly occupy herself with such lofty themes, Religion is content with a lower walk. The question then recurs, How did He manifest God? I answer, He made known the moral character of God. I am aware that when I thus speak I am translating the language of heaven into the language of earth. I am in some measure likening God to ourselves when I speak of his moral character, but it is not given to man otherwise to think of or otherwise to speak of the heavenly and divine. God in some way must be brought down to us, as we cannot possibly lift ourselves up to God. Now it is certain that men had for long ages puzzled themselves in vain about the moral nature of the Deity, and hence the contradictory attributes ascribed to their idol gods. Sometimes they ascribed to these the purest benevolence, sometimes the most malignant cruelty; sometimes they spoke of them as exemplars of justice and truth, sometimes they described them as perpetrating deeds so foul that even modern vice would cry shame upon them. Now it is plain that though we cannot know God in all his infinitude we may know whether He is kind or cruel—whether He is pure or impure— whether He is spiritual and transcends all sense, or is material, and may be shrined in a temple and sculptured in stone. To make this known to the world was the mission of Jesus.

Jesus Christ in his own person and character was a manifestation of God. He was a visible image of Him who is invisible. Every man is in a sense made in the likeness of his heavenly Father, in so far as he is endowed with Godlike faculties; but that likeness is too often marred by sin, and sometimes in the face of a fellow-creature we see not the countenance of a God but the features of a devil. But Jesus of Nazareth was altogether Divine. We must trace his life to see this.

His life divides itself into two quite distinct portions —his private life, which extends over thirty years, and his public life, which probably did not last more than three years.

Let us try and lift the veil which hangs over the thirty years when He was slowly being matured for his future work. We have several Gospels of the childhood of Jesus, stuffed with silly legends as to how He resuscitated a dead bird and carried water in a sieve, and ever and anon astonished his playmates by his miracles; but we know that these Gospels are spurious —they carry their falsehood on their face. There is nothing divine in such stories as these. We can believe however that He was a marvellously precocious boy, and that notwithstanding his precocity He was subject to his parents. We have reason moreover to believe that He was brought up in the bosom of a family— with younger brothers and sisters; for the legends of the Roman Church on this subject are not only groundless, but opposed to the Gospel narrative, and are designed to substitute false virginity and sour asceticism for home-bred piety. Here then is the first stage in the life of Jesus—a child among children. But is not the innocence and happiness of childhood emblematical of the heavenly and divine?

He slowly grew from infancy to boyhood, from boyhood to manhood, just as we do. And as He grew in stature He increased in wisdom and in all goodness. All his fellow-villagers knew him, and all loved him. There is reason to believe that He worked at his father's trade of a carpenter, and by making the rude implements of husbandry helped to support the household. He must have lived just such a life as any mechanic of the present day lives—making allowance for the change of times. But He was humble, industrious, and content,—content to do his daily work, to eat his humble fare, to remain in obscurity, notwithstanding that He must have been conscious of the great capabilities which were slumbering within him. And was not Jesus of Nazareth as truly divine and as truly doing his Father's work when He thus lived a village workman as when He afterwards blazed upon the world as a religious reformer? And are not these thirty years full of meaning to those myriads, in all countries and in all times, who must live in obscurity and earn their daily bread by their daily toil? This life at Nazareth, suffused with artisan religion, the religion of industry, honesty, truthfulness, devotion, had no trace of what is usually deemed heroical. No incident was worth recording. It was the ordinary life of a working man. No doubt, on the one side it was altogether divine, but on the other it was very human and very homely. Thus the second stage in this great life was that of a village workman.

When He was thirty years of age, this village carpenter appeared before his countrymen as a prophet. He had heard the heavenly call within him, and He had obeyed it. He summoned his compeers to repentance, declaring that the kingdom of God was at hand. He spoke to them of a higher religion than their ancestral one, which, though once full of life, was now sapless and fruitless, and wellnigh dead. The fierce light of public notoriety now shone upon him wherever He went. But in many respects He lived the same calm life which He had lived at Nazareth. There was nothing overstrained, nothing sensational, in anything He did. His four biographies have, of course, an Eastern colouring, but we clearly learn from them that He was not proud and domineering, but meek and lowly—willing to help all, heal all, save all. His whole life indeed was a life of earnest, useful, unselfish work, but at the same time it was not devoid of geniality and sociability, of private friendships and home-spun virtues. He had his friends, both male and female, whom He loved and by whom He was loved in return. He went to marriage-feasts and dinner-parties, and had his quiet evenings with Lazarus and Martha and Mary at Bethany.

How different this life from the legendary lives of the saints, with their asceticism, their ecstasies, and their artificial piety! How different from the mawkish biographies of some modern divines, who would appear from their diaries to have lived far above the low level of the Ten Commandments!

In such a life was there not a manifestation of God? Without accepting the pantheistic idea that Deity is visible everywhere and in all things—that He shines in the ruby, lives in the plant, and awakens into consciousness in man,—we may safely say that in all human goodness there is a manifestation of Divine goodness.

But Jesus of Nazareth, by his teaching as well as by his life, did much to manifest God. He emphatically declared his spirituality. The idea was not altogether new, but in every religious system of the then world it was forgotten. And having declared that God was a spirit, He drew from it the inevitable inference that all true worship must be spiritual, and thus revolutionised the religions of the world. All places and all times are alike holy. On Mount Gerizim or Mount Moriah, in mosque or cathedral or meeting-house, by the fireside or in the field, on Saturday or on Sunday, there may be worship in spirit and in truth of the spiritual God. Every aspiration after goodness is worship. Thus in the words of Jesus as He sat thirsty and weary by Jacob's well, and conversed with the Samaritan woman who had come there with her pitcher to draw water, we get a view of Divinity from which all the world might learn something; and we see no national Deity, no sectarian God, but the universal Spirit, the common Father of all mankind. The Gentile idea of God was grievously wrong. The Jewish idea was in some respects almost as far from the truth; but the Jewish and the Gentile ideas were alike corrected in the sublime virtues and blessed lessons of Jesus the Saviour.

While Jesus was yet a boy He began his work, and never afterwards did He flag in it. Even when He was working at his father's trade, as I have already said, He was also working the work of God. And so, when death overtook him, though it came early and came suddenly, it did not find him with his work only half done. At the early age of thirty-three, when most men are only beginning to think seriously and work hard, his work was finished, and when He expired on the cross He could utter the significant words: "It is finished."

Thus I have shown you how Jesus had a work to do, and how He did it. But the most important—because the most practical—part of my discourse remains, for I have yet to show that every Christian, like the Christ, has a God-given work to do.

It were well if every man realised the truth that he has a work to do in this world—that he is not meant to be, that he must not be, an idler in this busy hive; and it were better still if every man felt that his special work is assigned him by God.

The lots of men are very various. Some are born in the lap of opulence, and grow up in the midst of luxury, and have all their wishes anticipated and all their wants supplied by the ministry of others, without any exertion on their own part. Others are bred amid severe poverty, and their horny hands tell how hard is the toil by which, day after day, they gain their daily bread. But however different the spheres in which men move, and however wide their callings and their culture, all are alike required to be workmen for God.

Bear in mind that whatever the work is you have to do, that work is given you by God. Are you a shopman? Well, behind your counter sell your goods, and do your work as if it were God's work. Are you a lawyer? Well, work on in love to the great Lawgiver, defend the right and defeat the wrong, remembering that your calling is divine. Are you a labourer? a ploughman? a weaver? Well, steadily use your shovel—merrily drive your horses to the field—cheerily make your shuttle fly till the pattern stands out before you in the web, remembering that you are engaged in a Heaven-appointed task. You have a Master in heaven. If it were so, would not all trickery disappear from trade, all quirks and quibbles from the law, all eye-service, all unfaithfulness, all discontent, from the ranks of the labouring population! Depend upon it we in general take too low a view of our calling. We look upon our labour as merely drudgery: well, it may be so, but it is a divine drudgery. While we work we are doing good—and everything that is good is Godlike. Such a conception as this ennobles the meanest toil, and raises the poorest mechanic, the humblest tiller of the soil, into a servant of Almighty God.

I am afraid that some men—even good men—are discontented with their lot, and fancy that they are piously and properly discontented. They think they could do God's work better if their lot had been different. They think, perhaps, that an occupation so menial as theirs cannot possibly be the work of God. How can the loom, they may say, be connected with religion? How can a man by breaking stones on the roadside be promoting the glory of God? The poor man wishes he were rich, just that he might employ his wealth in the promotion of piety. My dear friend, let me ask you, If liberality be the virtue of wealth, are there no virtues peculiar to poverty? and were it not better for you to cultivate the virtues of the station which God has assigned to you, than vainly to pine after another station which never can be yours? The pious layman perhaps laments that his lips are sealed in silence, and that he cannot, as from the house-top, proclaim the praises of God; and accordingly he wishes he were a missionary, that he might publish to darkened idolaters the glad tidings of salvation; or at least that he were a minister of the gospel, that from the pulpit he might fulminate the thunders of Sinai, or speak in the softly persuasive whispers that come from Calvary. My good friend, you err, not knowing the gospel. Your work is as divinely appointed as mine: and your duty is to do it—to do it religiously and well. I know that some people foolishly think that clergymen alone are the servants of God—that their calling alone is divine—that they only, and such as they, promote the glory of God. My friends, I tell you that I believe that many a poor artisan who industriously and ungrumblingly plies his trade, that he may honestly support a wife and family, or that he may keep an aged parent from the parish, is more effectually promoting God's glory than many a pompous preacher of the Word. There is an eloquence in the pious resignation, the contented looks, the busy fingers of the one, which is not to be found in all the bombast of the other; and no man of this kind can calculate the influence for goodness and for God which he may exercise on society.

I know nothing which has exercised a more pernicious influence on religion than that unhappy divorce which has been effected between religious duty and the every-day duties of life. When a mother is faithfully tending her children, and making her hearthstone clean and her fire burn bright, that everything may smile a welcome to her weary husband when he returns from his work, it is never dreamt that she is religiously employed. When a man works hard during the day, and returns to his family in the evening to make them all happy by his placid temper and quiet jokes and dandlings on his knee, the world does not think—perhaps he does not think himself—that there is religion in anything so common as this. Religion is supposed to stand aloof from such familiar scenes. But to attend the church, to take the Sacrament, to sing a psalm, to say a prayer, is religion. Now

God help this poor sinful world if religion consists only in these things and not also in the other. We have devotional feelings, and by all means let us give them exercise and utterance; but have we not other feelings and other duties as certainly as these assigned us by Heaven? Why should we count the one religious and not also the other? Is religion to be shut up in the church, and not allowed to visit the house? Is she to attend us only when we sit at the Communion-table, and not also when we stand at our counter or sit at our desk? Why should we not think that everything we do is done religiously if it be done well?

I think I have known some people who have thus introduced religion into their every-day life. In the station in which they were, therein they abode with God. They were ever so honest, so industrious, so cheerful, so unrepining, so courteous to man, and so devout to God, that you could not but feel they were living that life of which others were merely talking. They were indeed living epistles of Christianity, known and read of all men.

Some men may think I have thus secularised religion. On the contrary I have wished to sanctify and make religious that which is usually regarded as secular. "That which God hath cleansed call not thou common or unclean." I wish religion to tinge everything with its own divine hues: and that whether we eat or drink, or whatsoever we do, we should do it to the glory of God. I wish every man to feel that whatever work he has in hand he is therein God's workman. I wish that as the sun bathes with his light not merely the mountain and the plain, but the tiniest plant that grows in the crevice of the rock, that as he shines not merely upon the carved cathedral, but upon the cottage home, so it should be believed and felt that the Sun of Righteousness illuminates with its soft radiance everything it shines upon, giving it the highest of all consecrations.

The work of the Christian is not really different from the work of the Christ. Every man has his mission, and it is to manifest God. Moving in different spheres, with different tasks assigned us, we may be called to do our work in different ways; but still this is our work. Every man should be, in his own person and character, like the Christ, a manifestation of God. The more virtuous, the more actively benevolent, the more zealous for all good we become, the more we manifest God. By discharging the duties of our station, or by honestly struggling to rise to a higher one, we perform our Heaven-allotted task, and so manifest God. In short, by living like Jesus and dying like Jesus, we manifest God. God, the all-good, shines out in every good word that is spoken and in every good work that is done.

Last of all, let me remind you that "life is short and time is fleeting." "Whatsoever therefore your hand findeth to do, do it with all your might." Jesus of Nazareth, according to tradition, died while still a young man, but before he died he felt that his work was done. How few at the early age of thirty-three have well begun their God-given work! How many with grey hairs on their heads are carried to the grave with their work but half done! I believe it often forms one of the bitterest elements in the cup of death that life has been wasted and opportunities of doing good allowed to slip past, and when the end comes nothing either great or good has been accomplished. It is a terrible thing to look back upon an utterly lost life. And why should it be so with any of you? All of you may live useful lives. Many of you might live noble lives; some of you might leave your mark behind you, and live a second life in the grateful memories of men. Remember there may be true goodness, and even true greatness—a manifestation of all that is most divine—in the discharge of the humblest duties, in the most obscure station, as well as in playing a grand part with the eyes of the world fixed upon you. How much to be envied the man who, when approaching the close of a well-spent life, feels that he has at least done some good in his day, and thus that he has so far fulfilled his mission, even though he may not have altogether finished the work which his Father had given him to do!

IV.

THE RELIGION OF LOVE.

BY THE REV. JOHN CUNNINGHAM, D.D., CRIEFF.

The love of Christ constraineth us.—2 CORINTHIANS V. 14.

"THE love of Christ constrains us,"—to what? To live not to ourselves, but to him who died for us. In other words, constrained by the love of Christ, and taught by the self-sacrifice of Christ, we ought to live unselfish lives. A consecrated love should be our motive, a Christian life should be our end.

I need not proclaim to you the old moral maxim, that merit is to be sought for in men's motives rather than in their outward acts; and hence the necessity, when judging of ourselves or others, of looking closely to the mainsprings of their conduct. Thus, supposing we live uprightly, what is it that leads us to do so? Is it the fear of punishment, or the hope of reward?—is it the pure love of uprightness itself, or the love of that holy Being who enjoins us to uprightness? Supposing you say the former, then I ask, Can there be any merit in motives so thoroughly selfish? Supposing you say the latter, then I ask, Is it possible for a creature constituted like man to love virtue for itself or God for himself? It is important for us as Christians to know these things, for Christianity consists as much in a well-ordered life as in an orthodox creed, perhaps more so. If it preaches faith, it also insists on good works. It involves a law to be obeyed as well as a gospel to be believed; and it seems to set before us a variety of stimulants to obedience—the hope of heaven, the fear of hell, and love in its multiform outgoings both toward God and man. Well, let me take it for granted that you are all living reputable lives, or, better still, active, useful lives: it is so far good; but behind that there is the question, What are the feelings which influence you to do so? Are they the feelings which the gospel sanctions and commends? That is the question which I wish to press home upon you.

Different men may do the same thing from very different motives; but I think that all human motives may be reduced under two heads—the love of self or the love of another. In other words, there may be a selfish virtue or a disinterested virtue. Which of these does Christianity teach and exact? Let us examine a little more closely these two great springs of human conduct.

I. We may do right from self-love.

In this sphere our selfishness may be so disguised as to be hardly recognisable even by ourselves. Indeed, so subtle is selfishness that it enters into almost every feeling of the mind, and in many cases it is only the very nicest analysis that can detect its presence. We may therefore quite honestly deceive ourselves and others in this matter, and imagine we are acting quite disinterestedly, while in reality our own interest lies at the bottom of our heart, and prompts our behaviour. The two great springs of action traceable to self-love are the hope of reward and the fear of punishment. Every reflecting person will at once discern how much of our conduct takes its rise from one or other of these two principles. Hope and fear are among the most powerful feelings of our nature; and, acting in opposite directions as they generally do, they lead to a behaviour in which the influence of both is to be seen, like those compound motions, the result of equal and opposing mechanical forces. How much do we do from the hope of reward! how much do we not-do from the dread of punishment! How steadily are we thus preserved in the straight path of duty from the pressure on the one side and the other of these two powers!

I need hardly say that human laws are framed with a reference to human fears, and that from this they derive their effectiveness. To every law there is annexed a penalty. The statute-book does not simply say, like the Decalogue, Thou shalt not steal; but it says, If you do steal, the detective will deliver you to the judge, and the judge to the jailer, and he will cast you into prison, and you shall not get out thence till you have paid the forfeit of your crime. We know that if we rob our neighbour's house or assault our neighbour's person, or slander our neighbour's good name, or in any other way disturb the peace of society and violate the letter of the law, we must pay the penalty. The fear thus inspired operates like a charm. It pervades the whole mass of society: though unseen it is felt; and even when scarcely consciously felt its influence is active, like some of those subtle agencies in the atmosphere which surrounds us, which tell upon our happiness, our health, and our life, though we are altogether unaware of their existence. It makes the thief honest, the slanderer silent, the turbulent peaceful. We are virtuous by compulsion. We do good because we dare not do evil.

While the legislature does not in general attach a positive promise of reward to obedience, yet society is so constituted that respect for law almost always meets its reward in some shape or other. Every man knows that the only way to get on in the world, to receive employment, to obtain promotion, to rise to a higher place in society, is to be scrupulously observant of the requirements of justice and truth. No one will employ or promote an unfaithful servant; no one will trade with a dishonest dealer; no one will trust the man whose character is bankrupt. It is impossible to calculate how powerfully this operates upon the whole community, reaching to every member of it, as the force of gravitation reaches to every atom of the system. Every man is, less or more, anxious to make head-way in the world. The workman is accordingly anxious for employment, the shopkeeper for custom, the agent for consignments, and each of these knows perfectly well, that if he in any way forfeit the confidence of the public, yea, if but the breath of suspicion blow upon his name, his chances are gone and he is a doomed man. This, then, equally with the dread of punishment, keeps men true to society, for they know that to be true to society is to be true to themselves.

It may not be denied that many of the religious

duties are performed under the same pressure. We live in a country and an age in which great respect is paid to religion and its observances. Notwithstanding the destructive speculations with which the air is filled, religion has not yet lost its hold on the popular mind; and accordingly a man with a character tinged, to some extent at any rate, with religion, all other things being equal, has a better chance of employment and promotion than the man who is notoriously irreligious. The truth is, we still like to see a man, with his wife and family, seated every Sunday in his pew in the church, cleanly clad, respectful, and devout. We are apt to say, That is a decent and deserving man. On the other hand, there is, in most quarters, a strong dislike of infidel opinions and an irreligious life. Your serious thinking people cannot help suspecting the very honesty of the man who never enters the church, never takes the Sacrament, and otherwise openly disregards the duties and the decencies of a Christian life. However well he looks, it is whispered that he is a scoundrel in disguise; being neglectful of religion, he may tamper with morality; seeing he does not fear God, he very probably will not regard man; and therefore he is by no means to be taken by the hand and helped on. He is rather to be left to rot in his irreligion. Opinion rules the world, and this opinion, deep-rooted and wide-spread, has an undoubted influence in creating an outward respect at least for religious observances. Many are pious, in short, or apparently so, just because piety is a passport to respect. It requires only a very slight acquaintance with society to know how much affected religion there is in the world, and how powerfully even fashion tells upon the Church.

It is probable that many of whom these things are true are all unconscious of it themselves, and would be honestly indignant if you charged them with anything like self-seeking or hypocrisy. Few men act under the influence of only one guiding principle, or one dominating passion. A multitude of motives—sometimes apparently opposing motives—combine to constitute and give colour to conduct, and often under the motives which are uppermost in the mind, there are others which lie buried alive in its lowest depths. As in material, so in mental chemistry, there are startling combinations with still more startling results. But no man is a good analyst of self. He does not care to cast his inmost thoughts into any crucible. But though we shut our eyes to the fact, it is nevertheless true that selfishness, in one shape or another, forms the basis of many of the virtues, and of much of the piety, which pass current in the world. We can only hope that it loses something of its native odiousness when it passes into these new forms, as we cannot detect the presence of tar in the glorious dyes which are extracted from it.

But is there no source of human conduct apart from selfishness? Are there no virtues wholly dissevered in root and branch from the vices? Is there no piety here below but such as is adulterated with worldliness? I think there is, and this leads me—

II. To investigate the other mainspring of human conduct—disinterested love.

I think there can be no doubt that love—love

not for self but for others—is a powerful propeller and regulator of human conduct. Some have indeed attempted to reduce all love into selfishness. I cannot at present examine these theories; suffice it to say, I do not believe them, and proceed upon the supposition, surely not a very unwarrantable one, that there is such a thing as disinterested love in the world. I care not whether it be instinctive or not; it is there, and wherever it is, it is beautiful and good. I have hitherto spoken of the hope of reward and the fear of punishment as two powerful incentives to a virtuous behaviour. But is there no other? Can you think of no other? For instance, are none kept in the straight path of purity and rectitude, because they know that any deviation from it would grieve and distress those whom they love? Are there not many who would rather do anything and suffer anything than cause a pang to a parent's heart? Are there not some who have been kept back from crime just by this consideration? I think I do no wrong to society when I say there are multitudes of young men, and young women too, who have no great regard for virtue for its own sake, who yet are virtuous, and that just because they would not by any conduct of theirs sully the sanctities of the old home-love. I believe that many a young man sent forth from the parental roof to push his way in the world, amid the blandishments of city life, has been kept sober, chaste, honest, only by the constraining love of those whom he left behind. God forbid he should do anything that would make a sister blush or a father avoid the mention of his name! He could be dissipated and reckless, and content to ruin himself, if it were not for this; but this he could not bear. And, my friends, if a member of a family has fallen, if a son has brought a blot upon his honesty, or if a daughter has brought suspicion on her honour, what is the most burning, maddening thought that fills her brain? It is not so much her own loss of innocence and peace as the thought of brothers, sisters, parents disgraced and grieved by her misconduct. What will *they* think? How will *they* feel? How will she be able to look them in the face? It is the love she bears to them, and the love she knows they bear to her, that makes her anguish intolerable. Affection itself becomes the avenger of her crime, and perhaps the very forgiveness it exhibits, and the caresses it bestows, and the renewed sacrifices it is willing to make, render her soul's agony all the more acute. Thus does love stand as the guardian of morals, and, by its powerful constraints, effects that which nothing else could,—no, not the dread of punishment nor the hope of reward. There are defiant natures which despise these things, and yet are subject to the sweet influences of love.

The whole superstructure of society, it has been remarked, is based on the family circle. This is true in every respect, and especially in this: that if you could destroy those ties which are knit by love among the different members of a household, you would thereby destroy all those virtues upon which society depends. Take away the affection of the parent for the child, and of the child for the parent, the regard of the brother for the sister, and of the sister for the brother, and you will remove the strongest barriers against crime, and the strongest incentives to a praiseworthy conduct. Every child which a man has, it has been said, is a pledge to the community for his good conduct. Nor can the son or the daughter easily throw themselves loose from the virtuous influence of family affections, which they feel to be holy beyond all others. The old home-feeling follows them wherever they go, flashing up into brightness when they happen to be brought into scenes or circumstances which contrast darkly with the peace and purity of childhood. I believe it is well known that a large proportion of our criminals, the pests of society, the tenants of our jails, are waifs and strays, who have never known domestic ties, who have none to care for them, none to vex by their crimes. And there are strange chapters in the history of some criminals who had friends who loved them, and whom they loved in return, times of relenting when they thought of these, tears streaming from eyes little accustomed to weeping, fond memories of affections forfeited, but never to be effaced, perhaps a resolution to return and cry, "Father, I have sinned against heaven and in thy sight, and am no more worthy to be called thy son: make me as one of thy hired servants."

I have hitherto spoken of love chiefly as restraining from evil; but it is no less powerful in promoting what is good. What would we not do for those whom we love! What burdens would we not bear! What hardships would we not undergo; what sacrifices would we not cheerfully make! History not unfrequently traces the heroic to such affections as this; and believe me, there is a humble heroism in many homes, which finds no record in the historian's page. There is sometimes a patient industry, continued till "the head grows dizzy and the eyes grow dim," for the support of an aged parent; there is sometimes a faithful watching for long months and years by the bed-side of a sickly sister; and, if a visitor there, you may see how carefully the drooping head is pillowed, and how anxiously the slow ebb of life is observed, and how gently every kind office is performed, and how no word of complaint is spoken, though there should be weary days and wakeful nights and an aching brow. Sometimes, again, how bravely is the battle of life fought in the face of poverty and misfortune, without flinching and without fear, with stout hands and a sturdy heart,—for there are little ones at home to be cared for; and what will the head and heart and hands of a parent not combine to do for these! These are good deeds, recorded in heaven though unnoticed on earth, and they spring from the constraining power of love.

Such is the influence of love in some of its many ramifications. It holds society together. It keeps the vicious in check, and spurs on the virtuous to be more virtuous still. It is more powerful for good than moralists and preachers. It is more stringent in restraining from crime than constabularies and penitentiaries. In truth, all the constables and judges and jailers in the world could not put down crime were it not for this, and the appeals of the pulpit are effective only when they touch a chord already existing in the human heart. Take away this principle, and vice like a rank and noxious vegetation would soon overspread society. It would be impossible to keep it down. But by its gentle and scarcely perceptible constraints love makes the bad good, and the good better; and it is universally felt that they must be very bad indeed who can overleap all its fences and violate feelings so peculiarly sacred.

We have now seen there are two opposite springs of human conduct: the one selfish, the other disinterested; the former embracing the hope of reward, and the fear of punishment; the latter resulting from the force of our love for some one. It is easy to see which of these sources of conduct is the purer, the nobler, the more divine; and it only remains for me now to inquire which of them it is which the gospel enjoins.

With my text, and other kindred sayings of Christ and his apostles in view, we cannot doubt that gospel morality is based on love—on unselfish love,— on the love which the Christian has for the Christ. "If ye love me," said Jesus, "keep my commandments." Here the great Master insists that a true love for him should lead to a Christian life. "The love of Christ constraineth us," says St. Paul in the text. This may refer either to the love which we have for Christ or the love He bears to us, or to both; and the effect of this reciprocal affection is to constrain us to live an unselfish, self-sacrificing life such as Christ lived; it hems us in and urges us on, so that we cannot but do as He did.

But it may be said, Other motives besides this are often set before us in the Bible. Both heaven and hell loom in many of its pages, and are pressed upon us by the preacher as motives to holy living; and salvation with all that it implies is frequently spoken of as a reward. All this is true. It is true, heaven is the appointed home of the holy, and hell even upon earth the natural doom of the unholy; and the belief of this must have its influence with men subject to hope and fear. In fact, these are the only things which have weight with some men. Nothing but the thunderings and lightnings of Sinai could awe the nomad tribes of Israel into subjection. Nothing but the pains of purgatory or the horrors of hell has influence still with semi-savages. But this is not the evangel of Jesus! And there is something good in the way in which your high Evangelical states the truth. "We keep God's commandments," he says, "not that we may obtain salvation, but because we have obtained it; we lead a Christian life, not that we may be saved, but because we are saved! Mary was forgiven much, and therefore she loved much!"

Much has been said and written regarding the pure love of God. It is a doctrine which leads directly to mysticism, but at the same time it is a doctrine which has had its confessors and martyrs, and the pious Fénélon put forth all his persuasive eloquence in its defence. Now, whatever we may think of the possibility of loving God—the spiritual—the absolute —for his own sake, and altogether apart from those hopes and promises which incline the heart to love, there need be no doubt in regard to the Divine man Jesus of Nazareth. If it be possible to love humanity in its highest form, we must love it as it is enshrined here. For during these eighteen centuries the image of Jesus, as first limned out in the Gospels, has so grown in the Christian consciousness that it is now the ideal of all possible perfection. To love Jesus is therefore to love the incarnation of all that is Godlike and good. Myriads can testify how they do love him with a love stronger than death.

Here then we have a powerful principle introduced into the Christian heart. I have already spoken of the power of parental and other human love in restraining from wickedness and stimulating to industry, honesty, and honour. How much more powerful this Divine love, this love of the self-denying Jesus! Every Christian knows it, feels it, can tell how it constrains him to live not to himself, but to him who loved him and died for him. Moses with his Decalogue could never accomplish what has thus been achieved by Christ and his Cross. The bonds of the old morality could, like green withs, be easily broken, but the ties of this new morality are strong, just because they are tender.

As this gospel morality is stronger in its sanctions, so is it purer in its motives, than any other. All other sources of conduct are less or more interested, selfish, and sordid. If we avoid sin merely because we dread its punishment, if we cultivate piety merely because we desire its rewards, our behaviour comes of unmitigated selfishness. We are utilitarians and economists, not Christians. But when the love of the Divine Jesus takes possession of our soul, when we love him and feel that He loves us with more than a woman's love, we are inflamed with a desire to imitate him in all things, and to make his all-perfect life the model for our own. It is thus the Christian saint rises infinitely higher than the patriarch or prophet of Old Testament times. Through the force of Christ's living example he has risen to a loftier plateau on the hill of holiness than was ever reached by the best of them. It is upon no calculation of the consequences of his conduct that he acts; it is from no balancing of profit and loss; he attempts not to make salvation a thing of barter, giving so much holiness, getting so much happiness, but he is pure, pious, devoted to God's service, submissive to God's will, because, filled with reverence for the human ideal of all that is Divine, he strives to imitate it. A lofty spiritual eminence to rise to, but not too high for Christian aspiration!

But still further, as the motive to this gospel morality is the purest possible, so is it less productive of pain and more productive of happiness than any other motive of obedience which could be presented to us. No man obeys so cheerfully as he who does it from love. A forced obedience is always a painful obedience. In France, after the great Revolution, there was a period known as the Reign of Terror, when the guillotine daily dripped with blood—the blood of the best and bravest and most beautiful in the land. The men in power were monsters of iniquity, and many of the laws they enacted were violations of all justice; but these men were outwardly honoured and their laws most scrupulously obeyed. Not a whisper was heard throughout all Paris—the tumultuous city—against either lawgivers or laws. Every citizen seemed more anxious than another to obey to the very letter, and to omit nothing in word or deed to show his perfect submission to the ruling powers. But all this while men's hearts were frozen with horror; the gaunt guillotine threw its shadow before them wherever they went; and when friends met they could only silently shake hands and part, for they dared not say what they felt, and they knew not if they might meet again. How different from this a community in which the laws are obeyed from a sense of their justice, and in which, accordingly, every face is radiant with joy, and in which neighbours and friends can freely interchange their thoughts without dread of a spy! Here then we have the reign of love contrasted with the reign of terror.

It is from the same circumstance that the love-allotted task is more lightsome than the same amount of labour exacted by fear. God knows how much is done for love, and how pleasantly.

So it is in the Gospel kingdom. The Christian lives not under a reign of terror, but of love. He obeys not from fear but from affection. He does not tremble like a slave, but he has the free, happy look of a child. And the duties of Christianity are not extorted from an aroused and alarmed conscience, they are the free-will offerings of a loving heart. We are willing workers for Christ, but labour in his service is felt to be no drudgery, for love lightens the heaviest burdens.

It is thus that the love of Christ constrains us. In other words, love to Christ, as the highest ideal of human perfection, the point where the human and Divine merge into one, is the basis of our Christian morality. That motive is the strongest that could be presented to us,—the purest, the happiest. With such a love in our hearts we cannot but live earnest, useful, holy lives, thus adorning the doctrine of our God and Saviour. May this love be shed abroad in your hearts! May it extend its influence over your lives! May it constrain you to devote yourselves soul and body to God's service! It was this love that moved St. John to write so touchingly, and St. Paul to labour so unweariedly, and St. Stephen to die so serenely; it has been the same love which in all ages has made the true Christian exhibit upon earth the beauties of a heavenly holiness, and which in the ages to come will subdue all hearts to virtue by subduing them to Christ.

V.

LAW AND MIRACLE.

BY THE REV. D. J. FERGUSON, B.D. STRATHBLANE.

> There was a man of the Pharisees, named Nicodemus, a ruler of the Jews: The same came to Jesus by night, and said unto him, Rabbi, we know that thou art a teacher come from God: for no man can do these miracles that thou doest, except God be with him. Jesus answered and said unto him, Verily, verily, I say unto thee, Except a man be born again, he cannot see the kingdom of God.
> —JOHN III. 1-3.

WHEN we read these words, our first impression is that our Lord's reply has little or no bearing upon the address of Nicodemus. The speakers appear to be moving upon lines that are quite apart: they hardly seem to be carrying on a conversation at all, but rather to be uttering abrupt and disconnected thoughts. There are many passages of Holy Scripture however, where the sequence of thought is real, though it may not be obvious. The connecting links may not obtrude themselves upon our notice, but we are not therefore to conclude that they do not exist. The present is a case in point. For the question implicitly before the minds of the speakers is, "What is the true criterion of a revelation of God?" In the one case, we have the answer that suggests itself to a nature of immature spiritual growth; in the other, the answer of perfect insight. Nicodemus based his belief upon the external fact of miracle: our Lord taught him that he must build upon a surer foundation; not upon outward, but upon inward facts, upon the truth of the impulse given to the inner life.

This, as it was an important lesson for the early converts from Judaism, remains an important lesson for the Church of to-day. According as the principle is accepted or rejected, our faith in Christ will have an intrinsic strength, or be insecure and dependent upon external support. It will either be able to overcome the world, and adapt itself to the conditions of modern culture, or it will be void of self-reliance, and, instead of looking to the future with confidence, its deepest yearnings will go out towards the "ages of faith" in the buried centuries.

That Nicodemus in his thoughts about Divine things should have laid exclusive stress upon miracle and sign need not surprise us. This is no more than to say he was a Jew. With many great qualities, the Jewish mind was essentially materialistic in its leanings. The nation as a whole were true sons of earth, devoted to its interests, placing their highest happiness in its successes, and in its misfortunes finding their sorest punishments. Prosperity was "the blessing of the Old Testament," just because it was the blessing they were best able to appreciate, and their religion had ever the aspect of a bargain between them and Jehovah. No doubt there arose among them Psalmists and Prophets of a very different stamp: men whose words have lost nothing of power and fervour, but find a quicker response in the mind of the Christian than in the mind of the pre-Christian age. But these were exceptionally gifted souls, raised by the force and originality of their religious genius far above their brethren. The masses were unspiritual in the last degree, and the religion of the Old Testament, based as it was upon signs and wonders, was the natural outcome of a disposition that craved external guarantees for spiritual truth.

In .the time of Christ, this habit of thought was especially remarkable, and the circumstances of the hour helped to confirm it. Not only had the minds of that generation been formed under the influence of the national myths and traditions, but a new and powerful element had been introduced in the religious speculations which were the fruit of contact with Oriental and Western thought. They were, besides, chafing under the Roman yoke, and the belief was widespread that a great catastrophe was at hand to usher in the Messianic kingdom. Take all this into account, and it is evident that under such conditions the Jewish craving for signs was not likely to decrease, but to become more feverish and intense. The contemporaries of our Lord, indeed, seem not to have been able to conceive of any other test of truth. "What sign showest thou?" was the cry on every side, and the weakness of their favourite proof was manifested in their continued unbelief. Nicodemus differed from his countrymen, not in that he could dispense with signs, but in his willingness to accept them as credentials of our Saviour's message.

The contrast between our Lord's method of teaching

and the spirit of the Jews is very striking. Christianity is based not upon the outward, but upon the inward. It makes light of physical portents, but seeks to quicken spiritual perceptions. Its moving principle is not a mere sense of wonder, or of prostration before infinite Power, but that trust in God which satisfies the cravings and stills the unrest of the soul. And hence our Lord laid little stress upon miracle and sign. He was habitually chary of their use, and over and over again rebuked the curiosity which so eagerly asked for them. According to the narrative, they became in his hands means of subjecting the material to the spiritual, and of leading the sensuous-minded multitude away from the seen and temporal to the hidden sources of Divine life in the soul. He emphatically pronounced his blessing, not upon the faith born of sight, but upon the faith which is the "evidence of things not seen;" and showed men that in their own natures there was a Holy of Holies, in which the voice of God might be heard giving an oracle of truth. The whole of his teaching took a nobler range than that of the law; and in breaking away from the material associations of the older faith, He opened up to his followers a new and fairer region of spiritual life and thought.

It is well for us, for the Church at large, that this is so. For the whole question is here involved, whether Christianity is capable of becoming the universal religion or not. Its elasticity and perennial freshness belong to its spiritual nature. From this source arises its power of statedly introducing reforms, and of subordinating or casting out altogether matters of doctrine and tradition, which are no longer necessary to the system; and to this therefore we owe it, that the religion of Christ is not to-day a faint echo of the past, but the greatest living influence among men. Indeed, it is impossible to see how faith could otherwise overcome the world. The life of Christ, left further and further behind us, would dwindle into a mere speck upon the horizon, and be swallowed up in the haze of distance. Faith in him would become the mark of a small and constantly diminishing band; it would altogether lose its power of expansion; and his religion, instead of rolling onward like a river fed from a thousand tributaries, would resemble a torrent which, however bounteous its source, receives no new supplies, and at length exhausts itself in the sand.

Christianity, then, is no rigid system of dogma, or of ecclesiastical forms, elaborated long ago, and incapable of growth or change. It is rather a living organism, drawing nourishment to itself from every side, and affected by the life-pulsations of every age. Look, for instance, what a vast difference between Christianity in the first and in the nineteenth century! Then, it was struggling for existence between Judaism on the one hand and Paganism on the other: now, it has conquered its position, and extorts recognition at least from its bitterest opponents. It has revolutionised the whole structure of society, and formed manners and customs and habits of thought. It has taught us that humanity, made in the image of God, is sacred, and that, belonging to man as the creature of God, there are inalienable rights which may not be trampled upon. It has given a new significance to the idea of duty. This it has taken out of the exclusive possession of the philosophic, and the resolute by nature, and bestowed upon the humblest soul whose hard lot is cheered by heavenward aspiration, and borne unmurmuringly for the sake of Christ. It has vivified and ennobled religious faith by giving a revelation of God at once human and removed from the weakness of humanity, and has thus shed a sanctifying influence over the intellect and heart of man. It has fused together the various elements of the body politic, and made a true national life a reality; it has trained and strengthened public opinion, marked out the course of legislation, and defined the limits of government. It is, in short, the atmosphere in which we live and breathe, and of which, unconsciously to ourselves, we sustain the pressure. "It is without us, and we are within its circle: we do not become Christians, we are so from our birth."

The importance of the change must not be overlooked, seeing it affects not merely the form, but the matter also, of our belief. For the law of action and reaction is as true in the mental as in the physical world, and in taking up into itself the whole circle of life, Christianity cannot but feel the influence of its changed conditions. It has to enter new fields of thought and knowledge, and adapt itself to the complex relations, and tendencies, and wants of the modern world. And as each generation necessarily holds its faith as the reflection of its own spiritual consciousness, its creed must no less be stated (or, what comes to the same thing, if not stated, interpreted) in its own forms of thought. Its religion, in a word, is moulded by that very real though impalpable power which we call the "spirit of the age;" and men are not only intellectually and morally, but spiritually also, the children of their time.

Within the Church itself, therefore, we have to recognise a historical process by which the faith characteristic of each successive age is determined. A current of life is thus introduced to prevent stagnation and decay; and the tendency makes itself more and more felt to distinguish between what is essential in Christianity and what is of passing value. The truths of faith are seen apart from the special form and local colouring which gave them vividness to the Jewish mind, and while the temporary falls away, that which is of permanent significance remains. We may indeed shut our eyes to the fact that the progress of history is a revelation of God, and refuse to acknowledge either its right or its power to modify the New Testament revelation. If we worship an infallible book and conceive of revelation as the publication, once for all, of a definite scheme of dogma, we shall naturally cling to the past, and forget that there is anything divine in the world of to-day. The apostolic age will alone seem sacred, and a secular era date from its close. But if, inspired by a worthier faith, we believe in a living presence of God in every age, the passing years will only bring into stronger relief the principles of our Saviour's teaching. In the history of the Church we shall see the process by which the spirit of Christ manifests itself and leads her into truth and freedom. The changes which must come in the presentment of the faith will then be to us the signs, not of decay but of health, not the forerunners of dissolution but the normal action and the proof of life. They will teach us how important and necessary it is to distinguish between the letter and the spirit, between form and essence, between what is local and temporary and what is universal and eternal.

Of the effects produced by this process of sifting and winnowing which goes on in history, we have a good example in the doctrine of miracle. In our own day, that doctrine does not occupy the prominent position it formerly had. It has fallen into the background, and lost its apologetic value; but, at the same time, its actual relations to the circle of Christian truth have been made clear. In the course of last century, on the contrary, the sharpest attacks which Christianity had to sustain were directed against this side. The contest raged round the credibility or incredibility of miracle, as if the whole of revelation depended upon the issue. In reality, however, no vital point of revelation was endangered. It was an affair of outposts altogether, and the work so energetically assaulted and defended had little importance for the citadel in the rear. Neither the philosopher who argued against, nor the divine who contended for miracle, was dealing with the essence of Christianity, and the complete triumph of either would have made little change. At the worst, a dogma of the Church would have been overthrown: but the dogmas of the Church and the religion of Christ are not synonymous terms.

Now to make belief in Christ depend, in any degree, upon the fact that He wrought miracles is to build upon the sand. It is to go back to the old Jewish belief of Nicodemus in the text, and to incur the implied rebuke in our Lord's answer to him. For by no act of power, be it ever so great, can we prove a spiritual truth. In the ordinary business of life, we should not point to a physical fact, or series of facts, as an evidence of a truth of consciousness. But when we enter upon matters connected with religion, it is more difficult to preserve the candour of mind which elsewhere stands us in good stead. A false reverence is only too apt to blind us, though the principle is as strong in the one case as in the other. Considered in themselves, miracles are signs of the possession of power; but whether that power springs from a deeper insight than common into the constitution of nature, or is strictly speaking supernatural, they do not tell us. Were they to be performed to-day, our conclusion would be, not that a divine being had appeared among us, but simply that events so startling challenged the closest attention and investigation; of the character of the worker himself we should judge from other and independent sources. And when we argue that the New Testament miracles prove the divine origin of Christianity, we are going upon the assumption that the possession of power over nature is the constant index of spiritual truth and wisdom—an assumption demanded by no necessity of thought, and contradicted by every-day experience of men's actions, an assumption, moreover, at variance with the teaching of Scripture itself, that a sign may be given, and yet the message be false. In other words, from premises that belong to the material world, we are attempting to draw a conclusion regarding the spiritual. There is, indeed, one supposition upon which a sign given in nature will be the evidence for a spiritual truth. The day may come when the old dualism of matter and spirit shall be resolved, and the interaction and interdependence of what we now call material and spiritual forces be made clear to thought. But in the meantime, while the gulf is still unbridged, we cannot pass from one side to the other. Until the junction is made, we must frankly recognise the secondary place of miracle in the Christian system. Granted the historical accuracy of the narratives in the Gospels, even then the argument from miracle holds, with regard to our Lord, a position similar to that which the argument from design holds with regard to the being of a God. The latter does not prove God's existence; it only proves the existence of a great artist working upon materials ready to his hand. And, in like manner, the former only proves that Christ was endowed with special power. About his doctrine it is silent.

If however, in the development of history, the evidential power of miracles has grown weak, it need not follow that the belief is to be thrown overboard, and the narratives deleted from the Gospels. The belief has still its place in the order of Christian thought: it continues to be of use, though in a different way, and in a more private sphere. We may not, as we have said, base our faith in Christ upon our reception of his miracles: conversely however, we may base our reception of his miracles upon our faith in Christ. The miracle is not the guarantee for the revelation, but the revelation for the miracle.

Such a change in the point of view necessarily brings us into a new circle of relations. The course taken by reflection lies away altogether from dispute and argument, and inclines towards the calm of meditation. Let the revelation be accepted, and the miracles fall into their true position, and speak to many minds, whose conception of Christ they enlarge and strengthen. Our Lord is then seen to be the revealer of the Father, not only in redeeming men from sin, but also in manifesting the Divine control over the universe. He not only speaks to the hearts and consciences of men, but also discovers to them their true relations to nature. And thus the miracles become the insignia of his office, and open up to us the secret of the external world. They tell us that the laws by which the universe is governed, and the physical conditions in which we live, spring from a hidden spiritual source, and are upheld by a spiritual presence. The constitution of the world is, they say, the expression of the beneficence of God, who has imprinted upon it his own goodness, and intended it to forward the happiness and wellbeing of his creatures. That his laws in their action do not always tend towards happiness, that on the contrary they often produce suffering and misery, is no doubt true. At times, they seem to work against and not in favour of man. There is much apparent waste and ruthless cruelty which we cannot explain. We have no key to the problem; and there are hours in which we seem to be the puppets of a remorseless Fate, rather than the creatures of a heavenly Father. Of the facts which may be brought forward in support of this gloomy imagination, some are invincibly shrouded in mystery, and there we must be content to leave them. They belong to the secret things of God. The tower of Siloam falls upon men not specially guilty; good and bad alike go down in the shipwreck; the pure and innocent are the helpless victims of disease. Before these and such like facts we can only bow our heads in silence. There are other cases however in which sin enters as a factor into the account; and here the miracles of Christ do vindicate God's goodness. They proclaim that in him power and love exist in union, and are the foundation of the system in which we have been placed, through which He seeks, and in obedience to which alone we attain, what is for us highest and best. To run counter to his will embodied in his laws is to plunge into suffering; yet the inevitable connection between disobedience and suffering is itself an expression of his loving care, his call to us to return, his effort to overcome our obstinacy and self-will. Refuse as we may, and as long as we may, to hear, He changes not, and nature in her calm uniformity bears the stamp of his fixed, unswerving purpose. We need no longer therefore stand in awe and helplessness before her, as with relentless step she moves on to crush rebellion; pitiless she may seem, deaf to all entreaty, and hard to exact the uttermost farthing of her due: but the miracles declare that the stern countenance hides a wise and loving heart, and in showing us a spiritual aim in her processes, bespeak for her lessons a more reverent attention. They teach us that the outer world is the "visible garment" of Deity, and our own frames the temples of his Spirit. They speak of a God not afar off, but near at hand; no yawning chasm divides him from his universe, his sustaining presence dwells in it, his righteous will controls it, his providence shapes its destiny. The miracles of our Lord, in displaying the moral basis of the whole creation, help us to realise more vividly the fulness of his revelation of God, to feel that we dwell in our Father's house, and with devout hearts to read, as expressed in material forms, the parables with which we are surrounded.

A belief like this is not to be accounted barren. Upon its own merits, it is fully entitled to take its place in the Christian scheme. But there is another aspect of the subject to be considered. Belief in the New Testament miracles, we have said, may rest upon belief in the revelation of Christ. We cannot however say, on the other hand, that belief in the revelation necessarily brings with it a belief in miracle. It cannot be denied, that in our own day, there are many, who, calling themselves by the name of Christ, shrink, avowedly or tacitly, from this particular dogma. They feel that the miraculous narratives of the Gospels, instead of being a help, are a burden to faith, and may therefore be quietly dropped out of sight. The impulse and support which, in their own spiritual life, they receive from Christianity, are not rendered stronger and more trustworthy by the thought that its first appearance was accompanied by signs and wonders. Its intrinsic value cannot be increased by any amount of miracles, and in this confidence they rest satisfied.

The influences which produce this reserve and unwillingness of mind are not so much to be traced to this or that definite source, as to be felt diffused throughout the mental atmosphere of the day. The silent changes of history have brought us into a new "climate of opinion," in which an easy and uncritical assent to dogma of any kind does not flourish so luxuriantly as in former ages, and which to the belief in miracle is especially unfavourable. Many movements of thought (which it is of course impossible to trace here in detail), in science, and philosophy, and religion itself, have combined to this result. Still there are three which have been so important as to demand a passing notice.

I. First of all, there is the scientific conception of the universality of Law. This may truly be said to be the revelation of our own age, not in the sense that it was unknown to our predecessors, but that in the present day the conception has been so extended and generalised as to dwarf its former proportions. It has passed out of the laboratory of science into the common possession of men, and is now one of the great truths so firmly established that they become truisms. We never stop to reason about them, and were any one rash enough to call them in question, we should not give him even a patient hearing. Moreover, the idea of Law is not to be confined to the material world with its indestructible treasury of force. It must be carried over into the world of mind, and be seen at work there also, not indeed with the rigidity of physical law, but within the large limits which freedom of thought and action demands. It is to be traced in the advance of civilisation, in the development of history, in the growth of religion, in relations such as those between morals and art, between society and government, between national life and literature. Now it is not difficult to see how such a conception must indispose men under its influence to look favourably upon miracle. In the idea of order everywhere supreme, calm, eternal, there is a sublimity which fills their imagination and stimulates their intellect. Any interruption of its uniform course, any breach of continuity, would be a blemish in the picture, and not an additional charm,—would be, indeed, a positive pain to thought, and instead of disposing the mind to reverence, would fill it with confusion and doubt. And it cannot be wondered at therefore, if, with the difficulty before them, they prefer to hold fast to a truth they certainly know, and to pass by what is so completely at variance with all their habits of thought.

II. A second influence adverse to the belief in miracle springs from the natural history of religion. When we compare the religions of the world in their origin and growth, it is remarkable that miracle is a constant element of them all. From the lowest fetishism upwards, this is a characteristic feature, varying, it is true, according to the genius of the nation, but expressing the same underlying conception. In the higher forms of faith, miracle is the special attribute of those who stand near to God, and mediate between him and their brethren. It matters not whether the teachers have themselves claimed the power or repudiated it; the deep impression they have left upon the minds of their countrymen is the fertile source of legend and tradition.

Thus for instance, the founders of Buddhism and Islam, the great historic faiths, which at the present moment dispute with Christianity the empire of the world, consistently protested against being thought wonder-workers. Yet in spite of their protests, the imagination of subsequent generations has encircled their persons with a halo of supernatural glory, and credited them with miracles that are equally marvellous with those recorded in the Gospels. It has been asked therefore, Have we not here a natural tendency of the human heart, to which we may trace the origin of miraculous narratives of every kind, even of the Christian ones? Must we not regard them all alike as the offspring of the religious imagination, and treat them simply as the poetical form in which great truths are vividly presented to us? There is here, observe, no question of imposture or wilful deception. From this point of view miracles are only representations, under material emblems, of thoughts and feelings which have been called into being by the spiritual teaching of a messenger of God—reflections, in the world of sense, of the workings of the mind—and to the multitude, ever eager for type and symbol, indispensable, the natural accompaniments of all religion. Hence it is too, that they linger lovingly round the point of origin of the faith, and gradually disappear as we travel onward. They cluster round the person and career of the prophet, and invest him with powers corresponding to the influence he has exerted. The results of his teaching are referred back to the time when it was first proclaimed, and feeling and imagination conspire to picture that as the golden age of the faith, the age when the gates of heaven stood open, and earth was bathed in a brighter radiance than the "light of common day." Miracles thus belong to the poetry of religion: they are a recollection of its fresh and buoyant youth.

III. The third influence adverse to the belief in miracles to which we shall refer comes from the realm of theology itself, when the authorship and constitution of the Christian records are brought into the discussion. By their very nature, appealing as they do to the senses, miracles address themselves to eye-witnesses alone. Whatever may be their value as evidences for truth, be it little or much, it is limited to the time of their occurrence. To succeeding ages, belief in them comes at second-hand, through the medium of tradition, oral or written; and the trustworthiness of the tradition is the measure of the stability of the belief. To establish the reality of events so rare and apart from ordinary experience, the clearest testimony is absolutely necessary; and therefore the reception of the New Testament miracles turns upon the position and weight allowed to the Gospels. With this question, however, we at once enter upon the domain of historical criticism; and whatever be the decision there, the title of that decision to be received depends exclusively upon the fairness with which the inquiry has been conducted; for the right to treat such topics critically can no longer be denied, and the right once conceded involves the possibility of different answers being given. Say with some, indeed, that the inspiration of the evangelists was such as to preserve them from all error, and of course the question falls to the ground. The mere fact that the miracles are recorded is of itself sufficient, and there is no room left for discussion. But putting aside such an untenable theory, surely no one who has regard to the origin of the Gospels—to their rise out of the mass of floating tradition, to their distance in point of time from the events narrated, to the freedom with which they treat the Old Testament Scriptures, to the temper of the age which we have already noticed,—surely no one who has regard to all this can maintain their character to be such as to exclude the possibility that they have received the impress of the modes of thought familiar to the early Church. The composite structure of the narrative forbids us to demand that the whole of the tradition shall be received without distinction, or to insist that the rejection of any part, no matter what, is at once a heinous sin and a deadly injury to revelation. It is the recognition of this composite structure which induces many to stumble at the miracles of the Gospel. They simply take up the position, that in none of the records which have been preserved do we possess the clear and sufficient testimony necessary to constrain belief in such events: and therefore, while they pay homage to the revelation with heart and understanding, and confess its power and beauty, in the miracles they only see the result of the prevailing tendency to embody spiritual truth in material form.

These then are, we think, three principal sources of the shrinking from miracle characteristic of our own day. And the question immediately suggests itself: What effect has the rejection of miracle upon Christianity? Is it possible at once to believe in the revelation of Christ, and yet to set aside what has hitherto formed so important a part of the historical narrative? To some, the answer will come without hesitation. To deny the miracles is, in their eyes, not only to impoverish the revelation, but to rob it of its distinctive features, and leave only a residuum of moral precepts. It is to sacrifice Christianity, and to put one's-self without the pale of the Church of Christ. A calmer judgment will hesitate to pronounce so sweeping a verdict. The change in the circumstances of Christianity has taught us to distinguish the relative proportions of its doctrines; and where, as among ourselves, its truths are the birthright of the community and its influence has created habits of thought, to suppose that its right of possession can be dangerously affected by the denial of miracle is to misapprehend its power and essence. The chief interest which the Church of to-day has in the signs and wonders recorded in the Gospels is a scientific one, lying in the direction of the philosophy of religion, in the field of historical speculation. The problem concerns the origin of the faith, and may be stated thus—How are we to account for the celestial radiance which enveloped Christianity at its birth, and was shortly afterwards extinguished? One answer is, that the tendency, rising almost to an instinct, of the human mind to make extraordinary phenomena in nature the attendants of every new moral and spiritual impulse, in proportion as the impulse is felt to be regenerative, is of itself sufficient to explain the miraculous narratives which have come down to us. On the other hand, it is said that, at that time, the continuity of history was broken, and the Christian severed from the Pre-Christian era; that Christianity was in fact an absolutely new beginning, independent of historical conditions, and witnessed to by special interferences with the ordinary course of nature. But these opposing views both belong to the theoretical side of Christian thought, and he who supports the former does not therefore deny the truth of the revelation. No doubt his creed will not formally correspond with that of his neighbour who holds the alternative opinion; the outlines will be filled up differently, and in quieter tones; in particular, the one will ascribe to the immanent power of God what the other ascribes to his extraneous and incidental action. Yet such a difference cannot be said to prejudice, far less to be fatal to, the interests of religion. So far as these are involved, a true faith in Christ may be modified by, but does not depend upon, belief in the miracles: it is in the immediate consciousness of his spiritual power, that the aim and scope of his mission are perceived, and that his word becomes " a light unto the feet and a lamp unto the path." And therefore to insist that no one who rejects the miracles of the New Testament may claim to be a Christian, is intolerance which ought to be resisted. It directly tends to drive away from the faith men who are neither vain nor uncultured, but reverent and thoughtful; men, however, who are so strongly impressed by the revelation of nature, that any teaching which is at variance with her already known truths is, unless it comes with irresistible authority, at once decisively rejected. Yet intolerance such as this is the natural result of a blind Bibliolatry which, refusing to distinguish between Christianity in itself and the New Testament its historical record, assumes that Christianity was necessarily purest near its source, and that lower down, we may only look for sullied waters. The very opposite is the fact. Near the source, the turbid stream of Judaism poured into the pure current of our Saviour's teaching, and the mingled waters were dark and troubled. It is only as we descend that the foreign matter then held in solution is gradually precipitated, and the river of the water of life flows on more clear. At the beginning, Christianity, deeply tinged with Judaic elements, was in the utmost danger of becoming merely a new form of the national religion. The feature of the apostolic age was the Church's struggle for independence of the Law; it was by degrees that her freedom was won, by degrees that she was successful in rejecting what was distinctively Mosaic. In spreading over large areas, it became necessary to speak to man as man, and not as a member of a particular nation; and therefore Christianity fell back upon the general principles essential to its existence, and allowed local disputes and Jewish prejudice to fade away unheeded. And the process is not yet complete. As the generations pass, we learn, as we have said, to see more clearly what are the divine and eternal, what the human and transitory, elements of the revelation. We become able to distinguish between what is essential and what is not; and as the latter drops into the background—whether it be miracle, or apostolic ordinance, or the clinging remnants of that Judaism which puts assent to dogma in place of faith—the grandeur, and beauty, and educating power of the revelation of Christ are felt only the more, and command a more reverent homage. The letter of Scripture opens up to disclose the spirit; the universal principles of our Saviour's teaching are made plain; its bold and generous outlines are thrown into relief and satisfy the mental vision; and the truth of his message is verified, not by any outward testimony, but by the communion of spirit with spirit, by the response of our own hearts to his revelation of the Father.

It only remains to notice very briefly the teaching of our Lord, "Except a man be born again he cannot see the kingdom of God." With these words, He excludes the appeal to outward tests of revelation, and refers us to a spiritual standard. The soul that in his presence becomes conscious of his influence has in itself a witness to his truth, beside which no other witness is once to be named. The life of Christ and the power of his Spirit over man are the great and the enduring miracles of divine revelation.

The secret of Christianity, let us remember, can only be "spiritually discerned." To be well acquainted with the Gospel history, and versant with systems of theology, is something quite distinct from being true followers of Christ. The belief that rests upon such attainments is purely intellectual, and goes into the same category as belief about Plato, or Cicero, or the tenets of the Stoics. It may be held without seriously influencing character, without evoking any personal devotion or sense of God's nearness, and from it we shall get no immediate or convincing proof of the truth of our religion. But when we come into contact with the Spirit of Christ, the revelation speaks home to us in a different way, and discovers its spiritual wealth; it meets the cravings of our nature, and tells us that these, far from being delusions, are the highest instincts of humanity. Under the burden of sin, and the felt discordance in our being, the soul of man cries out for the living God. The dream of the spirit is to be delivered from its weakness and unrest, from imprisonment in its present bonds, into a purer and fuller life, in which its haunting visions of holiness and peace and self-control shall come true, and achievement, no longer baffled by a recreant will and halting energies, shall follow hard on aspiration. That ideal has been realised in Christ; and the spiritual impulse which imagination and reflection could not by themselves originate has been given to humanity by the life and death of the Son of Man. To enter into fellowship with him is at once to be delivered from the overwhelming consciousness of infinite power, which, hidden in the depths of space, no cry can reach and no suffering move, and to find ourselves the objects of a Father's care; it is to be assured of the Divine goodness, and clemency, and sorrow for the sins of men, and to be taught that our highest life depends upon submission to the will of God; it is to learn that the whole course of God's providence and government helps forward the education of his children, and that the external conditions, against which we sometimes chafe and fret, are, in the very steadfastness of their laws, the pledge and earnest of his purpose to complete that education; it is, in a word, to know that our nature, hemmed in and sinful though it be, is yet akin to the divine, and can find its rest in God alone. A revelation such as this, which discloses the true relations between earth and heaven, can afford to dispense with outward testimony of whatever kind. The best witness to its truth is to be found in our own consciousness, in its acknowledged power to satisfy the wants and to develop the capacities of the soul. "The Spirit beareth witness with our spirit;" and in communion with God, delivered from the pressure of fear and the bondage of selfishness, the whole nature is strengthened, the balance of its powers is restored, and a genial influence quickens intellect and conscience and will. The faith which then possesses the mind does not rest upon argument, nor does it require to call authority to its aid. It has all the certainty and spontaneousness of instinct or natural endowment, and is at once the living spring of our conscious action, and the consecrating principle of our unconscious influence. It is a faith that cannot be overthrown; and amid the changes of history, amid the variations of dogmatic systems and ecclesiastical organisations, amid the "time and chance" of the human lot, its confident expression is in the noble words of the Apostle: "I am persuaded that neither death nor life, nor angels nor principalities nor powers, nor things present nor things to come, nor height nor depth, nor any other creature, shall be able to separate us from the love of God, which is in Christ Jesus our Lord."

VI.

THE VISION OF GOD.

BY THE REV. D. J. FERGUSON, B.D., STRATHBLANE.

Philip saith unto him, Lord, shew us the Father, and it sufficeth us. Jesus saith unto him, Have I been so long time with you, and yet hast thou not known me, Philip? He that hath seen me hath seen the Father; and how sayest thou then, Shew us the Father?—JOHN XIV. 8, 9.

IT takes little reflection or experience to make us aware that on every hand we are beset by mystery and contradiction. God has placed us within a system of rigid, universal law. He has hedged us in with conditions upon which our very existence depends, yet which we can understand only in part. We have hardly crossed the threshold of life before we find ourselves in a maze of problems, practical and theoretical, of action and of thought, through which we can see only a little way; we walk in twilight and must pick our steps. Duty seems to clash with duty, motive with motive, and the mind to be divided against itself. Truth is opposed to truth in bewildering confusion; and when we would follow out one, to what seems its legitimate issue, we find ourselves at variance with another not less important and not less sure. And it is when we try to reconcile such hostile principles, to apportion to each its own province, and hold them consistently together in thought, that we become most conscious, sometimes most painfully conscious, of the finite range of our faculties, and learn to spell out the alphabet of patience and humility.

Take, for instance, one of the great contradictions of our minds. At one time, we seem to ourselves to be free agents. We know that we are responsible for conduct, and have the power to choose our course of action. The conditions of life furnish so much material for the will to work on, and mould into definite form. But again, we seem no less to be bound down by an iron necessity. We are the creatures of circumstances and passively moulded by external influences. We are hurried along by currents of habit and instinct and predisposition, and act as if we were machines.

So too in the sphere of the religious life, we are met by the struggle between good and evil in our natures. It is the opposition between what the apostle calls the old and the new man, between Adam and Christ. The flesh lusting against the spirit, and the spirit against the flesh, give rise to a conflict which extends not only to outward action, but also to our inmost thoughts, and, in a most marked way, to our conceptions of spiritual truth. To give the higher elements of our being the control of the lower, is life and peace in a spiritual faith : in proportion as the balance is reversed, it becomes increasingly difficult to preserve any faith in the spiritual at all.

Belief in the spiritual runs like a silver thread through the whole tissue of life. It gives colour to our noblest thoughts, and inspires our highest hopes.

Yet the spiritual is bound up with, and practically inseparable from, our knowledge of the material; it always works in and through some external form. Therefore it is that we clothe it with a body, and give it "a local habitation and a name;" we limit and define it, and in this way there arises the common idea of personality.

So it comes to pass, that when we try to rise from the idea of finite spirit to the thought of God, the Infinite, "without body, parts, or passions," we find ourselves in a region where the ground seems to be slipping away from under us. The atmosphere becomes too rarefied for us to breathe freely; the exertion it demands brings too severe a tension upon our powers, and we sink down exhausted, and glad to return to the ordinary level of thought. It is as if we turned our eyes upon the sun, only to find that though himself "the very source and fount of day," his brightness passes into darkness, and makes us fain to be content with reflections of his glory.

It is easy therefore to understand why men in all ages have worshipped gods made after the likeness of humanity. The tendency to conceive of the Deity as a magnified man cannot be got rid of. Go to the classical mythologies, for instance, and the gods of Olympus are only projections, upon a large canvas, of the figures of their suppliants. Or turn to the Hebrew Scriptures. Jehovah is there represented as the great Potentate, who "sits upon the circle of the earth, and the inhabitants thereof are as grasshoppers." In a special manner, He is the God of Israel. He is swayed by human motives, and acts under the limitations of the national character. Anger and complacency, jealousy and favour, determination and repentance, are ascribed to him on every hand: and grand as is the conception of the Divine Being in the noblest of the ancient books, the basis of the conception is, in the last instance, the character of the pious Israelite. It is the especial glory of Christianity to teach that "God is a Spirit; and they that worship him must worship him in spirit and in truth;" and by that teaching to summon all nations to a common worship and a common faith.

And yet there are many in the Christian church who fail to grasp this, the central truth of Christ's teaching. To think of a person is to them the same as to think of certain lineaments and form: and therefore when they would meditate upon God, the Creator, Ruler, and Sustainer of the universe, they are forced to picture him in human likeness. Seated somewhere in infinite space, enthroned above the worlds, is, they imagine, the Eternal in the infinitely magnified form of man. Without some such concrete foundation, their thought of God could not maintain itself, but would vanish into thin air. And it is not strange, therefore, to find this faith developing in the direction of ritual or dogma. Of the earth, earthy, it cannot possibly lift itself above the range of earthly gravitation.

It seems to us that, in the passage before us, Philip represents this material tendency, and gives expression to the craving for a visible Deity. He had been of our Lord's company from the beginning, of the inner circle of the twelve. He had listened to the public teaching of Christ, and had been privileged to hear his Master's intimate discourse with friends. He had thus continually before him the holy life and character, the infinite power and sympathy, of Christ: and yet after all, he had utterly failed to grasp the spiritual nature of our Saviour's revelation of God. One of the apostles, entering into the scope of his mission, had already confessed him to be "the Christ, the Son of the living God." Yet here we have a brother-disciple, unable even at the end of our Lord's career to follow out the meaning of that confession, unable to rise above the realm of sense, and lift his thoughts into the sphere of spiritual life, and asking, "Shew us the Father, and it sufficeth us."

What was our Saviour's answer? "Jesus saith unto him, Have I been so long time with you, and yet hast thou not known me, Philip? He that hath seen me hath seen the Father; and how sayest thou then, Shew us the Father?" Could speech be more thrilling in its pathos? One can almost see the look turned upon the questioner; one can almost hear the disappointed, reproachful tones of that reply. And surely it was not the least bitter drop in the Saviour's cup, that at the close of his mission, when He felt his hours were numbered, He should know his teaching misunderstood by his most intimate friends. Not yet was He to see of the travail of his soul and be satisfied. He had to meet his doom, bereft even of the sustaining power of sympathy, with the conviction forced upon him, that they to whom He had specially ministered were still clinging to the present, valuing the material above the spiritual, the earthly above the heavenly, the seen above the unseen. If it be lawful to use such language, there is, in these sad reproachful words, a half-consciousness of failure.

Now there is one great lesson to be learnt from the text, viz., that our common human nature is the most perfect revelation of God.

The point of our Lord's answer evidently is that Philip, having had the life of Christ before him, should have been able to recognise in it a manifestation of the Divine. The purity and self-forgetfulness which it displayed were true reflections of the mind of God, and as such they would have appeared to the apostle, had he not been held in the bonds of sense. And thus our Lord has taught us, that what is good and true on earth is good and true in heaven, and that the moral and spiritual perceptions of the human mind are worthy of perfect trust. Justice and mercy and righteousness, as we know them here, are counterparts of justice and mercy and righteousness as they are in God. The Divine goodness differs from what approves itself to us as goodness, not in kind but in degree: "His ways are higher than our ways, and his thoughts than our thoughts." Doubtless it is said that He judges differently from man; but that is because He sees more clearly than we do, because all things are naked and open before him, and not because his justice is essentially different from ours. In short, our Lord has told us that, to the limit of its power, the soul of man is a faithful witness for God; and that the life which is governed by loyalty to truth and righteousness is in reality one with him, the dwelling-place of his Spirit, his continual revelation.

We need not therefore ask where we may find him, or fancy that if we could wing our flight through the infinities of space, we should at length come upon his sanctuary. God's chosen dwelling is the humble contrite spirit: the pure in heart, and they alone, can see him. Let our eyes once be opened, and, like the prophet's servant of old, we shall see that on every side we are surrounded by his presence. There are sanctities of life and duty, of home and affection, of sympathy and helpfulness, of penitence and prayer, which daily speak of him to those who will lend an ear. Let these be neglected or profaned, and we need not wonder if earth loses its consecration and speaks no more of God. Let them be reverenced, and wherever, in the history of mankind or among our fellows, we observe lives moved by high aspiration, cherishing loyalty to duty, and that reverence for goodness and truth, which speaks of the great destiny to be afterwards revealed, we must also acknowledge the revelation of the Most High.

But if in our common nature we get this revelation, it is in Christ himself that we get it in its most perfect form.

The types and metaphors we employ in speaking of the atonement must not be used so as to overshadow or distort the great truth that He came to show us the Father. By giving us this revelation, He became the mediator of a new communion between God and man. In the lives of the sages and prophets of every nation reflections of the Divine nature have been given. Therefore their fellows listened to them, and received a fresh impulse from them. Still, these have been only broken lights, single coloured rays which require to be gathered into one, before we see the pure white light of absolute goodness. Such a focus we have in the life of Christ. And therefore we turn to him, "the brightness of the Father's glory and the express image of his person," to obtain a true idea of what God is, and of what our relation to God ought to be. His holy life leads us into a nobler, tenderer, more humane faith in our heavenly Father, and challenges our reverence and admiration by the inherent power and beauty of goodness. In every department of life, but especially in the sphere of moral and religious truth, it is comparatively easy to apprehend and value, but difficult to originate and plan. In art, in science, in literature, there are thousands who can appreciate the masterpieces of genius, for one who is able to create and execute. This last is the test of the Divine fire. And so in like manner, the purity of Christ appeals to us. We cannot find it in ourselves; but, when it is presented to us, we recognise its claims to our reverent homage and obedience. It speaks to us of higher things, and shows us the possibilities in our nature of approaching God. And then the closer we draw near our Lord, the more does his character open up to our devout contemplation, and his revelation itself expand. We are told that while the planets are revolving round the sun, the sun himself, with his attendant train, is sweeping towards a point in space so remote, that the imagination fails to picture to itself the immensity of the curve. And so too, to the faithful follower of Christ, revelation develops into a nobler range, and teaches him to see the whole universe in ever widening cycles, centering upon God.

Finally, as it is our great privilege to keep the life of Christ before us as the highest revelation of what our heavenly Father is: so, on the other hand, it is our bounden duty to see that our religious conceptions do not run counter to his teaching. It is our bounden duty to cast out of our belief in God every element that could enter into conflict with his blessed life, and to reject any view of the relations between God and man, no matter how strongly upheld, which is at variance with the primary moral instinct of the human soul. If we have been accustomed to approach God with hearts mistrustful of the kindness of his feelings towards us; if our religion has been poisoned by fear, and the wings of our affections clipt by suspicion, and the understanding fettered by unworthy thoughts of his character and will; if, after the dictates of a cruel tradition, we have pictured him as an unjust despot, who brings myriads into being in order to consign them to utter darkness and despair; if this be the idol of our own imagination we have professed to worship, let us go back in all simplicity of heart to the life of Christ, and bring our belief into accordance with what we learn from it. There will be no need then for us to say with Philip, "Lord, shew us the Father, and it sufficeth us." We shall see him in the face of Jesus Christ; and our hearts will respond to the Saviour's answer, "He that hath seen me hath seen the Father."

VII.

CONSERVATION AND CHANGE.

BY THE REV. PROFESSOR KNIGHT, LL.D., ST. ANDREWS.

Far be it, far be it from me, that I should swallow up or destroy. The matter is not so.—2 SAMUEL XX. 20, 21.

Violence shall no more be heard in thy land, wasting nor destruction within thy borders.—ISAIAH LX. 18.

THESE two sentences taken together suggest a few thoughts on tendencies, which are threatening the old order of things, in Church and State alike; and which affect both our secular life, and our religious experience.

The saying of Joab to the wise woman of Abel, "one of the peaceable and faithful in Israel" who asked that captain of the host why he came to destroy a city—"Far be it, far be it from me that I should destroy,"—we may remove from its context, and regard it simply as a resolution not to overthrow anything in itself good. The other sentence from Isaiah refers to a period in the history of the Church when the harsh spirit of destructiveness would give place to the mildness, the moderation, and the sweet reasonableness of the Christian spirit. "Violence shall no more be heard in the land, wasting nor destruction within thy borders;" as a little further on it is said that a creative and constructive tendency would be substituted for the anarchy, the collision, and the dismemberment of the past. " They shall not hurt or destroy in all my holy mountain, saith the Lord."

It is usually rash for any one to say what the chief tendency of his own age is, trying to sum up, in a single proposition, so complex a thing as the spirit of a generation. For it is only at a distance, and in retrospect, that the main tendency of any epoch can be adequately measured; when the results of agencies that once were active are seen in what they have accomplished, or failed to accomplish. On the other hand, it is not difficult to estimate some of the forces that sway contemporary thought, and guide the action of one's own time. Many of these can be most accurately known, and are most easily criticised, just as the events themselves transpire.

We are told by some that we live in an idle empty age, devoid of heroism, an age of weak assents and timid compromises; and there may be some truth in the assertion. But if there is, this is not the chief characteristic of our time. Other influences are at work, both numerous and subtle, tending to break up and to dissolve. Schemes are inaugurated and movements started of which the watchword is destruction, and the successful issue of which would be the disintegration of society. If thought in many quarters is vague, latitudinarian, and indifferent, in others the tone and temper of society is headstrong, moving blindly and turbulently forward, it knows not whither. Everywhere "the old order" is changing, "giving place to the new." While every age is a time of transition, ours seems to be one of rapid movement and continual surprises. No one, who has any capacity for reading the signs of the times, can doubt that the tendency to acquiesce and to make compromise is not more dominant than the counter tendency to protest, to assault, and to revolutionise; and to those who discern this fact, it becomes a question of grave moment what their relation to the changing spirit of their age, and to the alterations that are being wrought upon its current beliefs, should be. Let us see then, whether in this, as in other things, our moderation should not be known unto all men.

The special tendency to which I refer—a tendency swaying certain sections of society, both civil and ecclesiastical—is one which fastens instinctively upon the defects rather than upon the merits of the past, and which would destroy the institutions which we inherit from our forefathers, because they now seem less adequate than once they were, and are somewhat injured by the wear and tear of time. And this is how it shows itself. It spends its strength in assault upon existing evils,—and sometimes in excitement for the redress of imaginary wrongs—rather than in the prudent use of circumstances, making the best of things as they are. It strives to abolish the imperfect by external assault, rather than to reform it from within by a new and higher spirit of endeavour. It is loudly affirmed in certain quarters that compromise of all kinds is an evil, that nonconformity—or the open expression of dissent from your fellow-men, when you chance to differ from them—is one of the first of duties; and that, as every party which happens to have ascendency for a time ought to tolerate a dissentient minority, and not concuss it into acquiescence, the minority should not only claim the right of recognition, but should incessantly and even noisily assert itself, endeavouring by all the means within its reach to become the majority.

That this kind of rivalry, or struggle for existence, has its uses is undoubted; because it stirs up slumbering energy, and prevents the supineness that might otherwise characterise large masses of society. It has always been the bane of conformity that it breeds indolence and acquiescence in things as they are, whatever they are. Narrow men of fervid temperament relish the excitements of controversy, because it supplies them with a stimulus, urging them along the bounded lines of their vocation, while those of broader vision necessarily care less for party organisation and the polemic schemes which agitate the masses of society. But they are singularly apt to misconstrue those movements with which they have no personal sympathy. It is well known that when clear vision is allied to a calm temperament there is a corresponding disinclination to the expression of difference, because of its accompaniments, the disturbance, the strife, and the turmoil of controversy. This, however, may be a sign of indolence, or even of pusillanimity; and if to teach the duty of moderation and conformity were to encourage an unreflective assent to current opinion,—no matter what the opinion might be,—rather than disturb society by debate, the collapse of interest in truth and of an earnest purpose in life would be inevitable.

Now, as in this world "all things are double one against another," it is wise to see the weak side of a principle, even while you are magnifying it, and indicating its strength, its value, and its adequacy. Let it be admitted, therefore, that the evil of compromise is its tendency to induce intellectual lethargy, and a repose that may be cowardly. So much of truth is seen to be associated with error, so much of good to be allied with what is evil, that for the sake of the true and the good, the error and the evil are not only tolerated, but deemed trivial. It is notorious that the practice of assent to traditional opinion has led to a habit of indifference. Even the virtue of catholicity has degenerated to the level of a moral weakness; and it will always do so, if, while the eye is trained to discern the good, the judgment be not simultaneously disciplined to reject the evil and the erroneous. In matters both of opinion and of conduct, it is as though a soft and dreamy haze overspread the landscape, blotting out the lines which mark off one object from another; and however pleasant such a state of weather after the blasts of controversy, and the storms of debate, a very slight experience of it will lead all healthy minds to wish for a return of the east wind, and the sea-breeze, which dispel the mist, and clear the firmament of its obscurities.

But then,—as the Preacher of the Exile reminded his generation—"*to everything there is a season, and a time for every purpose under heaven*; a time to destroy, and a time to build up; a time to rend and a time to sew; a time of war, and a time of peace." It would seem that the fluctuations of the weather, and the cycle of changes that occur in physical nature, are symbolic of similar periodic changes in the intellectual and moral life of men. Thus, a social revolution destroying the complacency of custom, a religious reformation breaking in upon the monotony of tradition, have their uses. They are as valuable as those periods of slow unconscious growth, which tend to mature individual character and to consolidate society. In the region of belief and action, however, we may not accept the changes that occur with the same complacency with which we receive and welcome the changes of the seasons. We are ourselves, in part, the producers of our own varying states; and if we inherit much from the past, we create and transmit as much to the future. We cannot, therefore, simply accept, in passive thankfulness, what the past has bequeathed to us. We must endeavour to refashion as well as to assimilate what it has brought us. And, to do this aright, we must have some knowledge of the temper and spirit of our time. We must understand its drift, whence its currents flow, and whither they are tending, if we are not to be its slaves.

Whatever its tendency, however, every wise man will welcome those changes which are the result of the natural processes of growth,—whether these are swift or slow,—and will resist those which are revolutionary, or rashly destructive of the past. More especially will those *Institutions*, which we have inherited from our forefathers, be reverently preserved and religiously fostered. While our individual opinions are being modified by all the light which an age of critical research is accumulating, we do well to be jealous of assault upon the social organisations which have come down to us from the past. Of these we are as much the guardians as the heirs. It is the merest commonplace to say that our opinions must inevitably change, that we cannot possibly conserve them in the old forms and frameworks of the past, that modification of belief is as certain and as necessary as the slower modification of physical structure, organisation, and life. And every one should be encouraged to subject his opinions to the free air of thought, to revise his convictions continually in the light of progressive evidence, verifying them by more and more adequate tests. That is wise, wholesome, beneficent teaching; because it is not possible for us to store up our convictions, with the view of preserving them, as exotic plants are cherished in a conservatory, by artificial heat. But while it should be the aim of each individual that all his beliefs should be vital—and therefore that, like every living thing, they should change with the life of the time,—when he looks abroad he finds himself in the midst of institutions which are the slow growth of ages. He is surrounded, in State and Church alike, by a vast and complex organisation, built up by long hereditary usage, which has ministered to the wants of many generations, and which still answers to the needs and requirements of to-day. These historic structures are, doubtless, also doomed to change. They must alter by the operation of the very same laws by which they have come to be what they are. They begin to change as soon as they begin to exist, because inherent fixity appertains to nothing on this earth. But because they have grown and consolidated slowly, they have a proportionate claim on the homage of posterity. They should in no case be rashly touched, or rudely dealt with.

Besides, they are full of latent possibilities. There is no fixed period of youth and of age, of rise, decline, and fall, for institutions, as there is for individuals. They, much more than we, may renew their youth in old age. We cannot detect the signs of decay in them, as we detect it in ancient trees or buildings, that have served their time; because there may be in all of them the slumbering powers of life, and adequacy for the new and altered conditions of another age. If they *are* to pass away, they should be allowed to do so by the process of fulfilment and superannuation, not by external assault or undermining. The student of history knows that they will all die soon enough, without our hands helping on the process; and to make it the labour of a life, or of a party, simply to assail institutions, to be iconoclasts by profession, is little better than being incendiaries.

The wise attitude, then, towards any institution which cannot be proved to be doing mischief is to hail the changes that are being effected upon it by the processes of internal growth and development, but not to seek its overthrow. Doubtless, the antagonism to every change, and the frequent blindness of leaders to the signs of their own times—so common in Church and State organisations,—go far to imperil their stability, and to invite the external assaults which attempt to lay them low. It is their want of elasticity and adaptability to new conditions of existence that has led many persons to be indifferent to their fate, and has deepened the currents of national life that flow outside their borders. But if those who assume the office of leadership are wise in their generation, this need never happen. If they open their eyes to the necessity of adjusting the institution to the times—as a living organism adapts itself to a new environment—it will not only survive the change, but will derive new life and inspiration from it. The social edifice, whether civil or ecclesiastical, will renew its youth; and the individual members, realising that they have only a temporary relation to the Structures into which they were born, will strive first to increase their efficiency and then to transmit them to their successors as little injured as possible.

It is a frequently forgotten element in the unity and solidarity of the race, that the present generation is bound to the past and to the future by ties as real and vital as those which connect the different members of the race that are contemporaries now. If, therefore, I may not forget that I am only one out of many, and have no right to carry out my individual liberty to the infringement of the rights of others, neither may we who live now assert ourselves so as to infringe the rights of those who come after us, or demolish institutions to which our successors have as good a title as ourselves. In other words, the unity and solidarity of the race apply, not merely to the whole area of the world now, but also to the whole history of the human family, past, present, and to come. It is comparatively easy for a party or a class to inaugurate the work of demolition, especially if a fanatical spirit is abroad; and under the guise of zeal for the common good, or for the glory of God, the most venerable structures, raised by the wisdom and piety of our forefathers, may be rudely overthrown. A revolution may accomplish in a few days the overthrow of that which it took centuries to bring to perfection; and institutions which have but half subserved their uses may be levelled with the ground, as a tree is smitten by a thunderbolt, or a city demolished by an earthquake. It is far more difficult to build up, to consolidate, and to confirm; because it requires the consent and co-operation of thousands, and the increasing purpose of generations of reverent men. The growth of human institutions is a long and laborious, a slow and silent, and mostly an unconscious process; and because it is so, what the human race thus accomplishes calls for the reverence of posterity and not its scorn; while it demands an earnest effort to preserve, sustain, and transmit it unimpaired.

Nor will it suffice for those who are always telling us that good comes out of evil, to suggest that such disasters as I have indicated only stir up the next generation to fresh creative activity. No doubt, in many instances, it is so. The sense of loss often leads to productiveness, just as necessity is the mother of invention. The destruction of Greek art, for example, and the burning of the great library of the ancient world, may have helped forward the revival of Europe *when it came;* because, while there were fewer precedents to appeal to, there was a greater demand for originality and inventiveness. But what of the long period of stagnation that followed the episodes of destruction and violence? what of the evils that ensued to the generations that were impoverished meanwhile? These disasters to humanity, these wounds to the human race in general, are the missing links in the chain of progress, which are forgotten by the advocates of revolutionary change. It is true that the race may ultimately gain from the destructive frenzy of a few; for such is the sweep of that all-pervading law of action and reaction that we cannot tell how much we are indebted even to the rude iconoclasm of the past for the constructive toil of subsequent generations. Such is the solidarity of the race in the direction indicated, so bound together are the successive generations, as well as all contemporary workers, that we can with difficulty estimate our debt to agencies and institutions wholly unlike those in which we have been nurtured, for the very impulses that are now inspiring us. But by appealing to the results which follow any course of action in the next generation, it is possible to defend almost everything that has happened in history. Every great crime stirs up society, awakens indignation, and leads to much reactionary good. But what of the evil it does in itself, and by contagion, or the force of example? The argument from results is a vain plea in defence of anything that occurs; because we are always liable to deception, both in tracing causes and following consequences; and we can never know that what emerges is not equally the result of other causes, co-operating with that which is most obvious, and on which the eye of the observer may be turned.

Besides, we have manifestly no right, from our detection of blemishes in an institution, which it requires no great acumen to perceive, to take part in its demolition. It is the easiest thing in the world to discover flaws, whether they be motes in your neighbour's eye, or beams in a sister Church, or tendencies that are unlovely and arrogant, or blind and headstrong, in the tone and temper of society. But if to detect these things is easy, and to rail at them does no good, to seek to destroy the institutions in which they exist, because we have been sharp-witted enough to see the evils that cling to them, is essentially fanatical. What institution could be put in the place of existing ones, that would be free from defect? It is sometimes in the interest of a fancied movement of reconstruction that the work of demolition is advocated. The overthrow is meant to be a process preliminary to upbuilding. But it is as impossible for us to devise a social structure that shall be free from blemish, as it is to construct a creed with the stamp of finality upon it. That which to our theoretic wisdom might seem superior, were its merits tested by practical existence, would soon be seen to be as faulty as its predecessor, many hidden evils being developed by experience.

In addition to this, it may be increasingly difficult to found new institutions, as society advances. Individualism seems more and more dominant, as time goes on; and if the corporate life of the nation—as embodied, for example, in the Churches of the State—gives way before this individualistic movement, it is difficult to see what can take its place, that will be half so salutary or half so enduring. What hope is there that any new organisation would be better than the old? that it would be worthier to live, or longer lived? Might not the destruction of the old hasten on the disintegration of the new? Our duty therefore seems to be, to let the institutions, in the midst of which we live, survive, so long as there is life in them, not only unassailed by us, but fostered and upheld. As already said, they cannot survive for ever; and they will all pass away soon enough. But our main business is to conserve and upbuild, in order that we may accomplish something positive; and what we thus conserve will, if it be genuine, take a silent and unconscious part in the demolition of that which ought not to live.

Then, should not mere modesty and diffidence, due to the fact that much error and illusion are inevitably mixed up with the convictions we entertain, lead to the same practical result? Let us see how this will operate. I suppose we are not wrong in saying that every one should see clearly and know accurately the character of things round him—what they are, and how they have come to be what they are—before he can know what his duty concerning them is. There should therefore be no toleration of opinions which cannot stand the day-light of evidence and the siftings of experience. The freer our thought can be the better, if its fetters are only custom, convention, and tradition. It should be the aim of every one to penetrate from the seeming to the real, and to be freed from illusions of every kind. But then, as it is certain that we all carry about manifold illusions mixed up with the truth we may happen to have reached, and also that we shall retain some of them to the end of life, *taking them for the truth*, the knowledge of that fact should make us extremely cautious in carrying out our convictions, if their practical issues are in any sense iconoclastic. It is as impossible for us to be entirely free from prejudice, as it is to be wholly free from the germs of physical disease. Add to this, that the deepest or most thorough knowledge we ever attain to—on practical as well as on theoretic subjects—is knowledge not of the whole, but only of a part of the question with which we deal. These two facts taken together should induce caution, and never permit us to be hurried into condemning an institution, if there are the signs of active life within it. In an age in which rapidity of change and transition are such marked features, an age in which it is the unexpected that happens, all neutrality of mind, irresolution, and indifference are to be condemned. But, on the other hand, intellectual indecision and tampering with conviction are not the only evils with which we are threatened, nor are their opposites the main virtues in an era of swift transition. When everything is being shaken that can be shaken, it is surely as much the duty of sensible men to hold fast by what has stood the strain of time and the shocks of controversy, as it is to be ready to abandon that which is palpably demonstrated to be worthless.

The open avowal of opinion, its emphatic declaration if intelligently held, is always welcome; but if its issues are in the main destructive, it should be advanced with reserve. It is true that we must speak the truth and do the right "though the heavens should fall." But then, if we speak the truth and do the right, no such catastrophe will follow, either really or metaphorically. It is true that we must change and progress if we are to continue to live, but we cannot move forward wisely, if we have no fixed relation both to the past and to the present.

Whatever our way of dealing with the great problems of human thought, the right relation to the great social and religious organisations of the world is obvious. There are those who place the very existence of a State Church amongst the agencies "that weaken the vigour of a national conscience, and check the free play and access of intellectual light." Surely, however, they fail to see the conserving and protective power of historic institutions. A National Church ought to be a reflection of the national character, and an organic growth springing out of that character. It ought, therefore, to tolerate within it many diverse types of thought and of practice, and to rejoice in each as a separate phase of that manifoldness, in the unity of which lies the strength of the national character. National Churches have not always done so to an adequate extent. But they have at least done so more adequately than others have done it. It is outside the State Churches, amid the rival jealousies of dissent, that aberrations of dogma and ritual are likely to be greatest, where they have no check from the national conscience, organised in the Church of the State. It is when bodies of men who might have remained within the national enclosure, are either driven out (from some peculiarity of belief or practice) or voluntarily go forth, and separate themselves, forming a new sect or taking independent root, that they, or their successors, are most likely to develop extremes of opinion and of practice.

Then, supposing our existing National Churches to be

broken up, the result would be neither the abolition of extremes of opinion, nor the unification of religious practice, but the intensification of sect life, alienation, and jealousy. And why? how may we with confidence predict such a result? Because the causes which have led to the development of diverse types of thought and of practice within the Church are permanent ones. *They* will survive, and create new types in the future; and each going on in its own way, may give rise to extremes,—if not more extravagant certainly more unsympathetic,—when they are released from the restraints they now experience. They are now controlled, both by the conscious and the unconscious influence of the presence of their opposites. It is not the variety within the Church that is to be condemned, for the more variety the greater the life; it is the want of toleration, of mutual sympathy, forbearance, and appreciation.

But, lest it be thought that in condemning the spirit that assails institutions, and in magnifying its opposite, there is any depreciation of the aims of our liberal teachers to find out what is true, and to proclaim it, though institutions should fall and crumble around them, I would repeat: Let criticism disclose to us more and more the origin of old beliefs, and explain the sources of illusion; let the laws of the universe and the causes of the rise and fall of systems of opinion be disclosed; let the habit of correctly weighing evidence, and correctly using words, be taught increasingly; let all error be tracked out and exposed remorselessly. These things never interfere with what is worthy of life, for it is thus that the leaven of the new ideas is instilled, to work silently in the body corporate, and to mould the thought of the world. But let no revolutionary hand be raised to destroy what has come down to us from the past, to remove the ancient landmarks of a nation's faith and piety, lest in rooting up the tares which unquestionably exist, we root up the wheat along with them. Change of opinion may be salutary and necessary. It may be the sign of life, and its very extent an index and a measure of life. But surely it is possible for our institutions to live, while our opinions change; for our social organisations to survive, while our former convictions are outgrown. Our institutions are deeper than our opinions, just as the race is wider than the individual.

Can we suppose that any future age of enlightenment will be able to dispense with the past, or discard the results of its accumulated experience? Have our fathers lived in vain, thought in vain, or built up the great structures of the past in vain, for their children's children? If the advance of knowledge and the widening of experience enable us to see that much in which they trusted is illusory, we cannot dispense with the experience we inherit, from that which the race collectively has outgrown. The child is father of the man, and the youth of the world is creative of its age. As we have still to deal with the same problems with which our predecessors wrestled, we may, on many points, come back to the conclusions of the past, after having moved from them for a time; and, on many others, we may discover that the new opinion is but the old one transmuted, reset in a fresh form, and clothed in the vesture or fashion of the day. When we have outgrown the ideas of late years, do we never return to the still earlier conclusions of our youth? or discover a hitherto unsuspected meaning in what was taught as the first lessons of infant piety?

Apply this subject, first, in our estimate of party and party movements; and secondly, in the formation of personal habits of modesty, reverence, and humility.

If you would find out the animating spirit of any party in Church or State, mark its attitude toward the past. Is it reverential? Is it docile? Is it conciliatory? Does it strive to base its forward movements upon the wisdom and experience of the past? Is it moving on the path of reform, with its face turned courageously to the future, ready to advance, but with its hand still clinging to the past? Then it is worthy of your esteem. On the contrary, is it noisy, arrogant, self-complaisant? blind to the wisdom and indifferent to the merits of the past; blustering in its assumptions, and confident of its superiority? Then it has deprived itself of any title to your esteem, by whatever name it may be known, and on whatever side of the conventional party-line it may happen to be standing. If a party, whether in Church or State, is full of the new wine, of revolutionary projects, it is self-condemned. If it is ambitious to progress, but to progress on the lines of the past, at once wisely liberal and wisely conservative,— and in no sense neutral because it shuns the falsehood of extremes,—then it is self-approved and self-attesting. It will be found that every institution shares the fate of the individual leader, and when its novelty is past, and its inevitable defects are seen, agitators arise who clamour for its removal. Others who see beyond the leader, to the Organisation which he leads, will seek to reform it from within, and to preserve its life by interior expansion and renovation.

Then as to individual character and habit. Have you got hold of a new truth? Hold it modestly, though firmly and with decision. Do not noisily proclaim it from the house-top. Let it silently ally itself with the truths you learned yesterday, and with those which you may live to learn to-morrow; and if they all grow up together, each will become more mellow and matured. When you learn any new truth, it is not intended that it should at once dethrone its predecessors. However true it is, it ought never to destroy the truths amongst which it comes, which have been there before it, and in the light of which you have hitherto lived. Above all, it should never be allowed to become a party watch-cry, or the badge of a narrow-minded activity. Now one of the chief merits of the conservative spirit, which scruples to assail what has come down to us with the seal and attestation of the past, is that it tends to habits of reverence, humility, and a wise discernment of the less obvious aspects of human duty, both towards institutions and individuals. I do not know how we are to attain to that delicacy of soul, which the old religious writers called "a tender conscience," but by habits of reverence, scrupulosity, and veneration for all that reaches us from the past, as well as for the fresh revelations of the day. True reverence for the past, for the voice of the Eternal, speaking in past institutions, events, "dispensations," will lead to a deeper reverence for the living Oracles of the present hour.

Reverence for the past, for all that has hitherto revealed the Divine character and ways, will develop in us that penetration of mind and alertness of soul that are quick to respond to the everlasting Voice, even in its faintest modern echo. Now to him, of whom, through whom, and to whom are all things, be glory, as it was in the beginning, is now, and ever shall be, world without end! Amen.

VIII.

THE CONTINUITY AND DEVELOPMENT OF RELIGION.

BY THE REV. PROFESSOR KNIGHT, LL.D., ST. ANDREWS.

They shall perish, but thou shalt endure ; yea, all of them shall wax old like a garment : as a vesture shalt thou change them, and they shall be changed : but thou art the same, and thy years shall have no end.—Ps. cii. 26, 27.

IT is singular how often we hear that the age in which we live is one of transition, and that we are passing through a *crisis* in religious belief. Doubtless "the old order" has changed, "giving place to new;" and it is altering, perhaps, more rapidly than at any former period. No opinion now passes unchallenged, because of its antiquity; no tradition is accepted, on the ground of authority; and, under the searching light of criticism, every belief is forced to show its credentials. There is, in consequence, a widespread feeling of unsettlement, as if the mental atmosphere were charged with electricity; and many are afraid lest the result should prove disastrous to religion. It is natural that when the fire is testing everything, we should endeavour to find out what is, and what is not, combustible; and only the ignorant or the callous will neglect to ask whether any of their convictions are of "the asbestos type."

But is this feature of the day a novel one? Is it original, or exclusively modern? It may be a mere illusion of our restlessness, that the characteristics of our age are in any sense exceptional; as if former times were not also transitional, or as if what we call the "crises" of history were not incessant. Every one knows that many things are real which are not realised by us when they occur; and to one who is even moderately acquainted with the history of opinion it may excite a feeling of surprise to be told that the men of to-day are exceptionally situated, or that in all the turmoil through which we are passing anything very extraordinary has happened. The opinions which men form and express as to the tendencies of their own time are indeed curiously inconsistent and conflicting. Each one's estimate, being a reflection more or less of his own temperament, is to that extent a biassed judgment. Some will tell you, for example, that the times are pre-eminently scientific; and that, while the sleep of tradition is past, all the knowledge and faith of the future must be critically readjusted from its base. Others assure us that we live in very degenerate days, in an age unearnest and unideal, given over for the most part to the worship of comfort and material prosperity. Thus, while many depreciate the present—contrasting it with the imaginary glories of the past—others exaggerate its significance, and magnify its crisis. It may be however that, a century hence, a halo will surround this age of ours, similar to that which now lights up the centuries that are gone;

while the supposed crisis we are passing through will seem a singularly small affair in the light of its sequel.

Be this as it may, it is altogether misleading to suppose that Religion is endangered in the nineteenth century any more than it was in the first. Religion lives now, just as it has always lived. Freed from the accessories, which have been so often mistaken for its essence, it is as true now as ever it was. If there be any analogy between the individual and the race, the religion of the world has now reached comparative maturity, and is necessarily stronger than it was in infancy, or during the period of its youth. Its historic origin may be undiscoverable in the past, but we find no period in which it has been absent; and during every century that has elapsed, it has struck its root deeper in the soil of human nature, while it has proved itself to be indigenous to every land. Its history is the history of progressive development, and of continuously unfolding life. Though now assailed in many ways—as it has always been—its most formidable foe is by no means a modern assailant. It is neither an antagonistic system, nor an opposing hierarchy. It is not even the tradition that has overlaid it, nor the "enemy in the household" that has so often destroyed its unity, in the strife of party spirit, or the clash of rival doctrines. It is a far subtler antagonist—one that is neither ancient nor modern, but a tendency permanently present behind the world's religion—associated with all its forms, and working underneath its symbols. This, which I call its most formidable foe, is now spoken of as Agnosticism. From it, religion has more to fear than from any form of explicit Atheism; because it refrains from direct attack—affirming that all the doctrines of religion belong to the sphere of the unknowable. Our modern agnosticism, however, contains nothing that is new, except the name; and the one great Dogma which it controverts contains nothing that is superannuated. A panic-stricken age is apt to forget that Criticism has always existed side by side with the Religion which it has endeavoured to test, and which it has perhaps protected as much as it has assailed. It is constantly forgotten that our predecessors felt the limits of the knowable, quite as truly as we do; and that the same intellectual puzzles, the same moral difficulties with which we are familiar, pressed upon the general mind of the race two thousand years ago, without extinguishing its reverence or destroying the worship of the Invisible. Neither our faith nor our doubt are things of yesterday. In every age religion has found a home in human consciousness, and in the face of all denial it has won for itself a sanctuary in human life. In every age also criticism has demolished some of the frameworks built around religion, which their authors fancied were part of its essence. But the breaking up of these frameworks has never injured the soul or spirit of devotion. On the contrary, it has set it free, giving it opportunity for new departures, to prove its immortality by development in fresh directions. Religious intuition never dies. Its activity is spontaneous and unceasing: while the labour of the understanding, working along with the spiritual instincts, invariably builds up some fresh scaffolding of dogma, which posterity destroys.

Two things, however, seem to excite periodic apprehension, and to suggest from time to time the instability of religion. The one is the possibility of explaining its origin by tracing its development, and detecting its presence even in the most rudimentary ideas and practices of the world. The other is the obscurity and ultimate mystery of the central dogma, on which religion rests. We shall look at these two things in succession.

As to the first, I have said that modern criticism does not assail religious belief. It only endeavours to explain it, by tracing its ancestry, and showing us the root whence it has sprung; by pointing out "the rock out of which it has been hewn," and "the pit whence it has been digged." But this explanation of origin is supposed to discredit the originality of what has thus been evolved; reducing it from a position of supremacy to that of one amongst a host of competitors, which have wrestled together for ages, and which still struggle for the homage of mankind. The truth or the falsehood of any particular opinion, however, is not dependent on the way in which it has come to light, or the stages of development through which it has passed, or on the precise point which at length it may have reached. It may have attained its present form by a process of very gradual growth, or by a rapid and apparently sudden disclosure. In both cases it may have equal evidence in its favour; and a doctrine may be proved to be true, either by an immediate demonstration of the reason, or by the continuous assent of the ages. It may have the evidence of a first principle, or it may be guaranteed by experience, *i.e.* by the constancy with which the instincts of mankind return to it, and the tenacity with which they cling to it.

It does not therefore follow that, if we can explain the origin of a particular belief, by tracing its parentage and finding that it has sprung from inferior elements, the validity of the belief itself is in the slightest degree imperilled. Nay, it is indisputable that if the human mind has grown at all, its religious convictions —like everything else belonging to it—must have changed. Our remote ancestors could not possibly have had the same religion as ourselves, any more than they could have had the same physiognomy, the same social customs, or the same language. Thus, the intuitions of subsequent ages must necessarily have become keener and clearer—at once more rational and more spiritual—than the instincts of primeval days; the clearness, the intelligence, and the spirituality being due to a vast number of conspiring causes. And, if the opinions and the practices of the race thus change, the change is due to no accident or caprice, but to the orderly processes of natural law. It cannot be otherwise; because, since no human belief springs up miraculously, none can be retained in the form in which it arises for any length of time. Thus, the "increasing purpose" of the ages must inevitably bring to the front fresh modifications of belief. If our theologies have all grown out of something very different, why should we fear their continued growth? Why should any rational theist dread the future expansion of theistic belief? If it has grown, it must continue to grow; and many of its existing phases must disappear. The controversies of our time are the phases of its evolution. But is it now so very perfect, that we would wish it to remain stationary at its present point of development? that its present phases should be permanent? May we not rather rejoice that "these all shall wax old as a garment," and that "as a vesture they shall be changed;" while the Object—of which they are the interpretation, or which they try to represent—endures, and of its immortality there shall be no end? It may even be affirmed that one of the best features in every human belief is its elasticity, that one sign of its vitality is its amenability to change. Were it irrevocably fixed it would have some secret affinity with death and the grave. Paradoxical therefore as it may seem, if religion be amongst the things that cannot be shaken, it must change. Its forms must die that its spirit may live; and the condition of the permanence of the latter is the perpetual vicissitude of the former. Curious it is, that some of its most ardent advocates cannot recognise it under a new dress, that even its disciples misconstrue it when it changes its raiment. They think it a foe if it is differently apparelled. But how often, in all human controversy, the combatants are merely speaking different dialects, while they mean the same thing. How often they are essentially at one, if only they knew it!

But granting that the opinion of the world is an organic whole, that all human conviction—with its present variety and complexity—has grown out of very lowly roots, and that our most sacred beliefs have emerged from others that are different, a further and a far more important question lies behind this admission. It is this: How are we to interpret the whole series from beginning to end? It is not enough to say that there has been progress; what meaning are we to attach to the term progress? Are we to think of it as simple succession and accumulation, the mere addition of new links to a chain of development? We know that men "rise on stepping-stones of their dead selves to higher things," and that the "individual withers, while the race is more and more;" but do the individuals and their beliefs only resemble beads which have been strung on a thread of endlessly developing succession? What has the race been *doing* during all this onward process of development? and has it at every stage been the victim of continuous illusion? Or, has it all the while been in closest contact with Reality, a reality which it partially understands, and interprets to good purpose? In other words, is the history of religious ideas merely the record of attempts made by men to project their own image outwards, to throw their thought around an impalpable object, which it has never yet been able to grasp? or, is it the story of successive efforts, more and more successful, to explain a Reality which transcends it, but to which it stands in a definite and ascertainable relation? Do the gropings of experience in the matters of religion record a long and weary search, with no discovery rewarding it? or are they the efforts of human apprehension to realise the divine, to get at the "last clear elements of things," with disclosure at every stage, and a steady approach to the goal which is continually sought and approximately reached? I think it is past controversy that if the religious education of the human race has been a purely subjective process, if it has been merely an upward tendency of aspiration, it is now no nearer its goal than ever it was. If we can only approach the Infinite by the journeyings of finite thought, or through sighs and cries of aspiration, the journey that way is endless, and the end is nowhere visible. But may we not find the object everywhere? may not the discovery have been as continuous as the search? and the two be simultaneous now? I think we may affirm that the human race has lived in the light of a never-ceasing apocalypse, growing clearer through the ages, but never absent from the world since the first age began.

And may we not also affirm as equally indisputable that it cannot now get quit of its belief in the Divine? that this conviction is a permanent element in its consciousness, I mean in the organic consciousness of the world? It has always been easy to controvert the statement that theism is, in one form or another, native to the human mind, that we cannot divest ourselves of it. Facts are quoted against us. An array of statistics is produced to show many blank spaces in the religious annals of the race, long periods in which the belief has been absent, and entire races in which it is now inoperative. But, if our former contention has any force, that the belief itself has passed through a vast number of phases, its absence may be merely apparent. If the laws of hereditary descent apply to religion as well as to language, to theological belief as well as to natural character and temperament, the continuity may be real while the genealogy is hidden. The assertion that theistic belief is innate is often travestied into the statement that the human mind cannot rid itself of some special theological doctrine, or theory of the divine nature. But the assertion is a very different and a much deeper one. It is that the intuition which gives rise to these doctrines remains, and that when our superstructures of theory are overthrown, a surviving instinct builds them up again, or replaces them by others that are better.

We must vindicate this assertion by explaining it a little further. The word *religion* has undergone many remarkable changes, alternately widening and contracting in popular use and wont; now involving less, and again including more, as the religious instincts themselves have narrowed or enlarged. Thus, the definitions of religion have been very various; and they may all contain some element of truth, while none are exhaustive. Probably we expect too much from definitions. It may be impossible to express the essence of religion either in a proposition, or through a symbol or a ceremony. It may be too ethereal for analysis, too delicate for our intellectual balances; but if it escapes our frames of theory, and defies all logical manipulation, that will be no proof of its inferiority, but rather a sign of its divineness.

Recall then some of the definitions of Religion offered for our acceptance. Suppose we say, with one, that it takes its rise in the sense of Dependence; or, with another, that it springs out of the consciousness of inward Freedom; with a third, that it is the apprehension of Power beyond the individual,—suggested by the phenomena which control or the forces which subdue him; with a fourth, that it is the apprehension of the Infinite, encircling the finite, yet revealed within it; or, with a fifth, that it is Morality sublimated, touched with emotion; with another, that it is that rational Insight which discerns the underlying essence and the fundamental unity of things, bringing man into harmony with himself and with the universe; with a seventh, that it is the pursuit of the Ideal, "the strong and earnest direction of the emotions towards an ideal object recognised as of the highest excellence, and rightfully paramount over all selfish objects of desire;" or, with yet another, that it is homage offered at the shrine of humanity, but directed to that other self, higher and wider than our individual selves, that divine Humanity, that human Divinity, in which we live and move and have our being. All these attempts to define its essence, and to express it in a theory, may be helpful to us more or less. They may be useful and fruitful in many ways. Religious thought and life have together assumed so many forms, that we cannot wonder at the variety of the definitions given.

But is it possible to find anything common, in all the religions of the world, which is a specific element in each of them, or a feature underlying them all? I think it is; although, in every instance, it may present a twofold aspect. As on the one hand a faculty or tendency of the human soul, and on the other the recognition of an object, it has always two sides, an inner and an outer. Call the former a faculty, or a capacity, or a tendency, it matters not. It is, in any case, a real element in human consciousness, a permanent power of apprehension, half intellectual and half emotive. But it is not enough merely to discover and to vindicate its existence as an inward tendency of the human soul. Every such tendency has an objective side that is quite as significant as the subjective. If it is a power of apprehension we must ascertain what it apprehends. In all cases this is an Object, external to the individual, definitely related to him; and, although very variously construed, it is recognised —both in the elementary and in the more advanced stages of religion—as having elements of kindredness with his own nature. Even in its subjective side, religion is not the mere opening of the flood-gates of emotion towards the unknown and the unknowable,— emotion awakened by the simple sense of mystery. It is also the intellectual recognition and the moral discernment of an Object. No theory of religion, which omits this fact, is complete or satisfactory. It meets us at every stage in the path of development. The records of religious history invariably disclose some effort of the human mind to penetrate further into the mystery of things, both by thought and by feeling, to rise higher in the apprehension of the Infinite, to descend deeper towards the eternal ground of things, —in other words, not only to feel the overshadowing mystery, but also to perceive the light that is within it. But, always associated with the effort to apprehend this object, there is a corresponding disclosure of the object itself. Divine revelation is accomplished simply by a removal of the things which had previously obscured the object it reveals. It does not bring the latter any nearer to us. It merely draws aside the veil, which had prevented the human eye from seeing it; enabling us to perceive what had been always present, but not always recognised. Thus, in all religion, there is first a subjective state of human thought and feeling; next, the recognition of an external object; and lastly, the discernment of that object in the act of revealing itself.

Try now to go back, imaginatively and sympathetically, to the rudest primitive age; think, for example, of our forefathers, in the grey morning of the world's religion, engaged at their tree and serpent worship. They heard the wind moaning mysteriously in the forest, while they saw the tree arise mysteriously from the ground. They observed its life come forth in the summer and retire in winter. They saw the serpent crawling mysteriously on the ground, by a power they could not understand; and in both cases were they awed in the presence of the mystery. What was exceptional and unintelligible excited wonder, and led to acts of homage. And, although the race has long outgrown the habit, the savage who first called upon his fellows to worship the tree,—as a symbol of the mystery of growth,—was really a prophet of religious ideas; quite as truly as, though much less articulately than, the founders of maturer faiths. If you consider the blank animal life out of which the former arose, in the long process of development, you will see how great was the advance which such a primitive worshipper made.

The sense of mystery in individual objects, such as

the tree or serpent, yielded by degrees to the wider and grander feeling of a mystery in Nature, as a whole: and the highest religion ends, not in an exhaustive explanation of things, but in a partial uplifting of the veil which only serves to disclose the wide horizon of the unknown. Pass over intermediate phases, and come down to its later developments. Our conviction of the Divine Fatherhood, for example, is immeasurably higher than that of the primitive savage, because we find a far loftier idea lodged within that symbol than any to which the savage mind attained. But our symbol does not exhaust the thing it symbolises. No analogy, figure, or metaphor casts more than a dubious light on the object which it represents. A symbol is in fact merely a ladder, by which we ascend from the ground of the material, but which we must in every instance cast aside when we pass to the sphere of the ideal and the spiritual. Thus, while there has been a gradual uprise of human apprehension in matters of religion, the mysteriousness of the Object apprehended has always made our explanations partial, and our definitions incomplete. Our present modes of thought regarding it are not ultimate. They will not suffice for our descendants, who may leave many of our symbols behind them, as we have abandoned those of a primitive and pre-historic past. But *religion itself* will not be left behind. Religion itself is deathless, because it is the outcome of a permanent tendency, and the satisfaction of an ineradicable want of human nature. It is indestructible, because it is the embodiment of a spiritual instinct, which survives in the general heart of the race; and which, if it ever seems to die, is immediately raised again from the dead, and lives on through a thousand changes.

If humanity stands in living relation to a Revealer, who is omnipresent and always communicative, the Christian revelation,—in the light of which we are now living,—is but the continuation and development of that which primitive worshippers enjoyed, in humbler manner and in lower form. Neither they nor we "can by searching find out God," or understand the Eternal as He is. We all have seen, through a glass darkly, the glory of the Infinite; but, between our purely animal ancestors, and the savage who was first subdued by the glory of the sky and the mystery of life, there was an interval as great as that which separates the latter from ourselves. In the whole process there has been revelation, the unveiling of secret things to hearts that were open and recipient. In all, there has been inspiration, at sundry times and in diverse manners, continuous, incessant, universal. All the stages of religious history have been graduated, —all are continuous; and if to the eye of omniscience there is as much meaning in the seed as in the flower, there was a spiritual significance in the earliest gropings of the world's remotest childhood, as well as in those of the maturest worshippers of Christendom. Do we not see as much in the lispings of our children, and watch their infantile apprehensions with as keen an interest as we take in the judgments of full-grown men? And can we suppose that the common Father of us all was less interested in the guesses of our remote barbaric ancestors than He is in ours? May we not rather say historically, that out of the mouth of the babes and sucklings of the world's religion He has perfected praise?

If our belief in the continuity of religion were more vivid, it would allay much of the panic and religious distraction that prevail. To a great extent this is due to our making religion too complex and artificial. If its essential simplicity were realised, its perpetuity would be apparent. We need to get quit of the illusion of seeking the living amongst the dead, of mistaking words for things. We need to get to the solid ground of reality, and then to lift our eyes to the eternal background that enfolds it, and the Supernatural will be discerned by us, as within the natural everywhere; not as an occasional force, sent down irregularly into the rents or fissures of nature, but as the inmost life of whatsoever is, or was, or yet shall be.

Whatever of its ancient strongholds religion may be compelled to surrender before the advance of criticism, this it will never give up; but, standing upon it, will compel the homage of the future. We may have to surrender the notion of creation out of nothing, the notion of creatures leaping on the stage of being, full formed, unevolved. We may have to abandon the idea of Divine energy slumbering for an infinity of ages, then becoming suddenly and stupendously active, again taking rest, and again awakening by fits and starts to action. We may find it derogatory to the notion of Deity to imagine that, as one asleep, He started up after an eternity of silence to work and sleep again. We may have to renounce the notion of a worker overcoming difficulties, devising and designing things after a human pattern, as one unworthy of the Infinite and the Omniscient. All our symbolic thoughts and word-pictures will more and more be seen to be inadequate, because, the moment the mind attempts to think of them as adequate, they vanish from its grasp. But no illusion of tradition will ever disenchant the mind of the belief that the Infinite is for ever revealing himself, that " God's great completeness flows around our incompleteness, round our restlessness his rest;" that God is within us as well as without, the soul of our souls, the life of our lives, the substantial Self that underlies the surface evanescent self. And it is one glory of the Christian religion that it has developed a new conviction of the nearness of God to man, their kindredness, their reciprocity, their relations of intimacy and fellowship. It has given rise to emotions more tender, intense, and reverential than were ever felt before, by its twin doctrines of the knowableness and the unknowableness of God; or, as I have already said, by its recognition of abiding mystery, and of the light that is within the mystery. God recognised as the interior essence of all things, the substance of all reality, revealing himself through all phenomena which are "the garment we see him by." If the finite for ever reveals the Infinite, the universe may from everlasting have lived and moved and had its being in God; and our humanity,—poor as we all feel it to be,—is not cut off from the Universal Life, by reason of our individuality and separateness from other things. Personality is not a fence dividing us from that Life, but only a fence which separates us from one another. Nay, at the core of our being we do not, and cannot, feel separated from one another, because we are one in relation to that Life. It is only on the surface that we are apart: in the deepest depths we are one.

So far, we have considered the first of the two causes, which excite periodic apprehension, and seem—but only seem—to threaten the stability of religion.

The second, which remains, may be dealt with more briefly. It is the obscurity and ultimate mystery on which the one great dogma of religion rests. That it should be difficult to prove the most radical truth pertaining to religion is perplexing enough. If the Divine Existence be the supreme reality within the universe, how, it is asked, should the human mind ever miss its evidence, or fail to realise it? Why is the stupendous fact not flashed in upon the soul on every side, with indubitable force, so as to produce an overmastering conviction? Should not the greatest truth be the most steadily luminous and self-attesting? equal in its obviousness, at least to the phenomena of nature, or the laws of mathematics? Why, in other words, it may be asked, should clouds and darkness surround a Nature that is, in its inmost essence, light?

In answer, this last peculiarity may be sometimes due to a defect in the eye of the beholder. God may be light, and in him may be no darkness at all, but the light may shine in the darkness of our natures, while "the darkness comprehends it not." An explanation may be found in the characteristics of our own optic nerve,—just as many of us are morally colour-blind. Again, the atmosphere which surrounds us may be so dull and cloudy that the light cannot penetrate it. Both our moral and our social state at times project a shadow far beyond themselves. But there may be other reasons additional to these, springing out of the very nature of the case, and the course of education we are passing through. If we lived in the cloudless light, the conditions of moral discipline would be very different from what they now are. If all religious truths were as obvious as those of science, there would be no room for spiritual trust; and our moral life would become a process of mechanical development. If the "doubt, hesitation, and pain," to which our best achievements are due, disappeared, the achievements themselves might cease to be. Nay, if we lived in the light, alone and always, we might see the Divine object, without perceiving it: we might hear its voice, without recognising it. But with light and darkness intermingled and successive, with glimpses of the object seen through the openings of the cloud which close again and conceal it, we are in a region of experience, in which the discipline of trust is rendered possible; and the ventures of faith are realised. Thus, what we sometimes think an obstacle to faith may be an aid to our vision of Reality. And if it be so, all the variety in our interpretation of that Reality—the different conclusions of our different theologies—may be merely due to the particular angle at which the light reaches the eye of the beholder, to the point at which the cloud has broken, and the way in which it has disclosed the Object behind it.

With this conceded, we may be in a position to see how the theistic solution helps us, in the presence of the mystery which remains, after all our solutions have been given. That the theistic explanation of the world is bordered round about with difficulty is admitted by every one, who has thought to any purpose on the question. But then, all our knowledge—even the most luminous portion of it—recedes, at the last, into the unknowable; and no conceivable revelation, in this or any other condition of existence, reaching us from any imaginable quarter, could enable us to understand "all mysteries and all knowledge." Under its most ample disclosures, we should but stand as now, on a little sunlit promontory, with the immeasurable ocean before us, and the horizon of our knowledge would still be girdled by a line of mystery. But then, the theistic doctrine does not leave us baffled before the enigmas which it recognises. We are neither intellectually prostrate nor morally helpless before them, because it supplies us with a key, which partially unlocks the mystery. It gives us at least a definite, coherent, and rational explanation of things; while it leaves a score of puzzles unexplained. If it lightens "the burden of the mystery"—which still remains to elevate the worship it evokes,—that surely is much. If it keeps our puzzles in the background of intellectual experience, and does not suffer them to obtrude upon the forefront of the moral life, that surely is more. If it turns the unceasing sense of mystery into a solemn discipline in reverence, that assuredly is most of all, to us who see everything through a glass darkly. If the darkness which may be felt moderates our confidence, and checks dogmatic arrogance, the light that is associated with it elicits our enthusiasm, and inspires us with new hope. It forbids despondency. It rouses us from listlessness to earnest life and trustful endeavour. We have at least *some* light to guide us; and, while we wish we had more of it, we are grateful for what we have. Thus, walking in the light, to the upright it ariseth, " shining more and more unto the perfect day."

IX.

THE LAW OF MORAL CONTINUITY.

BY THE REV. WILLIAM MACKINTOSH, D.D., BUCHANAN.

Whatsoever a man soweth, that shall he also reap.—GAL. VI. 7.

In the sphere of practical religion, there is no more far-reaching nor more controlling principle than that here laid down by St. Paul. Like most other great principles, it admits of being placed in many lights, and expressed in many forms. Popularly, it is spoken of as the doctrine of the spiritual harvest; in ethical science as that of the continuity of the moral life. It is the doctrine that every action, good or bad, confirms and perpetuates the disposition from which it springs: that the life hereafter will correspond to the life here: that the reward or punishment, which comes home to us inevitably, instead of being fixed by arbitrary decree, is but the natural consequence of our well or ill doing; and that our future grows out of our present, just as a plant out of the seed, while our present is but the fruit or summation of all our past life.

In speaking of the continuity of the individual life, it is not necessary to take into account the cognate fact, that the life of the individual is more or less influenced by the lives of past generations, and is indeed, to a great extent, their product. That involvement of the spirit in the flesh, and that bias towards egotism—the sources of evil,—which mark the starting-point of the moral development of the individual, and which, on psychological, altogether apart from dogmatic grounds, we take to be a phenomenon of the child's life, are no doubt largely modified from that source; but the *developed* form of evil in the parents does not reappear in the child. Its moral life is not a continuation of theirs, and does not begin where theirs left off; but takes a fresh start, a new departure for itself. At the most, the ancestral evil only appears in germ in the child, and gives concreteness to the otherwise abstract point from which the development of the individual life would take its departure. It seems to us, therefore, that the influence of ancestral good or evil does not import any additional complexity into this subject, and may be left by us out of sight.

The doctrine of the text throws light upon the nature of human responsibility, as well as upon the mode of Divine judgment. A man may be said to bear his own burden, and to be responsible for himself, just because he reaps what he has sown; and God may be said to execute judgment by the natural operation of this same law of reaping and sowing. It is not by connecting physical and social evil with that which is moral, that God can be said to decree righteous judgment, inasmuch as there is no exact correspondence between these two forms of evil; that which is physical being in no way commensurable with that which is moral. The relation, whatever it may be, in which, by Divine arrangement, these two are actually placed to each other, is not arbitrary, just because nothing is arbitrary in the Divine government, but, so far as purposes of judgment are concerned, is disciplinary, economical, and apparently provisional. We cannot so much as form a conception of a finite world in which pain and evil do not exist; and though sin has a tendency to aggravate the evil, and draw it down upon itself, yet this tendency is only general, and indeterminate, so that the evil does not infallibly and invariably find out the sinner himself. He may escape all or most of the subsidiary effects of his sin, which may overtake not himself, but his innocent children or neighbours. His frauds may not come to light. By the use of remedial measures, or in virtue of a vigorous constitution, he may never feel the bad effects of intemperance. His station in society may give him impunity in crime. A great moralist has said, that there is almost no calamity from which a man may not extricate himself in part or in whole, by plunging more deeply into the spiritual evil by which he incurred the risk of it. The spiritual consequences are the only ones which can never be escaped, except by repentance and amendment, which, in their turn, have no virtue to revoke the temporal and physical effects which sin has incurred. It is by suffering men to reap—in the taint or hue which it impresses on the texture of the soul—in the formation and bias of the inmost character—the very evil which they have sown, not a different kind of evil, that God, the Judge of all the earth, may be said to do what is absolutely right, and to render to every man according to his deeds. If there be a punishment of sin additional to this, it will consist chiefly in the inward misery and self-dissatisfaction, caused by a perception of the growing interval between what we are and what we should be; and of the opposition in which we are placed to an eternal order on which we are yet absolutely dependent.

The recognition of the principle here laid down is not an element or dogma distinctive of Christianity, or of positive religion generally. On the contrary, it may claim to be regarded as an element of natural religion, whose evidence is not, it may be, an instinct of the religious consciousness, but is derived more properly from experience. It is a fact or principle, moreover, which even the widest experience could have revealed only to a deep spiritual insight, to an eye that could penetrate to things not seen. For, as we have just implied, good and evil are unequally and partially distributed in that world of sense which is open to common observation; and "it is in the world of spirit only that every one receives his due," in that world which, to most of us, is veiled in impenetrable mystery, though it lies all about us.

We do not pause to reflect how largely this principle falls in with one of the grandest generalisations of modern science: viz., that every force propagates itself under the same or some other form: that no action fails to produce its adequate effect; and that, in the physical and social worlds alike, there are no abrupt or violent transitions, but everywhere progress of connected growth,—a conservation and interaction of forces, moral as well as physical. Just on account of this coincidence, the mind of the present day may probably be prepared to ascribe to this principle a theological range and importance greater than has been ascribed to it hitherto. It is more pertinent to state, that in almost all ages, some minds have been able to come upon the traces of this principle, without the aid either of scientific investigation, or of external revelation. Hints of an acquaintance with it have been left on record in varied language, by the poets and philosophers of heathen lands, and by ancient founders of religion and lawgivers, who owed nothing to such sources of knowledge.

The tendency of crime to generate new crime was one of the great themes of Greek tragedy, and was recognised as the true curse and penalty of crime,—as the most tragic element of life. Four hundred years before the Christian era, one of the great dramatists expresses the idea that there is nothing arbitrary, nothing partial, in the judgment of God, but that all is according to law and justice. "He that deviseth mischief is overtaken by mischief." "While God reigns the law holds good, that what a man does, that he also suffers." At a later period, we find the greatest of Greek philosophers expressing the idea, that the penalty of injustice is not "death nor stripes," but the fatal necessity of becoming more and more unjust. These remarkable utterances, and many like them scattered through the writings of classical antiquity, record the impression, made by experience, on that remote age; and show that men were reaching forth as by premonition to the truth of which St. Paul afterwards laid hold. The meaning is substantially the same: viz., that a man's principle of action is what determines his fate; and that he falls under the operation of that law, whether of love or hatred, by which he elects to regulate his life.

If we go back to an age somewhat more remote than that in which the poet formulated the doctrine of Nemesis, we come upon the founder of one of the three principal religions now existing, who seems to have been inspired to his great enterprise mainly by his marvellously keen perception of the eternal law which rules the destinies of men; the law of recompence, or, as it has been called, "the indissoluble chain of cause and effect in the moral world, according to which, the blessing of every good act, and the curse of every bad act, pursues the soul in the whole course of its wanderings, as a shadow follows the body." Buddha had, it is evident, a profound insight into the fact, that the individual in every moment of his existence is substantially nothing else than the fruit or product of his former deeds. He held that the fate of the individual depends in no respect on the decree of higher powers, but is the consequence of his own acts,—the fruit of his own sowing. The only salvation, or means of salvation for man, which he knew of, was the extirpation of selfishness and the conquest of sensuality. "To cease from all evil, to practise all good, and to subjugate the passions: this, according to an ancient formula, was the doctrine of Buddha." Recognising the existence of the law to which we are referring, the problem for which he sought the solution was to devise "a pathway of salvation" adapted to it, without taking any account whatever of a supreme lawgiver, or acknowledging the need of help or mediation of any kind. Fantastic as was much of his religious system,—if that could be called religion, which was without God, and without faith, except perhaps in the nature of man,—yet the fact that, in utter sincerity, he founded his plan of salvation upon this doctrine, shows how firm was his grasp of it.

In the Old Testament, especially in some of the Psalms, in the Proverbs, and in the Book of Job, there occur some distant approximations to the same great idea. The author of the latter book is seen to be groping for a solution of the riddle presented by the calamities which often overtake the righteous. The ideas current in his time upon the subject do not satisfy him. Instead of regarding calamity as necessarily a punishment of sin, open or secret, he tells us in his prologue that adversity may befall the good man as a test and trial of his integrity, but that in the end his integrity is vindicated, as we see in the epilogue. Manifestly, however, this solution does not tally with experience; and the riddle can only be solved by taking into consideration, that, apart from sin, calamity is of small account, and that the real punishment of sin is the degradation which it stamps upon the soul: that sin itself is the true evil, the real disease of the soul for which there is no comfort, and no compensation; while over every other form of evil, the upright soul may elevate itself in triumph, and make it ministrant of good. Unable to reach this solution, the author after many attempts sinks back baffled, and brings his drama to a conclusion, in which little else can be seen than a confession that the riddle is insoluble, and that his speculations have led to no result, but have just brought him back to the point from which he started,—a proof that, with all the glow of his genius, and the fervour of his emotion, his insight and inspiration fell much short of that to which Buddha attained.

We may take for granted, then, that the knowledge of this principle may be and has been arrived at independently of any external revelation. And we now add, that it underlies Christianity, as much as does the existence and unity of God, or any other article of natural religion. It is a part of that foundation which cannot be shaken or removed by any subsequent revelation. We feel that here we touch the solid ground of fact: that here we have one test in addition to many others, by which we may try the claims and check the extravagances of any dogma, or system of dogmas, and that we should be justified in bending or modifying into agreement with it any creed which may otherwise have claims upon our reverence.

St. Paul does not advance the doctrine under the seal of apostolic authority, nor say that he has received it in the way of supernatural illumination. He appeals for its truth to our rational nature, and to experience, though not the experience of every day. He evidently regards it as a truth, which however attained, yet being once stated, can hardly be questioned. He presumes that we must all feel with him, that there is an analogy between the world of nature and of spirit: that the one is but the type and shadow of the other; and that the great spiritual law which connects our past with our present, and our present with our future state, is but an application or department of one of those great general laws which run through all existence. Partly through experience, partly through inward discernment, we come to understand that there is a spiritual as well as a natural husbandry; and that when we speak of a spiritual harvest, our language is more than a figure of speech: it is an analogy, which in view of the unity and harmony which pervade the universe, carries in it the force of demonstration.

Here then we have the great law by operation of which God executes judgment: the law of moral sequence, by which an effect corresponds to its cause in the moral as in the physical and natural world; the law by which we proceed from less to more, whether of good or evil; the order by which good action leads to greater good, and evil action to greater evil; the principle which insures that it shall be well with the righteous and ill with the wicked. Divine judgment in this sense follows human action with undeviating regularity. There is nothing arbitrary, nothing artificial in that judgment; but all is natural, as natural as the successive stages in the growth of a plant. The present is the seed-time, the harvest will follow; and the analogy between the spiritual and the natural harvest requires that as we sow we shall reap. As every seed produces' fruit after its kind, as wheat produces wheat, and tares produce tares, so the good we do brings a harvest of good, and the evil a harvest of evil. Our good deeds form into habits, and our habits of well-doing become a second nature. Our evil deeds form into habits of evil-doing, and these become inveterate. It is thus and thus alone, that our Lord could say, that for every idle word that men speak, they shall give account thereof in the day of judgment. No word so fleeting, but it will leave its trace upon the soul of the speaker. In the language of a great living writer—

> "Our deeds still travel with us from afar,
> And what we have been makes us what we are."

Notwithstanding all appearances to the contrary, this law is of universal force, incessant and invariable in its operation. To see that such is the case, and that what are called exceptions to the law are only apparent, we must emphasise the sameness in kind between the seed which we sow and the fruit which we gather. It is not enough to say, that we reap evil if we sow evil, and that we reap good if we sow good, but we must add that the good which we reap is the same in kind as that which we sow. A man cannot reap wheat if he sow tares, but as little can he reap one kind of grain, such as wheat, by sowing another kind of grain, such as barley. For "God hath given to every seed a body of its own," which it cannot put off or exchange, even when it dies and is quickened again. Even so a man can as little sow one kind of good and reap another kind of good, as he can sow evil and reap good. A man cannot be sure that by sowing moral good, he will reap physical good, or inward happiness. A fair reputation, mental repose, and abundance of the things of this life are all good in themselves, and greatly to be desired, but they are not the true or highest good for which we must "labour;" they are uncertain of continuance, unsatisfying at the best, and not to be compared with that enduring substance, on which we must set our hearts. The inferior good is generally "added" to those who seek first the kingdom of God; there is in general a more or less palpable or subtle connection between the higher and the lower good; the latter is a more or less probable contingent or accessory of the former, but not its necessary sequel. The connection is often dissolved, or even reversed, at least in the experience of the individual. "There be just men, to whom it happeneth after the work of the righteous, and wicked men to whom it happeneth after the work of the righteous." An upright life may be rewarded with poverty and loss; comfort and high estate may follow in the train of intense selfishness and great criminality. The inflexibility of a man's virtue may doom him to defeat and disappointment, while the easiness and pliancy of another man's morality may be the very thing which enables him to make the best of this world. As the great poet says, "Some rise by sin, and some by virtue fall." A man may carry a guilty secret in his heart, and through obtuseness of the moral sense, or a reprobate hardihood, he may be able to derive full and unquestionable enjoyment from the fruits of his crime. Whereas the very first step to repentance, the first acknowledgment or discovery of his guilt, may involve for him the loss of all earthly happiness, comfort and respect, though it may also be the seed or starting-point of a new and better life.

The apostle's meaning, therefore, is not that a man will derive physical comfort, and outward, or even mental, happiness from following the right; for a man's desire of happiness may be thwarted by the mere fact of his obedience to the requirements of his higher nature, by a scrupulous adherence to the golden rule. But the meaning is, that according as a man sows a good or a bad life, he shall reap a better or a worse life. His good or evil deeds wax into habits, and produce corresponding states of mind, which bring harmony or disorder, freedom or enslavement, into the inner life. The only certain, as it is the highest and most sufficing, enjoyment arises from the mind being consciously at peace within itself, and in harmony with the divine and universal order. To pursue our separate and individual aims is to bring us into conflict with that order, and to land us in misery.

Emphatic reference is frequently made in the New Testament to the principle of judgment, or of recompence as now explained. It is what St. Paul had in view when he says in his Epistle to the Romans that God "will reward every man according to his works." In the Epistle to the Colossians he says, by literal rendering, "He that doeth wrong shall receive back the wrong which he did." The very wrong which he did returns upon the doer. The spirit which vented itself in wrong-doing is intensified in him. And our Lord said, "Blessed are they that do hunger and thirst after righteousness, for they shall be filled,"— filled with that very righteousness for which they hunger. It is just by the operation of this law of recompence, or of continuous development, that God rewards men impartially, that a righteous judgment is passed upon all men. It is by this all-embracing order that God trains and judges the rational creation. This is the true Theodicy, and if there be any other form of judgment, it is quite secondary, or auxiliary to this.

We may still make use of such words as reward and punishment; but such words, however familiar to our lips, and however descriptive of human means and modes of discipline, must be applied with much caution and reserve to the consequences of our actions as regulated by the Divine order. Those consequences which seem to answer most truly to the ideas expressed by such words are nothing, as we have seen, but the fruit or natural development of the good or evil we have done, and are neither extrinsically superadded nor arbitrarily imposed. These same ideas are often associated in men's minds with good or evil fortune, in cases with which they have no proper connection. Thus, striking calamities are of frequent occurrence, in which physical and social evils concentrate themselves at certain points, and these are popularly called judgments of God; acts of his punitive justice. But both Science and Scripture warn us to be cautious in the use of such language. Those on whom the tower of Siloam fell were not, therefore, greater sinners than all other men; and scientific investigation has taught us to trace physical evil to physical causes, to perceive that, as some one has remarked, "plagues are not, as Bishop Porteous said, the ghastly ministers of Heaven's wrath, but simply the result of neglecting sanitary conditions." In many cases, no doubt, such calamities may be said to be judgments in an intermediate or secondary sense, just because they are instances to a greater or less extent of the law of retribution. Dissipated habits undermine the health. As surely as a disregard of cleanliness and decency tends to induce epidemics, so immoderate self-indulgence tends not only to weaken and deprave the corporeal powers, but also to vitiate the mind. And such inflictions are truly beneficent, because they act as auxiliaries of the moral order, and are suitable to a state of discipline, serving to repress transgressions of that order, and to promote the observance of it; and thus operating in a general way to the same end as the law of moral · continuity, by the direct and infallible action of which, without the intervention of any supplementary or epicyclical contrivance, God judges the world in the true and full sense of the word.

The views here presented have not only obtained a wide currency in later times, but are able also, as we believe, to bear the most rigid scrutiny; and if it be an axiom or first principle of theology, that we ought to accept no dogma which contradicts the sure conclusions of reason, it seems to follow that we may have to modify the popular belief of Christendom concerning a day of final judgment to decide irrevocably the destinies both of the good and of the bad. Turn it over in our thoughts as we may, it is difficult to bring the ordinary idea of such a day into harmony with the doctrine of the spiritual harvest. By all who accept the doctrine of a future life, it will be admitted that the departing soul will carry with it into that life the same moral state which it has formed for itself here. Its works, whether good or bad, will follow it thither; each of them will have left upon the soul its stamp and imprint. At the moment when it is ushered into another world, every soul will have reached a certain stage of moral development or of moral degeneracy. And the belief common amongst us is, that on the day of judgment one class of souls will not only be acquitted from the consequences of all the evil that yet cleaves to them, but will be suddenly perfected in holiness and freed from all remaining taint and infection of sin. Upon the other class, a sentence and a transformation of quite an opposite character will be passed, though, confessedly, the day of judgment will find the characters of both classes compounded both of good and evil. It has been said, indeed, that the difference between the two classes is one in kind, because sin has lost that dominion in the one class which it retains in the other. But this difference, even if it be one in kind, and not, after all, in degree only, does not account for what is supposed to take place. In the life to come, the dominating power, whether good or evil, in the case of any individual, can only determine, or form a factor in, the further development of that individual, just as it does in the present life; but it cannot achieve for itself a total and immediate triumph, as is supposed. It is obvious, therefore, that though we may and do connect the idea of such a day of judgment with the language of the apostle, yet the two ideas are quite incompatible. So far from being an exemplification of the principle involved, such a day of judgment would much rather be a violation and a subversion of it. If the judgment be final, and the extinction of evil, which co-exists with the good, be complete and sudden, it is evident that the gradual and natural process of moral amelioration, which began here, would be foreclosed and precipitated by a supernatural fiat of Almighty power. That moral discipline which is in harmony with human responsibility, and with the idea of moral development, would be suddenly arrested. A Divine decree would complete the work already begun, and supernatural action would be introduced into a scene where it would be as much out of place as in the present order of things.

The subjects of this astounding transformation will, by supposition, occupy very different stages in the scale of moral development. In some, the development will only have commenced; in others, it will be far advanced; and if a Divine fiat may thus at any point interfere with the natural course of things, it is hard to see why it might not have interfered at the very first to prevent the incursion of evil into the world. Such interference on the day of judgment is as inadmissible, because as inconsistent with human liberty, and with an inviolable order, as at any other crisis in the history of man.

It can never be of little moment to bring our ideas of religious subjects into harmony with the truth and nature of things. A divergence of our theories from reality is apt sooner or later to avenge itself by leading to some practical error, or by entailing the loss of some practical influence. And it seems to us as if the idea of a day of final judgment exposed us to a risk of this kind. It is the substitution of an artificial for a natural conception of Divine judgment; of a human and imperfect for a Divine procedure. On a mind little trained to reflection, the notion of a day and a throne set for judgment will make a vivid, because a definite, impression. But to a reflecting mind the notion of a continuous and progressive judgment, before as well as after death, is much more impressive, and much more powerfully operative as a check and counterpoise to the solicitations of lust and selfishness. In the one case, life is regarded as a mere trial or probation, which being successfully endured is rewarded by perfected holiness, and an immediate cessation of all sinful motions. Impressed by such an idea, the soul will strive to undergo the ordeal, and hope that its failures under trial will all be made good. In the other case, life is regarded as an education; and the problem of life is to extirpate the evil in our nature by degrees, in actual personal conflict. In this latter case there can be no thought of getting rid of evil by any forensic act or sovereign fiat of the Judge. If, by an act of sovereign power, God may bring the halting course of moral development to its destined period, even the impenitent, provided their faith be strong enough, may hope—not without reason—to impetrate the exercise at any moment of such a power in their behalf; while those who have entered the narrow path may be tempted to slacken their pace, or to relax their moral effort, if they are taught to expect that their shortcomings, more or less, may be cancelled at last by a sudden translation to the goal.

It may be said, that if such views be generally accepted, the cause of morality and religion will lose that leverage which it derives from the dogma of a final and irreversible doom, determined by our condition at the moment of our departure from this life: that if time and space for repentance may be looked for after death, the natural tendency to levity and procrastination will receive a fresh accession of force. But, is then that loss so great, or the aggravation of this tendency so certain? Is it not an undoubted fact, that the common doctrine, though addressed to our fears, and calculated, as it may seem, to strike terror, and to call to immediate repentance, yet fails most signally, in the case of large numbers, to give impetus to effort, or to produce that moral earnestness, which is currently ascribed to its influence? Do not the inherent incredibility and injustice of a penalty utterly disproportioned to the sin beget, in the case of multitudes, a merciful scepticism, and a not altogether ignoble determination to brave the unknown terrors of the other world? That doctrine again, according to which the present and the future life are connected by the law of continuity,—though it may be less fitted to keep us trembling on the brink of despair, and to subject the mind to a state of all but intolerable tension, though it may even annul one urgent motive to immediate repentance,—yet tells us, that by a continuance in sin, we, day by day, surely consolidate about us the walls of a prison-house, from which we shall "by no means come out, until we have paid the uttermost farthing;" that the burden of sin will continue to oppress us, and be the source of misery to us there as here, until, by a discipline of unknown severity, the cords which bind it on our souls are undone. And surely such a doctrine as this cannot, if well considered, give encouragement to indifference or levity.

We are far from saying that the popular idea of a day of judgment is positively or altogether pernicious, but only that it is less influential, especially for men of thought and culture, than that of an ever present judgment. We do not deny even that there may be an important truth underlying the popular conception. It is quite in harmony with the idea of an inviolable moral order, that for the individual soul its entrance into a new stage of existence, and for the whole race the end of the world, may be a point or crisis of immense significance and range in determining the further development of the individual and the race. A new motive power may thus be called into existence simply by what the Scriptures call the revelation of the righteous judgment of God; the revelation of that inflexible moral order in compliance with which alone the race and the individual can reach the goal marked out for them, but which in the present mingled scene men have such difficulty in apprehending. If amid new conditions that order reveal itself more distinctly to human vision, it is conceivable that the further development of some may be accelerated, while a turning-point may be gained for others whose course hitherto has taken the wrong direction. How this may be so we shall yet see when we come, in speaking of the renovating power of Christianity, to consider the mode in which an accession of light operates on the mind. The revelation of the judgment of God will be but a supplement to that which has been made to us in Christ, and will enhance its operation in delivering us from evil.

We understand, then, that the judgment of God is only another name for the natural and inevitable consequence of our lives. That judgment will be executed, not once for all, as we have been taught to believe, by a separate Divine decree or verdict in each individual case, but by the operation of a universal law established from the first by the Governor of all. It has begun already for every one of us, and is going on continually, leading on gradually to higher and ever higher issues. As the harvest of this year furnishes seed for the year following, so the chain of moral sequence, good or evil, is carried on in unbroken continuity. We may not see clearly the process, while it is still going on, the growth of habit and of tendency being for the most part insensible. Amid the hardships of our moral warfare, and amid the apparent freedom and intoxication of present indulgence, we may long fail to see that the tyranny of acquired habits is but the fruit of past indulgence; it may only be on rare occasions that we have the bitter feeling that we are reaping the reward of our evil deeds. But the Scriptures speak of the revelation or full manifestation of the righteous judgment of God, when, the whole process being transferred to a new condition of things, it may stand forth in clear outline before the universe. That law, hitherto revealed only to a select few, may then reveal itself to every soul of man, as the outcome of his earthly experience, and constitute by its revelation a new motive power in the education of the race.

No doubt, it is impossible for us to imagine how moral discipline can be continued under other conditions in a future state. But this is no objection to the views now stated. For St. Paul himself, and Luther in his usual frank and outspoken manner, besides many others best qualified to give an opinion on the subject, have confessed themselves quite unable, on the old dogmatic lines of thought, to form any conception of a future state. The whole subject lies utterly out of our field of vision, and beyond our comprehension, whatever view be taken of Divine judgment; and all we can be sure of, all that for the purposes of present discipline we need to be sure of, is that law will continue to assert itself there as here, and that God, the Judge of all the earth, will do right.

We have seen that upwards of two thousand years ago, the principle of moral continuity, if not thought out, was at least divined by a few gifted spirits; yet we must admit, that until a comparatively recent period, almost indeed until the present age, the apprehension of it by all but a few, if not even by these few, was only approximative. The moral sentiment could hardly emerge as a conscious and authoritative factor of human life, without the discovery being made at the same time that virtue is in some sense its own reward, and that, in the words of the Wisdom of Solomon, "wherewithal a man sins, by the same shall he be punished." But language such as this, which abounds in every literature, is far from involving a distinct and adequate recognition of moral sequence. The great medieval poet, in whom "ten silent centuries found a voice," intended in his *Divina Commedia* to represent in action the principle of recompence, founding for this purpose on the legendary materials and popular beliefs of his period. But as *we* read the lurid imaginings of his *Inferno*, and compare them with the real drama of Divine judgment, we feel that they do not turn to burlesque, only because they pass into allegory. They survive for us as a splendid creation of poetic fancy, so elastic in its truthfulness as to shadow forth an idea of recompence more true and spiritual than the poet himself intended to embody. Only in these later times, when science, in its researches into the material world, has lighted everywhere upon the traces of an all-pervading continuity, has the existence in the moral and spiritual worlds of an analogous principle been confidently postulated. And if it can be shown without prejudice to the religious sentiment, that the principle of continuity obtains in the moral sphere no less than in the material, and rules the succession of religious as of other phenomena,—that the judgment of God upon human action is immanent in the action itself,—this will be a step toward that reconciliation of faith with science, the conscious or suspected lack of which is the specific danger of our age, the source of its universal unrest, and of its all but universal scepticism.

X.

THE RENOVATING POWER OF CHRISTIANITY.

BY THE REV. WILLIAM MACKINTOSH, D.D., BUCHANAN.

Whatsoever a man soweth, that shall he also reap.—GAL. VI. 7.

FROM these words of St. Paul, and from other passages of Scripture, we collect that the gospel does not profess to exempt us from the law of recompence; or, which is the same thing, from the law of moral continuity. It is to the infinite credit of Christianity, that so far from seeking to magnify itself, by professing to make this or any law void, it asserts the validity for all time of whatever is law. But if this be so we have to ask, What the gospel is good for? What title has it to that designation? What service does it render? From what fear does it deliver, from what burden does it relieve us? The law of the spiritual harvest is that evil is the natural product of evil; that nothing either good or evil ever perishes of itself, but must in some way influence, or enter as an element into, the future. Conscious of the evil that is in us, we feel that our faith and our hopes are vain, unless by some means good can come out of evil, or take the place of evil, even though it may be that the evil that passes may leave its trace in the colour and character of the good that abides. The final result of the evil may be only to differentiate the good, which in this differentiation will carry within itself the data or evidence of its history and growth. It is by the harmonising of such differentiated elements that the process of self-development, by which man becomes the builder up of his own highest self, is saved from insipid uniformity, and the moral sphere is impressed with that variety and shading of character in which the manifold wisdom and goodness of God loves to mirror itself in the spiritual as in the natural world. Now, though we have no hint of anything of the kind in the text, this is just what the gospel does teach us to expect and look for. We feel indeed that unless the good could supplant, could get the better of, the evil that is in us, there could be no such thing as a gospel or message of gladness to man. The gospel is what it is, and what it professes to be, just because it shows us the way from evil to good; just because it delivers us from the one and brings us to the other. But it is necessary to know in what sense and how far it accomplishes this, that we may not be led astray by a mere form of words, or misconstrue the method by which the gospel confers this benefit upon us.

Undoubtedly there is much difficulty in conceiving how there can be room for amendment and conversion, side by side with the existence of a law of moral development, and with the idea of moral continuity. It seems as if by insisting on the tendency of every action to confirm the disposition from which it springs, we go far to deny the free agency of man, the possibility of repentance, and the power of Christianity or of any other influence to initiate and effect a renovation of human life. But it must be remembered that the difficulty exists of conceiving how good may spring up, as confessedly it often does, in the midst of evil, whether we adopt that idea or not; and that it exists moreover for the physiologist no less than for the moralist and the theologian. The physiologist admits the persistence of force and the law of moral sequence, but affirms none the less that the evils arising from past indulgence may be neutralised by the exercise of self-denial; that pernicious habits may be and often are overcome by reversing the process by which they have been contracted; and that a spiritual force, latent in every one of us, may be summoned forth to counteract the tendencies to evil which have been fostered and strengthened by long use and habit. It is not, however, with the mere theoretical difficulty involved in the conception or rationale of that force that we have here to do, but rather with the practical and objective difficulty involved in the effort requisite for calling up the force to counteract the evil that has possession of the heart, and to give impulse to the endeavour after the better life.

In modern phraseology a sense of the painfulness and difficulty involved in the earnest and successful exerting of that force has found expression for itself in the saying, that men never change, they only develop; which, if it be received with certain qualifications, represents an undeniable fact, but which is too often an utterance of the direst and most hopeless scepticism.

The same feeling was expressed in ancient times by Job, "Who can bring a clean thing out of an unclean?" and by Jeremiah, "Can the Ethiopian change his skin, or the leopard his spots? Then may ye who are accustomed to do evil learn to do well." To both these thinkers it seemed that to change the tenor of a life was equivalent to a physical impossibility; much as it seems to any one who takes the law of moral development and continuity into account. The conception of that law does not aggravate the difficulty, but only gives expression to it, or explains its nature. Our Lord also seems to have been painfully, almost despairingly, sensible of the same difficulty, as for instance when He said, "O generation of vipers, how can ye being evil speak good things?" or when He declared that "a corrupt tree cannot bring forth good fruit." To say this and yet not to despair of man was no small evidence of his faith in man's Maker. In man, no doubt, there is a will to do good, but how to perform is the difficulty; and in the presence of the evil bias, and by comparison with it, that will to do good seems to be the weakest of all things. The sense of its weakness, contrasted with the magnitude of the issues depending on it, seems to have filled even St. Paul with "wretchedness;" and the question which long after his conversion continued to haunt and to agitate his mind was just this: how that which was thus weak could confound that which was mighty; how a man could struggle against that to which he is naturally inclined, and overcome that which is strongest in him; how the will to do good, which was as if it were not, could bring to naught the things that were, and counteract that gravitation to evil which is a power indeed in the soul.

St. Paul was confident that the better will, when reinforced by Christian influences, could and would triumph; but to conceive of these influences as an exertion of supernatural grace, as he is generally supposed to do, is little else than to explain away the difficulty, and really to deprive the process of conversion of all its value and all its mystery. We have rather to seek the explanation of it in the latent capacities of our nature; in the balance of good and evil within us; in the vitality and spontaneousness of a spiritual force, of a higher nature within us, to which the gospel appeals; and in the action of the Divine idea, as the gospel presents it, upon the reason of man. We say that this spiritual force, though held in durance and oppressed under the weight of evil, yet, if touched and brought into sympathy and *rapport* with the power of goodness " not ourselves," leaps forth into light and gathers strength, despite of prevailing evil, in a way which, to men who are inwardly conscious of it, has often seemed to be nothing short of miraculous and divine. In thus ascribing to an interaction between the longing or aspiration within us, and the tendency of things without us, an effect of such decisive importance to our spiritual life, we are led into proximity with the esoteric doctrine of Brahminism, which a great Orientalist has recently expounded, viz., that there is no hope of salvation for man, except by the individual self recognising the true and universal self and finding rest in it.

However much a man may give himself up to the

service and practice of sin, yet the dominion of sin, notwithstanding its self-perpetuating and self-intensifying power, never becomes absolute and undisputed. When we say that an evil habit is self-perpetuating, we speak of a tendency, not of a necessity. The better principle has within itself the potency of a reactive force, the possibility of a new life, which may encroach on the dominion of evil, and even establish its own supremacy, though seldom without a struggle by which the soul is almost rent in pieces. The painful effort which it costs to loosen the hold with which habits of sin have fastened on the soul is the penalty which we pay for past indulgence; a painfulness which is familiar to the experience of many of us, and which in the gospel is symbolised by the cross, by the strait gate and narrow way, and in primitive Buddhism by the struggle of the elephant to extricate itself from the swamp. For the truly religious man there is no escape or dispensation from such efforts, except indeed in those rare cases in which the sense of Divine love and the beauty of goodness take immediate possession of the soul, or in which a new affection suddenly lights up the heart with a triumphant joy.

The judicial tendency of action to intensify the spirit from which it springs, and so to perpetuate itself, operates either for good or for evil—a duplicity of operation which holds true of every law of our nature, and every part of our constitution. As fineness of organisation makes us at once susceptible and vulnerable at every point; as our senses may be to us the source of exquisite pleasure or of exquisite pain; as one and the same organ makes us sensitive to harmony or to discord; as we can only enjoy a benefit in one direction by being exposed to the possibility of injury in another; as one and the same discipline may mature a virtue, or develop a germ of vice, so the tendency of the moral life to perpetuate itself operates for evil as well as for good. But the tendency in either case is relative, not absolute; and it may be noted as an indication or pledge of the ultimate triumph of good over evil, that this universal and two-edged tendency is on the whole and by preponderance beneficent, inasmuch as it makes for good more than for evil. The empire of the latter, however firmly established, always runs the risk of being overthrown; feelings of remorse and penitence may be awakened by the greatness of a crime, or by a sense of inward desolation, and evoke an insurrection of the soul against the sway of evil; whereas it is seldom indeed, if ever, that a man repents of what is good. And hence the continuity of the moral life, though it may be such as to exclude the possibility of a lapse from virtue which has reached a certain stage, does not exclude amendment and conversion from a life of sin. From the observation to which we have thus been led, it would seem as if there were indeed, in the nature of what is good, a substantive character which is wanting in what is evil; and as if that were the true theory of the nature of the latter, according to which it is not an actual entity but a mere privation, or, as it has been expressed, "an undeveloped good."

Hence, too, it is our belief, that though the law of moral sequence be of absolute validity, so that the past can never be extinguished, yet that evil as such will gradually be eliminated from the universe. We are fully alive to the mystery which rests upon this subject: how inconceivable it is that in accordance with that law, and with due respect to the freedom of his creatures, God can yet eliminate evil from their hearts. But we do not believe that there is any sin absolutely beyond forgiveness; that there are "forms of evil so vital, that no repentance can fully blot them out;" or, as it has been otherwise expressed, that there are "acts which may have such irretrievable effects on character, that for them there can be no place for repentance." That many acts, and many forms of evil, do appear to men to be thus fearfully irretrievable, irreversible, we acknowledge. But we rest here on the words of Christ, that what is impossible for man—impossible for man even to conceive—may be possible for God, and for the benignly transforming operation of that Order, which is but another name for God. That there are passages in Scripture which seem to bear out such a hopeful and cheering prospect, it is not necessary to say. If for long ages the Order may seem to operate indifferently for evil or for good, yet its preponderating tendency in favour of what is good will finally issue in the transformation of what is evil.

The soul is a scene of conflict between good and evil. Explain it psychologically as we may, it is a fact of daily experience that the soul may struggle with itself; the higher with the lower nature. The animal and selfish propensities, which have sole possession of the child, are not evil in themselves, but only become evil when they retain the upper hand in spite of reason and conscience, and obstruct the rule and growth of the higher nature, of that spiritual principle which, deposited in the soul as a seed, is, by inherent right and destination, the governing and controlling power over the whole man. In proportion as we live in subjection to our lower impulses, we sow to the flesh; in proportion as we obey the higher impulses of our nature, we sow to the spirit. According to the apostle, we may do either; and there is probably no man so much a slave to carnal and egotistical principles but oftentimes acts in deference to the higher and better principle. The more a man so acts, the more does he invigorate that principle, keeping it at least from utter torpor. The more again he obeys the motions of his fleshly nature, the more does he strengthen its hold and confirm its dominion; and all this happens according to that moral order, in which Divine judgment executes itself.

When evil habits have once been confirmed, these can be overcome seldom or never by the call of duty, or by a sense of moral obligation, but by the power of some new hope, some new interest or affection, and most of all by the power of that affection which is called forth by the revelation of Divine grace. The revelation to our mind of the paternal character of God, and of the gracious relation in which He stands to us, produces a complete revolution in our feelings and relations towards him, and thereby elevates us to a higher level of the religious life. Before that revelation is made to us, our religion consists in the effort to propitiate God, and to deserve his favour, a task we all feel to be of impossible achievement. But thenceforth our endeavour is not to merit or deserve, but to show ourselves sensible and worthy of the unmerited, priceless, and unalterable favour and good-will with which He regards us—a distinction of immense practical significance. In the former case, we are actuated by fear and other mercenary dispositions, the very consciousness of which is enough to lame and frustrate our efforts; in the other, we are stirred by gratitude, and all the higher impulses of which our nature is susceptible.

The problem of human life—the task appointed to us—is our deliverance from the sway of our lower nature, our surrender to the control of our higher nature. The powers by which we are enabled to accomplish this task are three. *First*, Our own higher nature itself, which is never wholly effaced, and which reacts against the evil, and makes us receptive of all the higher influences that may be brought to bear upon us from without. *Secondly*, The complex of all these higher influences—the beneficent constitution of things in general, their tendency in favour of what is good, which operates upon us more or less, even when we are unconscious of it. We do not mean to say that this tendency operates in spite of us, or that it approaches its aim or purpose independently of us. A philosopher or man of science may feel himself at liberty to hold such a view, but the teacher of religion cannot. For were this the case, as extreme evolutionists would have us believe, it would be equivalent to the death or extinction of all religion, and obliterate that which constitutes the highest distinction of the rational creature; that relative freedom of will by which he is, like God, though in an inferior degree, *sui causa*, the maker of himself. That "man is man and master of his fate" is the witness of the inmost consciousness. He is man *because* he is master of his fate, and not the absolute thrall or slave of circumstance; and it has been shown over and over again that to set this witness aside would end by landing us in infinite absurdities, or in universal scepticism. To this witness, therefore, we must hold fast, in spite of all ratiocination to the contrary, however unanswerable it may seem. It is matter of wide experience that one and the same discipline may, as we have already remarked, foster virtue, or develop the germs of vice in us. But which of the two it shall be, must depend more or less upon the rational subject giving himself up to the influence for good or the influence for evil, even though he may have no distinct apprehension or consciousness of the existence or nature either of the one or the other. A man may not be conscious of the several influences, good or evil, by which he is surrounded; and yet it is by acts of volition, however obscure, that he surrenders himself to this class rather than to that.

With this explanation, we say that the tendency of human relations in favour of what is good, so far as it exists in excess of the opposite tendency, being impressed by God on the creation, is an evidence of his design to secure the triumph of what is good, and to deliver us from evil. After being hidden from human vision for long ages, or only partially surmised by other teachers, this design was at length brought fully to light, and presented to our faith by the founder of Christianity. In consequence of this tendency, it might be said in all ages that "God meeteth him that rejoiceth and worketh righteousness; those that remember him in his ways;" and it is not fanciful to suppose that their insight into this tendency was what encouraged the great religious teachers of ancient times, and pre-eminently Christ, to believe and proclaim the paternal character of God; and from the vantage-ground of this new idea to discern more clearly than ever that all things work together for the ultimate good of man. That tendency is the outward revelation which offers itself to the interpreting power of the pure in heart; and these two factors, the outward and the inward, explain to us the otherwise inexplicable nature of that Divine instinct by which humanity rose at length in Christ to the thought of God's absolute goodness; while the necessity that exists for the latter factor co-operating with the former, in order to the perception of that truth, may explain to us how the hold of it on the part of mankind is even yet so slender, precarious, and uncertain.

Thirdly, These two factors for the accomplishment of the Divine purpose are consummated, or brought into full operation by the revelation to our consciousness of that which was implicitly contained in them, but of which we had otherwise remained unconscious; by that revelation, we mean, of the Divine good-will, or paternal relation towards us, by which Christ has reinforced our better nature, enabling us to be intelligent fellow-workers with God in our conflict with evil, and giving a higher aim to our life. The deeper insight which Christ has thus given us into the character and purposes of God has advanced us to a higher level of religious development. For it is the view which a man takes of God, and of the world, and of the relation in which he stands to both, which, upon the whole, determines his life and actions; and if he believes, no matter how he comes by the belief, that God loves him and designs to further the triumph and dominion of the higher nature implanted in him, this conviction is the very highest that can be given him to reinforce his efforts in that conflict with his lower nature. It is through the apprehension of the grace of God by that higher reason which is faith, that grace becomes operative in us; so that not only our service of God (Rom. xii. 1), but the action, at its highest, of the Divine mind upon our minds is "rational," as being exerted through our rational nature. It is, we say, through our reason, through our conviction that God wills the triumph of our better nature, that we are animated to a triumphant forth-putting of its latent energies. All this may be brought to the test of experience. Let any man lean upon this thought and see what will be the effect of it; whether it will not make of him what the apostle calls a new creature; whether it will not suffice to advance him to fellowship with God, to extricate him from the dubious struggle with his lower nature, and in a manner to raise him above himself.

In passing, we may remark that unless a man be possessed by this consciousness,—and unless the consciousness stands in some historical connection with the impulse given by Christianity, he can scarcely be called a Christian,—but he may yet be a pious and religious man, accepted of God. The life of God in such a man may be developed by the second of the factors enumerated, that is, by means of the discipline supplied through the Divine order, in the midst of which he stands, and to the influence of which he unconsciously yields. Such, no doubt, is the case with many in heathen lands, and with many also in Christian lands, whose minds are closed against the direct teachings of the gospel.

To correspond with what has now been said, the gospel can only be regarded as a revelation or discovery to man of a method of salvation which had always been possible in the nature of things, though, it may be, hid from the beginning, potentially though not actually in operation from the first. It is the discovery of that sole and only possible method of salvation which is determined by the nature of man and of him in whose image man was created; not an arbitrary "divine contrivance" as it is sometimes popularly called; nor an invention of something absolutely new. Some minds seem to be so constituted as to have no difficulty in accepting the idea of such a divine contrivance, while to others such an idea is wholly inconceivable. The Catholic Apostolic Church, one of the most recent of the sects, and one which owed its origin to men of apparently high culture and of liberal education, is said by a seemingly well-informed writer to be founded on the idea, that after the death of the original apostles, and owing to the want of faith in the Church, God changed his original plan and purpose; and that after eighteen centuries of abeyance, He has made a new revelation and given a new organisation to his Church. The idea, thus perhaps somewhat brusquely stated, is so manifestly extravagant, that we have some doubt whether it will be accepted by the Catholic Apostolic Church itself as a fair or accurate representation of its principles. But there can be no doubt that this idea, if it be really entertained, is, at bottom, a mere exaggeration of that on which popular Christianity rests. Popularly, and even theologically, Christianity is regarded as a late contrivance; as the disclosure of a "second intention" in God's government of the world; as a contrivance which was conditioned and brought late into action by means of unique and altogether exceptional events in the history of man.

If we keep in view that law which has engaged our attention, it will be distinctly apparent that the gospel can be a means of supplanting evil by good, only by discovering and evoking powers which had always existed, though it may be latently, in man's nature. The gospel deserves its name simply because it teaches and persuades us to cease from evil and to do well; to change the seed which we sow, and thus to obtain a better harvest. It affords to us helps and encouragements to repent of the evil we have done, and to enter upon a new course of life. It appeals to that aspiration towards what is good, which, according to St. Paul (Rom. vii.), is never quite extinct in any soul of man; while it reinforces that aspiration by announcing that the Divine complacency in our endeavours to do well is none the less because of the evil that is past, and that there is joy in heaven over the returning penitent. It proclaims forgiveness for all past failures, and so clears the way for the daily renewal of our lives. The power of a new life resides in the conviction that the past has no claim upon us; that no objective atonement is necessary; that all we have to do is to shake ourselves free from the evil that cleaves to us; and that the obstacle to our deliverance lies wholly in ourselves and not in God. By his death on the cross, Christ may be said, in a figurative sense indeed, to have expiated our sins, or to have purchased their remission; it being important to observe that the figures vary. But what He did, in the strict and literal sense, was to reveal to us the infinite placability of the Divine nature. The faith which He thus kindles in the hearts of men produces no change in God's relation or intentions towards us, but is only the recognition and apprehension of a relation always existing. Yet so surprising to those on whom it first dawned was this revelation, and so transforming in its effects ever since on human hopes and character, that in every age men have been constrained to give expression to that of which they were conscious, by speaking of the great event as not merely a manifestation of the changeless love of God, but as the efficient cause of an utter revolution in God's relations to man.

The forgiveness of sins was no absolutely new doctrine, though it was uttered with new emphasis by him who, at the same time, elevated the standard of human duty by his teaching and by his example in life and death, and thus became the founder of our faith. The faith or hope of Divine forgiveness for

M

faults committed, must have been implicitly contained in the prayers and sacrifices of every religion in which the ethical element was in any measure developed. Without some faith or hope of this kind, such religion would have been impossible, or been but another name for despair. The prayer for forgiveness was in fact heard in all religions, though but seldom did it ascend anywhere in the confidence of a favourable answer. Probably in Israel did men first rise with any distinctness to this faith, for there it was that a clear and simple conception of a moral law first prevailed. The idea of a righteous judgment involved in such a law left no escape from despair, except by way of the idea of a free and complete remission of sins, or of that Divine grace which could not but reveal itself to man, when he discovered the "weakness of the law," that is, its unfitness to become a power unto salvation. Of this evangelical idea, therefore, we find traces everywhere in the Old Testament, and notably in the Psalms and in the Books of Jonah and Ezekiel. To take but one example, Ezekiel represents the people as asking, "If our transgressions be upon us, and we pine away in them, how should we then live?" which is just as much as to ask, If we have sown the evil, how can we reap the good? To men in this desponding state of mind, God bids the prophet say, "As I live, I have no pleasure in the death of the wicked; but that the wicked turn from his way and live: turn ye, turn ye from your evil ways; for why will ye die, O house of Israel?" That is to say, Ye can escape death only by turning from it; by forsaking the way that leads to it: ye can escape the harvest of evil only by sowing the seed of a good harvest. And then follows the encouragement which men have to apply to this work. "Therefore say unto the children of thy people, The wicked shall not fall by his wickedness in the day that he turneth from his wickedness; neither shall the righteous be able to live by his righteousness in the day that he sinneth. When I say to the wicked, Thou shalt surely die," that is, Thou shalt reap the evil thou hast sown, "yet if he turn from his sin, and do that which is lawful and right, he shall surely live and not die. None of his sins that he hath committed shall be mentioned to him." These utterances of one of the great prophets of Israel were the result of that deep religious insight which had been gained through centuries of experience by a succession of the highest minds of the nation: of an insight which possessed the few, but was not possessed even by them except with difficulty and in moments of rare illumination. Christ, on the other hand, a greater than all the prophets, seems to have enjoyed this insight from the first; and being in full possession of it, He laid it, supremely confident, as the foundation and corner-stone of religion for all time and for all peoples; and so ushered in the kingdom of God, "not by changing the will of God, but simply by revealing it to us." Just as in other fields of thought and action, every advance made by humanity has been effected not by any change in the Divine order, but by the discovery of laws which have always been in existence, by the reception of these laws into the circle of human thought, and by an adjustment to them of human life and conduct; so has it been also in the field of religion, and in respect especially of the great advance first from nature-religion to the religion of law, and then from the religion of law to the religion of grace, as we now have it in Christianity.

The object of most of our Lord's teaching was to show the way by which evil might be made to give place to good in men's lives, and to encourage those who were reaping the harvest of sin to begin to sow the seed which might ripen into a better harvest. He taught men as plainly as could be, that no time was too late for repentance, and no sin too great to be forgiven; that though the evil they had done would certainly bear its fruit in the difficulties which are thereby laid in the way of return to a better life, yet that the heavenly Father was ever ready to receive the sinner into his fellowship; and that the confidence of a final triumph might spring up in the felt presence of indwelling sin, from the conviction that God's will is our salvation. He sought to train all about him to seek the true good as an end, and to practise it as a means of greater and of growing good, and thus to proceed from less to more under the eye of him who despises not the day of small things.

As we ascribe such a transforming power to the forgiveness of sin, let it be clearly understood what we mean by that word. We do not thereby designate an act of God's sovereign pleasure, but only an act of that supreme goodness which is the universal character of his government of the world. His power to forgive is a power which resides in his love. When we say that He alone is able to forgive sins, we do not mean to claim for him a dispensing power, or a prerogative to extinguish sin, to annihilate its effects, and to break the continuity of the moral order by an almighty sentence. For God to vie in this respect with the prerogative claimed by his earthly vicegerent is, to our way of thinking, as impossible as it would be to subvert an arithmetical proportion or a geometrical law. But what we mean is, that God alone has the heart to forgive, which man has not. Man is not able to forgive, because he is unloving and vindictive. But God is able, because He is love. Though infinitely higher in degree, yet God's forgiveness is the same in kind as that of an earthly parent. He loves, nay, forgives the sinner, even while He leaves him to bear the punishment of his sins. "Thou," says the Psalmist, "forgavest their iniquities, but thou tookest vengeance of their inventions." Even in punishing God forgave the Israelites. He punished because He forgave. The Divine end was the same in both: namely, their repentance. God seeks man's salvation even by the operation of the law of recompence, and welcomes the first faint symptom of repentance. And sin is effaced by means of an inner process, of which the motive power is the perception of Divine love acting on the spiritual nature of the percipient.

In accordance with these views, we define forgiveness to be the persistence of Divine love in spite of our sins. But it would be illogical to infer from this definition that our sins have no effect on God's relation to us; that He is indifferent to our sins; or that "the deep law of resentment, as modern sentimentalism would have it, is expunged from the Christian code." God aims, through his moral order, unremittingly, unswervingly, at the removal of our sins, and at the remedy of the evils caused by them. This aim He pursues, not with anthropomorphic and relenting fondness, but with that inflexible persistence, which is essential to the nature of the Divine order, and which, because it is inexorable, may, to reluctant man, seem even to be pitiless. The same merciful discipline—the same purpose of leading men to repentance—runs through the severity and the goodness of God, but none the less on that account is his severity felt to be real. By the operation of the law of continuity, in which Divine love, so to speak, disguises itself, sin becomes more and more intolerable, and the soul makes ineffectual efforts to throw off the sin which oppresses it. A revelation therefore of Divine grace is needed to encourage the hope of deliverance and to give new vigour to repentance. We obtain strength for true amendment, by accepting that forgiveness, which God, as made known to us by Christ, is always extending to us, and by our confidence in his sympathy with our efforts to break the dominion of sin. The reactive power of our higher nature, of which we have already spoken, is stimulated into energetic action by our belief in Divine sympathy. It is only through the apprehension of that sympathy, through that intercourse with God which is thus made possible, through the conviction that the Supreme is on the side of the insurgent good, and rejoices in its triumph, that we may mount to higher and ever higher stages of the moral and spiritual life. The more common virtues, social or civil, may be practised without such confidence. But the higher ideal of

Christianity can be set up as an aim by those only who believe in the persistency of Divine love; in the fact that God's forgiveness is ever at the door, ready for their acceptance, so that, with his entire concurrence and good-will, they may begin anew, and start afresh after every failure. In the apprehension of that fact resides the power of an endless growth.

Even while the soul is dead in trespasses, given up to the practice of sin, God is still placable,—in the language of Scripture, He waits to be gracious; but his grace is in abeyance, or at least appears to be so: and even when the soul struggles to turn from its sin, without having yet risen to the idea of Divine love, that grace remains inoperative; inasmuch as it is only through faith and the apprehension of Divine grace by means of it, that, in accordance with the laws of our rational nature, grace can become fully operative in us. When the soul yearns for deliverance from evil, the only barrier to the satisfaction of its yearnings lies in its ignorance of Divine grace. There need be no element of uncertainty as to the forgiveness of its sins. For no special acts of pardon need to be passed, any more than, as we formerly remarked, there need to be special acts of judgment. All happens according to the operation of unvarying law in the one case as in the other. To say so is almost a truism, when we admit, what is indeed the case, that Divine forgiveness is only a form of Divine judgment. The sovereignty with which God dispenses forgiveness is just the sovereignty of law. The idea of a sovereign, in the sense of an arbitrary dispensation of forgiveness as of judgment, is altogether excluded: and there is no third form of its dispensation. The specific consciousness of the Christian is given expression to by St. Paul, when he says, that we are not under law, but under grace; but the law of which this is said is law in the special sense of the word,—as an external commandment which condemns the sinner—in which sense it is opposed to grace: whereas law, in the more general acceptation of the word, as but another name for an immovable order, must regulate the grace of God itself. To think otherwise, one must have a strangely childish notion of the Divine infinitude.

In opposition to the view of Divine forgiveness here advanced, it may be said that evil once done not only tends to reproduce evil in the doer, but also calls forth the reprobation of the Judge; and therefore, as the consequences of our deeds cannot be evaded, this reprobation, as one of these, ought to remain: in other words, that our sins do not admit of Divine forgiveness. But in answer to this objection, we reply, that the forgiveness of the sinner is quite compatible with the reprobation of his sin. The reprobation which is merited by our sins remains in their very tendency to reproduce themselves: it is reflected in the terrible self-dissatisfaction of the sinner himself: in the pressure which they increasingly put upon the soul, and in the barrier which they raise to his repentance. These are the strongest proofs of the Divine disapprobation: the penalty which we pay for our indulgence in sin; which the drunkard, for example, feels weighing upon him to his infinite distress, when he struggles, too often in vain, to be temperate. In the hardness of that struggle, the sinner may be said, *figuratively*, to expiate his sin and to endure its penalty; and at the same time he is strengthened for that endurance, by his faith in the goodness with which God sympathises with him in his struggle to escape those very toils with which He has beset the path of sin, to make it painful.

To meet the hardships connected with a course of amendment, we need a great encouragement; and that encouragement we derive from the knowledge that God is in alliance with our better nature, that He wills our deliverance from evil. But how do we obtain such a knowledge? The tendency of sin to beget new sin is a law of Divine appointment, and might seem to prove that it is God's design to hold us to the sin we have committed, and to punish it by riveting it upon our souls. But then this law is only the reverse, or negative, of that propitious law by which *good* action tends to become habitual. We cannot separate even in idea the one from the other. Here, as elsewhere, it is, as we have already said, one and the same law which works both good and evil in our lives. It is one and the same organ which makes us susceptible both of pain and pleasure; and so the same Divine constitution of our nature, which is intended for the furtherance of our spiritual life, may also minister to its hindrance. It is the same moral order which encompasses, sustains, and controls men however they may act, whether well or ill; and it has been justly said that man is no more independent of God and of his order, when he transgresses, than when he obeys the Divine will. The operation of this law, in the case of the sinner, is sooner or later to make sin intolerable, and to awaken in him the desire for deliverance from its burden. Instead, therefore, of being a proof of God's will to hold the sinner to his sin, and to hinder his repentance, it is rather a proof that God is on the side of his efforts to escape the bondage of sin; a view of God's relation to the sinner, which expresses itself in the doctrine of forgiveness; and which, when apprehended, oftentimes fills the sinner with joy, and becomes the pledge and instrument of his victory over sin,—the motive power of a true and thorough repentance.

Nothing is more conspicuous in Christ's teaching than the confidence which He places in man's ability to choose the better part, however degraded he may be, however far he may have strayed. Christ's faith in God was also, it is evident, a faith in man. None knew better than He how hard it is for a man to enter the kingdom of God; in other words, to grow strong in his weakness; as we may see from what He said of the camel passing through the needle's eye. But none the less unhesitatingly, none the less authoritatively, did He enjoin men to seek first the kingdom of God, to keep the commandments, to take up the cross. One who was steeped in sin, He enjoins to go and sin no more. He credits even the most depraved with some spiritual power; with some capacity for goodness, however weakened it may be, through long disuse, torpor, and self-indulgence. He believes in a spiritual force in men, latent it may be, yet powerful enough to raise them above themselves, and all the help they need, or can possibly obtain, is to be encouraged to exert that power; and this encouragement He places before them partly in his own example, and partly in the assurance which He conveys to our souls that the forgiveness of sins may be confidently laid hold of by all who desire encouragement in the endeavour to forsake them. For others —that is, for those who live without aspiration, who only wish to obtain a discharge from the consequences of their sins—forgiveness, we need not say, is a mere nonentity, if it be not a snare. It may lull the conscience into a false security, but it can have no effect whatever in releasing such persons from the deadliest consequence of their sins, the tyrannous presence of sin itself in the soul. What Christ's teaching amounts to is: that nothing stands in the way of those who desire to break off their sins by righteousness, except the outward and inward opposition, which has been arrayed by the law of recompence against their better endeavours. And that law, which has seemed hitherto to operate against them, will begin to operate in favour of those who honestly seek to grow in righteousness. After the remarks already made on the subject, we do not need to say now whether there be such a thing as expiation for past sins, in the sense of an objective atonement. But this at least it is desirable to say, that we can, in none but a highly figurative sense, apply the term "expiation" to that amendment, however painful and laborious, of which our faith in the Divine good-will is the motive power. To make such an application of the term (as some theologians seem inclined to do) is to infringe upon the great evangelical idea of the freeness of the grace of God; to throw us back into the religion of law, and to bring us once more under the dominion of the servile spirit.

The beginnings of good which we are encouraged to make in the midst of evil are necessarily small and contemptible in all eyes but his who accepts the first faint indications of the better will. But it is none the less true that good may thus spring up, and that the evil which is not fed at length ceases from remembrance. And though what we reap is the same in kind as we sow, yet what we reap is more than what we sow. For it is of the very nature of seed of every kind to yield increase, to return more than itself; so that, under favouring circumstances of soil and climate, it may produce an hundredfold. Just so, under the beneficent scheme of providence revealed in the gospel, the good which a man does may yield an hundredfold into his own bosom. All things work together for good to him who takes courage and sets himself in singleness and simplicity of heart to do the will of God.

We see, then, that the guilt which we contract is not a fate riveted upon the soul, but an incubus, a burden which may be rolled off, though oftentimes with painful effort, from our shoulders. God desireth not the death of the wicked, but rather that they should turn to him and live; that is, attain to the true and pure and higher life. He will judge the world in righteousness, and render to every man according to his deeds, but He pities and forgives the penitent, and extends to them his hand that they may walk with trembling, faltering steps in the ways of holiness. By virtue of the gracious constitution of things, which we have depicted, there is a curative and reparative power by which evil is transmuted, defects remedied, and new openings made to good. And even the disabling and enslaving effects of sin upon the soul, that most deadly of its penalties, may be eradicated by the exercise of that liberty and privilege to which the gospel invites the sinner, of turning to the supreme good.

Such is the theory of the religious life, and of the gospel scheme. All the rest is mere form, phrase, and pragmatism, to which we are in danger of attaching too much fully more than of attaching too little importance. Ritual and dogma may be so skilfully elaborated, so cunningly adapted to the frailties and likings of the mass of mankind, as to form the strength of the Churches, while they prove the weakness of our Christianity—the cause, direct or indirect, for example, why the non-Christian nations can discern in our civilisation so little to admire or to copy. Stripped of dogma, a creed may seem to be scanty, but not too scanty if it serve to lift the moral life of man into likeness and fellowship with the Divine. Catholic theologians, in the name of religion, demand more than this: namely, that men should pay honour to God by the profession of an elaborate form of faith, and by the practice of an unproductive cult or ritual. But it is a question, whether such a view of religion can be consistently held by Protestants. The Reformation was a protest, before the Diet of Spires, against the degradation of Christianity. Luther broke with Rome solely because it had lost its power to lift the life of man; because it trafficked with souls, and sanctioned all enormities. He made no attempt, it is well known, to create a new *theology*. A sentiment of the deepest reverence for the purely theological portions of the ancient creed was what gave impulse to his reforming zeal. He took exception to such portions of it only, as seemed to him to be at variance with the formal and material principles of Reformation, and to lie at the root of the growing vices and corruptions of Christendom. But the second Reformation will start with a more sweeping principle, and proceed more thoroughly to work, for it will not only discard whatever of the popular creed is hostile to the higher life, but it will be a protest against making of any faith or dogma, which is not necessary for the lifting of human life, a condition of salvation. Men are gradually feeling their way to this point; and we are blind not to see that we are already in the midst of this second Reformation, a Reformation all the greater, because it cometh not with observation.

We are led to the conclusion, that both ritual and dogma should be simple, ministrant and unobtrusive, that they may not encroach too much on the proper sphere of religion, or be substituted in its place, or exhaust that spiritual force in man which should be reserved for it. Enough if, in the necessary acts of common worship, and of private devotion, these give a popular, flexible and vanishing expression to the religious consciousness. But that consciousness itself is fed from the deeper springs of reverence and sympathy, of personal love and trust; which, welling up first in the soul of Christ, have been derived from him to all who have yielded to the attraction of the

Cross, to an attraction which propagates itself from one to another, even "without the Word" (1 Peter iii. 1), by signs of a hidden life, not artificial, which the heart can decipher.

If it be thought that we have attributed to the doctrine of the spiritual harvest a value too dominating, and a sweep too wide, or that we have drawn from it inferences of a nature too negative and destructive, we reply that it itself is the most positive of doctrines; that by the unassailable and commanding position which it occupies among the doctrines of religion, it supplies a sufficient basis for the inferences which have been drawn from it, and acts as a dam against that dogmatic flood, which threatens even now from Rome and Oxford, as by a final effort, to carry all before it. By holding to this fact of the spiritual harvest, we at once reduce the dimensions of dogma, and make it to be felt, that dogmatise and spiritualise as we may, we cannot escape, by a single jot or tittle, the responsibility which clings to us, and that the help which dogma and ritual give us to meet that responsibility is the exact measure of their truth and value.

Well may we reverence the memory of Christ, as Mediator between God and man; because He it was, who from the depths of his own experience, imparted to men the knowledge of God as our Father in heaven; whose property it is to forgive the trespasses of his children, and to incline their feet into the path of righteousness. But let us reject those dogmatic exaggerations of the doctrine, which in the hands of that Church, which is strong in the indisputable possession of historical right, have been as a hammer to forge the chains of the "most formidable spiritual despotism which the world has ever seen;" and by the retention of which, in spite of their inconsistency with her own principle of life, the Church of the Reformation has not only enfeebled her protest and her claim to a higher right than the historical, but carries within herself to this day the seeds of dissolution, and exposes herself to the risk of disappearing again beneath the rallying tide of Romanism.

But indeed, the views expounded lead us to regard with very moderate respect, if not with much suspicion, all rigid ecclesiastical organisations, which necessarily have an ineradicable tendency to retard the progress of the race, even when not avowedly altogether hostile to human liberty and culture. If the generally accepted necessity for such organisations may scare us from a disparaging view of them, the irreconcilable feuds and mutual intolerance of the Churches may go far perhaps to justify such a view. The common life of man is the true form in which, and through which, religion has to shine and show itself. Such is the purpose of God. Whereas the idea of the Church, as supplying the form for a religious life, a life within the life, separate from the common work-day life, rests ultimately on a dualistic and unchristian basis; and is a fugitive device—a devout imagination of man's heart. We may rest assured that the world would not be better, but a great deal worse, than it is, if a conventual, ascetic, ecclesiastical, or pietistic air were to pervade all its doings and institutions.

The formation of a truly noble and manly character and individuality depends on our keeping in mind that we are responsible for our actions, and on our resolutely accepting that responsibility. If we imagine that our responsibility may be transferred to other shoulders, all we can expect to issue from such a doctrine is an effeminate and spurious sentimentality; a piety artificial, even when not divorced from life and practice; a religion which, if sincere in the sense of being without hypocrisy or dissimulation, is not sincere in the sense of being pure and undefiled. The hope of escaping responsibility for our vices and our mistakes is what makes a devotee, not to say a saint. But only he who feels that a necessity is laid upon him of bearing his own burden, and helping others to bear theirs, may hope to grow into that noblest work of God, the simply honest man, the genuine disciple of Christ.

In conclusion, there is no occasion to fear that the apprehension, in the form of scientific truths, of the law of continuity, and of the Divine good-will implied in that law, will make the act of faith less necessary to give to both their practical influence over the life. We are at one with those who regard faith, not as supplying the lack of evidence to truths imperfectly authenticated or understood, but as lending to truths which are theoretically received, and more or less understood, their proper power over the life and conduct. Our endeavour has been to show what modifications of the popular construction of Christianity are needed to bring it into harmony with the laws of mental physiology. We regard Divine judgment and Divine forgiveness, which is but a form or species of judgment, as both alike regulated by law; and law itself as identical with the will of a living God. To stop short of this would be to disown the light which science sheds upon human destiny; to go beyond this would be to leave no room in human thought or practice for that religious principle which is essential to our nature. The defence of popular Christianity—and it is a sufficient defence—is, that it is popular; a figure or an allegory of the absolute truth, which is enshrined in it. But the more that science spreads and establishes its claim to rule human thought, the more will it become necessary to discriminate between the figure and the thing itself; and to acknowledge frankly the subjective and symbolical character of the Dogma. In making this acknowledgment to ourselves, while provisionally retaining the popular and dogmatic forms of expression, we shall but act upon the germinant suggestion of Luther, that things which we do not fully understand, we may yet represent to ourselves under images, even though they may not exactly tally with the images of which we make use for this purpose.[1]

[1] "Wir müssen alle Dinge, die wir nicht kennen und wissen, durch Bilder fassen, ob sie gleich nicht so eben zutreffen, oder in Wahrheit also seein, wie es die Bilder malen."—LUTHER, *as quoted by* WEISSE, *in his* Zukunft der evangelischen Kirche.

XI.

AUTHORITY.

BY THE REV. W. L. M'FARLAN, LENZIE.

Prove all things.—1 THESSALONIANS v. 21.

THE court in which our faculties of observation, reflection, discrimination sit as judges is recognised by an increasing number of persons as that before which it is our right to test the validity of all opinions presented for our acceptance. There are still, however, on the other hand, some who refuse to acknowledge the supremacy of the court thus constituted, and who maintain in opposition to the claims of the judges within the breast to be supreme in all matters of belief, the right of powers without it finally to decide for us what is true and what is false. In other words, the old controversy between the rights of private judgment and the rights of authority is still unsettled. Any contribution consequently towards the settlement of it, which a Christian minister has to offer, may not be unacceptable to the members of a Christian congregation.

I propose, accordingly, in the present discourse, to vindicate the claims of the individual reason to supreme authority over the beliefs of the individual.

In my vindication of them, I shall confine my observations to one sphere exclusively—that of religion. It is unnecessary that I should defend the rights of the individual reason in any other department of human knowledge than the theological or religious, because in all other departments these rights are acknowledged, theoretically at least. We attribute, no doubt, a certain authority to experts in the various sciences. Most of us are content to take pretty much at second-hand our astronomy from the astronomer, our chemistry from the chemist, our physiology from the physiologist. Or, to come down to homelier matters, most of us when attacked by disease intrust ourselves, with a confidence more or less implicit, to the physician. Warned again by the proverb, "He that is his own counsel hath a fool for his client," we put our case in the hands of the lawyer when we are forced in courts of justice to defend our rights or to redress our wrongs. But while we thus permit the professional man and the scientific specialist to exercise a certain authority over our beliefs and over the conduct which is dependent on our beliefs, the authority which we concede to them is merely provisional. We change our medical or our legal adviser so soon as we have or think that we have sufficient cause for believing that the advice of the one or of the other is erroneous. We do not place ourselves absolutely at the mercy of those who popularise for us the various sciences. The credence which we have given to the statements of a lecturer on chemistry would be shaken were we to learn that they were contradicted by other competent chemists. Nay, we always conceive it possible that we may become chemists ourselves, that we may yet acquire such knowledge of the science of chemistry as would enable us intelligently to follow and justly to appraise the arguments by which the statements and counter-statements of the conflicting professors of it are respectively supported. We do not therefore concede to professional practitioners in law or medicine, nor to the professed teachers of any science, an authority which is more than provisional; neither do we, avowedly at all events, recognise in any of our fellow-creatures a right to dictate to us our political beliefs. Practically many of us, as to these beliefs, may be blindly led by our favourite newspaper, or we may tamely submit to the prevalent opinion of our class, or to the traditions of our family. Theoretically, however, we all assert that in regard to our political, as in regard to our scientific opinions, we are not in bondage to any man.

There only remains the sphere of religion, it thus appears, in which it may turn out that men consciously submit to an authority which is more than provisional, and disclaim the right of proving all things. To this sphere, therefore, I shall restrict my remarks. In it we shall find that the only supposed claimant whose claims to supremacy over our beliefs, in opposition to those of the individual reason, it is worth our while to consider, is the Bible. The spiritual descendants of the most strenuous of all the Reformers, we recognise neither in Church nor Council, Pope nor priest, the right to impose upon us theological dogmas. With the Covenanters most of us thoroughly sympathise, in so far as they refused to accept, at the bidding of the Stuart Princes, a doctrine, a worship, an ecclesiastical polity, which were distasteful to them, and indignantly declined to be "of the King's religion," to borrow from the great French autocrat—whom Charles and James were anxious to imitate—a phrase which he was fond of using. In a country in which dissent is rife and multiform, no dissident minority has occasion to dread on the part of a tyrannous majority interference with its "freedom to worship God." Neither then on behalf of the Church, nor of the State, nor of public opinion, are claims to an absolute authority over our religious beliefs openly urged in Protestant Scotland. No doubt there is not a little of social intolerance amongst us. Those who avow what are called infidel opinions are ostracised. The Socinian even is regarded with a certain suspicion and dislike. Nay, there are still circles in which every departure, however slight, from the dogmas of the Westminster Divines, or at all events from some such modified creed, let us say as that of the Evangelical Alliance, are denounced as sinful. As the counterpart of the impatience thus manifested towards those who venture to diverge from the prevalent orthodoxy of the day, we find in Scottish society a tendency to accept blindly the theological traditions handed down to us from the past, and to receive as doctrines divine the opinions of the doctors in divinity whom we have been accustomed to revere. This practically is the attitude of a large number of Scotchmen towards the creeds of the past, or the popular theology of the present. Theoretically, however, they disclaim all title, whether on the part of the Puritan divines of the seventeenth century, or of the Pan-Presbyterian doctors of the nineteenth,—to impose upon them their theological beliefs. They derive these they say direct from the Bible, the only rule of faith and manners. If they condemn misbelievers, it is, they assure you, because misbelievers despise the authority of the sacred Scriptures, not because they reject that of any uninspired theologians dead or living.

It is only to the Bible, then, that an authority superior to that of reason and conscience is attributed amongst us—in theory at least. To the Scriptures Protestants have conceded the infallibility which they have denied to the Church. The utterances of Scripture may in some cases, it is avowed, be incomprehensible by the ordinary human faculties. They may awaken no response in the higher reason of man. They may excite repulsion even in his conscience. Still they proceed, it is alleged, from the eternal reason. They express a knowledge which exists in the Divine mind. They are truths which have been supernaturally communicated to the specially guided or the specially gifted. They ought therefore to receive unquestioning assent from all who would be of the household of faith. Not only must all that the Scriptures teach about morality and religion, about man's relations to God and the duties which he owes Him, be thus without question accepted,—there must be no cavilling, either at anything they have to tell us in regard to the era or the manner of the world's creation, the chronology of primeval times, the history of the judges and the kings of Israel, the origins of Christianity and the controversies of the primitive church. All their statements alike must receive implicit credence, for all alike were written by penmen who had access to the mind of Omniscience, and were in contact with it when they wrote. Human reason may be legitimately employed in examining the evidences of the Divine authorship of the Scriptures, and in interpreting their contents; but it cannot be legitimately employed in calling in question the veracity of any statement within the boards of the sacred volume whose meaning has been ascertained.

Such are the claims to an absolute authority in all matters of belief which are urged on behalf of the Bible by those who hold the theory of its plenary inspiration and verbal infallibility. I have stated that theory in all its "rigor and vigor," but I do not think that I have caricatured it. It may seldom be obtruded upon us in these days in its most uncompromising form. No preacher of any pretensions to intelligence and culture now speaks of those who wrote the Scriptures as though they were mere mechanical instruments of the Holy Ghost, automaton penmen as it were, who performed the parts arranged for them just as the automaton chess-players and card-players of whom we read perform their parts in the manner designed by the cunning mechanists who have formed and who work them. It is the fact, nevertheless, I believe, that some such theory of inspiration as that which I have described above is maintained by all who regard the whole Bible as the Word of God, and therefore as entitled in all its parts to an authority over the reason of man which is absolute and final.

Is this theory, we have now to ask, of the infallibility of the Bible valid? Can we discover in the

Scriptures an external authority which shall supersede the internal authority of reason and conscience ? That we may be able to answer these questions, let us examine the grounds on which those who claim for the Bible an absolute authority rest their claim. Their argument, I take it, may be thus briefly stated : Miracles are the credentials granted to those to whom a Divine mission is intrusted. But it is attested by persons who wrote within thirty or forty years of Christ's death, and who suffered for their testimony, that Christ and his apostles wrought miracles. Therefore we may conclude that to them a Divine mission had been intrusted. Now, persons intrusted with such a mission must, in executing it, speak with absolute authority. In executing their mission—in discharging their function, *i.e.* as religious teachers sent from God, Christ and his apostles, it is recorded by the credible witnesses mentioned above, claim for " the law and the prophets," *i.e.* for all the books of the Old Testament, it is assumed, a Divine authority similar to that which their own words possessed. Hence it follows that the entire Scriptures both of the New Testament and the Old are authoritative, and true because authoritative. Such, in brief, is the argument by which the theory of the infallibility of the Bible is supported. The argument seems logically valid. If the premises of the various syllogisms into which it might have been developed are all statements which can be verified, the desiderated conclusion is unavoidable. The misfortune is that the premises in the concatenated argument presented to you above cannot be verified. They cannot be verified otherwise than by an appeal to human authority, to the authority of the learned in our own day it may be, or at all events ultimately to that of Fathers and Councils of the Church which Protestants, by the necessity of their position, disclaim. The ordinary reader of the Bible, if he is to accept the argument in support of its verbal infallibility at all, must accept it from beginning to end, must accept it entire on the authority of the erudite. He cannot verify for himself the statements that the Gospels and the Book of Acts were written within forty years even of Christ's death; that the record which they contain of the miracles, alleged to have been wrought by Christ and his apostles, is one on whose truthfulness we can implicitly rely; that the report which they give him of their sayings in general is thoroughly accurate,—that their report of the words in particular, in which the divinely commissioned teachers of the New Testament affirm, it is supposed, the infallibility of all the books of the Old Testament, is a correct representation of their teaching on that subject. On all these points the ordinary reader of the Bible is dependent on students who are learned and leisured. How can he satisfy himself that the learned men, on whose authority he rests his belief in the Bible's authority, are the most learned men he can find? There is no consensus of the erudite in regard to that theory of an infallible Bible, to which he is asked to pin his faith. Far from it. The theory aforesaid, which, by dint of much erudition, one school of theologians think that they have established, another school of theologians affirm that they, by dint of greater erudition, have demolished.

If therefore the ordinary reader of the Bible is to accept the theory of its verbal infallibility, he must accept it by attributing a practical infallibility to the divines of the school to which he has arbitrarily given the preference. More than this. The learned men themselves who have formulated the theory in question are ultimately dependent upon human authority for their belief in it. The right of each of the books which make up the Scriptures to a place in the sacred canon can be established only by the authority of the early Councils of the Church—by the authority indeed of the early Fathers of the Church, whose opinions in regard to the date and the authorship of the various books in the Bible were adopted by the Councils which decided as to the canonicity of each. It is only on the authority of these Fathers, therefore, that they rest their belief in the early date of the Gospels and the Book of Acts. It is only on their authority also, it follows, that they can satisfy themselves as to the accuracy of the narratives which contain records of the miracles wrought by Christ and his apostles. Now these miracles, according to the theory we are discussing, are the attestation of the Divine mission of the Founder of our religion and his immediate followers. The conclusion therefore is inevitable, that the advocates of the infallibility of the Bible must ultimately accept on human authority the proposition on which the whole stress of their argument in favour of it rests,—the proposition, namely, that it is proved by the miracles which Christ and his apostles wrought that they had such access to the mind of Omniscience as made them absolutely infallible in all they said and wrote. Whatever therefore may be said in favour of the theory which represents the Bible as true because authoritative, it cannot be affirmed of it that it is consistent with the principles of Protestantism.

The Reformers entertained no such theory in regard to the Scriptures. They appealed from the Church to the Bible, no doubt. They professed to derive all their theology from the latter, and not from the former. But they regarded the Bible not as true because authoritative, but as authoritative because true. Luther's views in regard to the canon were what many in these days would consider lax. Well-informed persons are aware that he was inclined to exclude from the canon the Revelation of John. Every one knows in what contemptuous terms he spoke of the Epistle of James. The Westminster Divines adhere to a doctrine which was substantially identical with that of the great Reformer. These astute logicians perceived that had they adopted the opposite doctrine, and maintained that the Bible was true because authoritative, they would have been compelled ultimately to submit, in one form or another, to the dictation of the Church, whose right to dictate to men their beliefs they and their spiritual progenitors had so strenuously denied. They therefore held that the Bible was authoritative because true. " The authority of the holy Scripture," they say, " for which it ought to be believed and obeyed, dependeth not upon the testimony of any man or church, but wholly upon God (who is truth itself), the author thereof;" and again, " Our full persuasion and assurance of the authority of Scripture is from the inward work of the Holy Spirit, bearing witness by and with the word in our hearts." This is remarkable language. When it is translated out of the dialect of the seventeenth century, which the Divines of Westminster spoke, into that of the nineteenth century, which we speak, it amounts I think substantially to this: that the Scriptures are authoritative only in so far as they are true. The distinction between the human and the Divine elements in Scripture was not of course so distinctly recognised, either by the Reformers or the Westminster Divines, as it is by thoughtful theologians in our own times. That distinction had not been forced upon the attention of the former as it has been forced upon the attention of the latter, by the discoveries of men of science and the investigations of Biblical critics. Still, they assert, we have seen, that the chief assurance which we—we, the elect in the dialect of their day, we, the spiritually susceptible in the dialect of our day,—have of the " divine authority of Scripture is from the inward work of the Holy Spirit, bearing witness by and with the word in our hearts." And this language they must have perceived was totally inapplicable to such portions of Scripture as the descriptions of the dimensions and furniture of the tabernacle in Leviticus, the genealogies of Chronicles, the historical narratives even, of the Old Testament, in their details at least, the purely historical and the apocalyptic sections of the New Testament itself. We may claim therefore to have the Westminster Divines with us, when we assert that the Scriptures are authoritative because true, and only in such portions of them as awaken a response in those in whom reason and conscience, the faculties by which alone truth can be discerned, have been duly developed.

This doctrine of the Westminster Divines in regard to the Bible is really that of all simple and devout souls. They find in the Bible manifold revelations of God, which awaken a response in their conscience, and confirm those prepossessions of their spiritual nature, loyal trust in which alone deserves the name of faith. Finding in the Bible many revelations which need no testimony from without as to their truth, they probably speak of the Bible as a whole as the revelation of God. Quite possibly they employ phrases borrowed from that theory of verbal inspiration which is, we may say, an article of luxury fabricated by those who are at once learned and leisured for their own use and delectation : but that theory in reality has over them but little influence. Its phrases upon their lips are not scientific propositions to be interpreted with rigid accuracy. They are the mere hyperboles of affection, its fervid exaggerations. For simple and pious souls in our own day, as for the Psalmist of old, the law of the Lord, his word, his testimonies, his statutes, his commandments, in which they rejoice and take delight, finding them more precious than gold, sweeter than honey, and the honey-comb, are not the whole Bible, but those portions of the Bible only which they have found in their experience helpful to their souls. All who have a love for the Bible which is that of the heart and not merely of the lips, that of the closet student of it, and not of the platform spouter about it, have their favourite books and portions of books, and these alone are to them Divine revelations. Through these portions of Scripture God speaks to their souls with authority, but in their souls they feel that they are divinely authoritative only because they are divinely true.

This is the manner in which men and women, who are pious without being learned or leisured, regard their Bibles; so long at least as they remain unsophisticated in spirit by the votaries of the fine-spun theories we have been discussing. In a manner essentially similar, men and women who are more highly educated, though they do not pretend to great erudition, regard their Bibles. What the former class of persons vaguely feel, the latter class of persons intelligently discern. After much reading and more reflection, they have satisfied themselves that the theory of the verbal inspiration of the Bible, in vogue during the last and the first half of the present centuries,—the theory, that is, which attributes to every utterance in the Bible an absolute authority *ab extra* over the minds of men,—is untenable. The Councils, they hold, which settled the canon, have failed to prove irrefragably that the Gospels and the Book of Acts were written before the close of the first century. Consequently they cannot be certain that all the words in them attributed to Christ and his apostles were really the words they spoke, undiluted, undistorted, unexaggerated. Neither can they be absolutely sure that the miracles ascribed to them were actually wrought by them. They cannot, therefore, accept the words which Christ is reported to have spoken, nor those which the apostles unquestionably wrote, as the utterances of teachers, who can be proved by the miracles they wrought to have had such access to the mind of Omniscience as made them absolutely infallible in all they said and wrote. The argument for the infallibility of the Old Testament falls with that for the infallibility of the New, for the argument for the infallibility of the former rests either on assertions of it in the latter, which are attributed to Christ and his apostles, or on predictions concerning Christ, which predictions the former contain and the latter allege were fulfilled.

But while the intelligent and open-minded Protestants of whom I speak at present cannot recognise as valid the argument in favour of the verbal infallibility of the Bible, they cherish for the Bible a profound reverence. The Scriptures contain, they believe, a revelation to man of those truths which it most concerns him to know. Even though, as the advanced critic alleges, none of the Gospels were written before the second century—though, consequently, they cannot feel certain that any of them report with absolute accuracy Christ's words, or record, without adding some elements of the legendary and mythical, his deeds—they yet recognise in many of the sayings and discourses attributed to Christ the words of a Divine teacher, in his works as a healer of disease a Divine beneficence, in his life as a whole a Divine life. Many of Christ's words as reported in the Gospels are so remarkably illustrated by many of his deeds recorded there, his character harmonises so wonderfully with his teaching, that they are forced to regard the narratives of the evangelists as substantially truthful, in so far as they present to us a picture of the personality of Christ. And that personality, they think, is a revelation to man as to what God is, as to what he ought to be. Through it there was introduced into the world, they hold, at once a purer conception of the Divine character, and loftier ideals of human life and conduct. Christ's personality as presented in the Gospels introduced these truths into the world, they further perceive, as his teaching by itself could not have done. For

> Truth in closest words shall fail,
> Where truth embodied in a tale
> Shall enter in at lowly doors.

Thus in the Gospels especially do those who are forced by the investigations of the Biblical critic to reject the theory of verbal inspiration, or any approximation to it, yet find a revelation of Divine truths. But in all Scripture these highly-educated Christians, as well as simpler Christians, find scattered here and there similar revelations. In the Psalms and the discourses of the prophets, in which Christ's teaching concerning the righteousness of God, God's care for man, the purity of heart and life which He demands of him, are anticipated, as it were; in the writings of the apostles, which not only reinforce Christ's teachings, but which present them in new lights, we may say, and show how his ideal of the Divine life can be realised in circumstances more closely analogous to our own than those of the Galilean peasants to whom He first proclaimed it—in the Scriptures, that is, which stand on either side of the Gospels—they find a revelation of Divine truths. They reverence the Scriptures as a whole, because there is so much more in them than in any other book which "finds them," to use Coleridge's well-known phrase, "at the deepest depths of their being." But while they recognise a Divine element in the Scriptures, they recognise a human element as well. They do not attach an equal value to all portions of them. They do not place the Books of Esther and Daniel on the same level with the Psalter. They do not claim for the writers of Chronicles an inspiration equal to that of the second Isaiah, or even the first. They do not pretend to find in the historical books of the Old Testament as much edification as in the letters of Paul, nor in the theological disquisitions of Paul himself so much furtherance of the higher life as in the more practical portions of his Epistles. They do not affirm that the common-sense philosophy of the Book of Proverbs, serviceable though it be in many respects, is of equal worth with the spiritual teachings of Christ. While they admit that there are important truths of morality and religion embodied in the Pentateuch, they admit also that its authors attribute an importance to the ceremonial parts of religion which is wholly at variance with the loftier conceptions of the Divine requirements entertained by the prophets; and that they, in common with the authors of all the historical books, and indeed with the prophets themselves, both in their estimates of human character and their interpretations of the Divine dealings with man, sometimes fail to set before us an ideal of life and conduct which is pure and elevated.

Enlightened Christians in the present day feel that in this manner they are entitled to deal with the

Scriptures. They claim the right to judge each of their utterances in the light of their own Christian consciousness, and to deny Divine authority to any of them which fall beneath the ethical standards which, as men illuminated by the spirit of Christ, they have set up for their own guidance. They deny all Divine authority, I may add, to those portions of Scripture which treat of matters which belong more properly to science and history than to religion. The Christian consciousness, in the light of which they claim to judge the Scriptures, they admit has been developed chiefly by the Scriptures. It is a spiritual inheritance which belongs to them as men christianly educated, as men, besides, who are descended from generations of the christianly educated. There is nothing, however, in this admission on their part, that the Scriptures have been of highest service to them, which is inconsistent with their denial, on the other hand, that the Scriptures as a whole are infallible, and therefore in all their utterances authoritative. It is not the Scriptures as a whole they maintain, but the higher teachings in them only, which have generated the Christian consciousness in themselves, in the society to which they belong. Nothing, they are persuaded, has done so much to retard the development of the Christian consciousness in the Protestant sections of Christendom as the superstitious reverence for the Bible prevalent among Protestants. It is one of the strongest arguments, they think, against the theory of verbal inspiration, that by inducing its readers to attach a like value and a like authority to all portions of the Bible, it has had this injurious influence on society.

Gratefully recognising all that the Scriptures have done for the race,—perceiving how they have introduced into the world the purest conceptions of the Divine nature and the loftiest ideals of human character which it has known, going to them, therefore, with a profound but with no superstitious veneration,—the enlightened Christians, of whom I have been speaking, discover in them ever fuller and deeper meanings. Holding the views in regard to the Scriptures which they hold, they may be unable to deduce from them, in the shape of a dogmatic system, a theory of the Universe which they can impose upon their neighbours as complete and final. They do find in them, however, and in the Christian consciousness in the formation of which they have had the chief part, a working theory of life which is most helpful. Reading in the light of that consciousness the Psalter, the Prophets, the Epistles, the sayings of Christ, they never fail to find in them that which all earnest men and women most want,—help amidst life's practical difficulties, comfort amidst its sorrows, the assurance of the forgiveness of its sins, quickening of its loftiest aspirations after the divine. The Bible, they acknowledge, is thus full of revelations to the devout soul: but they hold that those portions of it only are revelations to them, which awaken a response in the conscience and higher reason. Such is the attitude assumed by many enlightened Protestants in our own day towards the Bible. It is an attitude, I believe, essentially similar to that which was assumed by the Reformers in the sixteenth century. The modern Protestant may assert more boldly than the primitive Protestant that the Bible is authoritative only in so far as it is true. But true Protestants, both of the earlier period and of the later, agree in maintaining that the Bible is authoritative because true, and not true because authoritative.

With these conclusions, at which many enlightened Protestants in our day have arrived in regard to the Scriptures, I agree in the main. The doctrine which they hold in common with the Reformers, the doctrine that the Scriptures are authoritative because true, I heartily accept. The only authority, I must maintain, which we can attribute to any of their utterances is that of its inherent reasonableness. I can discover no better.

This proposition seems to me much more reasonable than the counter proposition of the advocates of the Bible's verbal infallibility. These theorists assert in effect that men cannot be sure that light is light, until some one armed with authority tells them that it is so: that they cannot know that truth is truth until the speaker of it is accredited by signs from heaven. Such an assertion, whatever semblance of humility it may wear, is really dishonouring to God. Those who accept it pour contempt upon their Maker, by refusing to put forth, on the highest and grandest subjects, the powers which He has conferred upon them for the discernment of truth. The human faculties, I am aware, are finite, and fallible as well as finite. Still, limited though these faculties are, and liable to error, they are the only instruments by which men can grapple with knowledge and make it their own. In refusing to apply them to the grandest of all questions which can occupy the attention, they virtually express their disbelief in any Divine illumination granted to all sincere seekers for the truth. They have placed themselves, they say, under the guidance of the inspired penmen. But their belief in the inspiration of the sacred writers rests not on the inherent reasonableness of the statements they make, but on the authority of some ancient doctor of the Church, who assures them that the books which bear the names of lawgivers, and apostles, and prophets, are entitled to a place in the sacred canon. This, I hold, is to abandon the Protestant position. It is to acknowledge the authority of our fellow-men speaking without, as superior to that of reason and conscience speaking within. It is to call some other than God father, some other than Christ master.

There are many departments of knowledge on which we must to a considerable extent be dependent, provisionally at least, on our fellow-men for our opinions. In regard to theology, however, the case is different. It suggests questions which none can be content to answer at second-hand, without damage to their spiritual life,—which none can succeed in answering at first-hand, without manifest advantage to their spiritual life. What is the chief end of man? What is God? How does God enable man to attain the true end of his being? These are questions which serious-minded men and women cannot allow theological experts to answer for them. They cannot lazily accept as their replies to them, the replies which have been made by an Athanasius, an Augustine, a Calvin, nor even those which have been made by the evangelists who profess to report the words of Christ, nor by a man of such profound spiritual insight as Paul. Help they may get from prophets and apostles, from ancient saints and doctors, from the divines of the sixteenth century, from the theologians and philosophers of the nineteenth, in their attempts to answer the questions enumerated above. It is sheerest folly to reject their assistance, or to treat with contempt the conclusions at which the great and good, the devout and thoughtful, have arrived on the greatest of all subjects. Still, serious-minded men and women cannot accept in any blind and unintelligent submission to the authority of celebrated, or even of sacred names, the answers which have been made to the great questions in theology. They must work out its problems, which are the problems of life, for themselves. They must prove all things for themselves, grappling with the difficulties which modern speculation suggests, and with those sorer difficulties which are raised by their own experiences of suffering and sorrow, of the evil which is within them and around them. Not, it may be, till after long struggle with these difficulties shall those who engage in the intellectual and spiritual warfare of our age be able to answer the all-important problems of which I have spoken, or to give any adequate account to themselves of the meaning of their lives in this strange world. They shall, however, through toil and storm, reach at length the serener air. They shall come at last through the conflict with doubt, to call something like a faith their own. The certainties of that faith may be few, but they are sufficient to form a working theory of life, and they are more helpful than the most minute and elaborate creed taken up at second-hand.

But is it not dangerous, some one asks, to abandon the theory of verbal inspiration, and to deny the existence of any authority superior to the reason and conscience of man? There can be no real danger, the genuine Protestant replies, in following truth whithersoever it may lead us: and if there be no authority in which men can more implicitly trust than the christianly-enlightened conscience, it is well that they should recognise the fact. After all, the courageous Protestant goes on to urge, men need not be under any alarm because they are forced to abandon the notion of a verbally infallible Bible. To simple and devout souls the Bible will still be the Book of Life, whatever theory in regard to its inspiration the thoughtful and the cultured may adopt. From its higher teachings they will continue to receive counsel and consolation, guidance amidst the perplexities of their daily life, and strength to bear its trials. The divine element in it will now, as heretofore, quicken their spiritual life. The human element in it, with its admixture of error, will probably cause them less and less of pain and disturbance, the more completely they are enabled to free themselves from the superstitious conception of plenary inspiration. To men of mind less simple than those referred to above, to men who from natural temperament crave for systematic completeness in their views, the destruction of the doctrine of verbal infallibility may prove a rude shock. That shock may prostrate them. They may lose in consequence of it all intellectual nerve, so to speak.

Unable any longer to feel themselves in possession of fixed opinions on many matters about which men naturally desire to be certain, they may grow morbidly impatient. In their impatience they may betake themselves not improbably to Rome, and become the slaves of its spiritual despotism. This conduct is not unnatural in men of their peculiar intellectual temperament, but it is unmanly. It is a cowardly abandonment of the field on which the good fight of faith is fought. Men of firmer intellectual fibre, who feel that with the demolition of the doctrine of the Bible's verbal infallibility the entire theological system which had seemed to them an intellectual home and place of safety is reduced to ruin, adopt a different course. They accept the new position. Driven from the dogmatic structure which had sheltered them so long, they throw up an earthwork of personal conviction to screen them from the assaults of that practical atheism, which is deadly to the soul. Of the two courses, that of the pervert to Catholicism, and that of the man who is resolved to have no theology which he cannot base on personal conviction, the latter is the nobler and the manlier. It is the safer one too, for that matter. It is better for all who have in them any capacity for a lofty intellectual and spiritual life to be out in the open, than to be confined within the dogmatic fortresses, which are in fact prison-houses, dungeons of the soul. Let them stand fast behind their temporary shelter, and having done all, let them stand. They shall be enabled to advance ere long to a stronger position, which is still one which a freeman need not be ashamed to occupy. Meanwhile let them stand,—let them cleave to whatever convictions they may have made really their own, should they be only these —that righteousness is blessedness, that integrity is worth retaining, that there are things pure, just, honest, lovely, which a man should think of and follow after. To those who cleave to these simple convictions, others will be added. They shall find these words true in their experience: "If any man will do the will of God, he shall know of the doctrine whether it be of God." They shall discover for themselves that there is a Divine authority in Christ's doctrine, that man has a Father in heaven, who is righteous with a righteousness which He intends to be theirs,—who is seeking to make them righteous with that righteousness,—perfect as He is perfect. To those whose appetite for dogma is large, this creed may seem meagre and unsatisfying. It is more genuine and more serviceable, however, than that of those who accept, in submission to the authority avowedly of their Church, or professedly of their Bible, all the decrees of the Council of Trent, or all the articles of the Assembly of Westminster. It is the creed of one who can say with the old Hebrew seer and poet, "I have heard of Thee with the hearing of the ear, but now mine eye seeth Thee." It is the creed, consequently, of a man whose Protestantism has in it a genuine intellectual and spiritual life.

XII.

THE THINGS WHICH CANNOT BE SHAKEN.

BY THE REV. W. L. M'FARLAN, LENZIE.

That the things which cannot be shaken may remain.
HEB. XI. 27.

THAT the old theologies are being shaken by the new sciences is a fact which is patent to the most superficial observation. The assaults which are made by the students of the sciences, natural and biblical, upon the dogmatic theology of the past, are dealt with in different ways by observers of different classes. They are angrily denounced by one class as the wanton attacks of the wicked upon the religion of Christ. They are soberly welcomed by another as instrumentalities, somewhat rough in their operation, by which the religion of Christ is being purified from the corruptions which have attached themselves to it. They are enthusiastically hailed by a third as agencies which will effect the destruction of the religion of Christ, viewed by them as an obsolete superstition. What the position is, which is occupied by observers of the second or middle class, I shall endeavour in the present discourse to define. This class includes within it many of the religious teachers in all the Churches. To what extent, we have to inquire, do such religious teachers admit that the old beliefs in which they were indoctrinated are endangered by the new theories which, it is alleged, must supersede them entirely? They admit, I may venture to reply for them, that in so far as these beliefs were embodied in the dogmas of scholastic theology, they must be abandoned or greatly modified. The sections of that theology which treat of sin and salvation they regard as specially untenable. These sections comprehend the following dogmas:— (1) the descent of man from the Adam of the Book of Genesis; (2) the fall of that Adam, from a state of original righteousness, by eating the forbidden fruit; (3) the imputation of Adam's guilt to all his posterity; (4) the consequent death of all men in sin; (5) the redemption in Christ of an election according to grace; (6) the quickening in the elect of a new life—(*a*) at their baptism, Catholics affirm—(*b*) at the moment of their conversion, most Protestants allege; (7) the eternal punishment and perdition of those who remain unregenerate. These sections of the traditional theology of Christendom,—originally elaborated by Augustine, amended and developed by the schoolmen of the middle ages, adopted wholesale by the Puritans,—dominated the Christian intellect for centuries. They have ceased to dominate it. They no longer press on the minds and spirits of men like an incubus. At the Reformation, the whole of the mighty theological fabric which the subtlety of the schoolmen had reared, began to be subjected to a process of disintegration as it were, a trace of which may be detected in the Protestant modification of the Catholic doctrine in regard to the moment at which regeneration takes place, to which allusion has been made above. Ever since the Reformation, the spirit of free inquiry has been destroying, bit by bit, the structure of scholastic theology. During the last quarter of a century she has been attacking it with hands more than ever bold and busy. In consequence of her attacks the ancient structure is now apparently tottering to its fall. It is no longer, at all events, an impregnable dungeon fortress of the mind, a kind of spiritual Bastille, so to speak, in which the Christian intellect is hopelessly immured. With comparative ease men can break that hoary prison-house, and find the liberty which they crave, to interpret Scripture for themselves, to think for themselves. We observe accordingly that conclusions of the school divines, which the Reformers did not venture to question, are denied outright by the leaders of modern theological thought, and that many Protestants of the nineteenth century reject theological dogmas of theirs, which almost all Protestants of the sixteenth century unhesitatingly accepted.

Among the discredited dogmas of the schoolmen, those in regard to the origin and the nature of human sinfulness have, as has been already stated, a foremost place. Various causes are conducing to the rejection of those ancient ecclesiastical beliefs. It seems, in the first place, to an increasing number of intelligent persons, that science has established her right to claim for man an antiquity so great as to be wholly incompatible with the scriptural account of a first progenitor of the human race, who was created, and who sinned and fell, some six thousand years previous to the present date. It seems to them, in the second place, that all investigations into the condition of man during these millenniums, many more than six, throughout which the human race has occupied the earth and left vestiges of its occupancy, prove that the path trodden by mankind has been one upwards and not downwards;—disprove, in other words, the doctrine that the race has lapsed from a state of paradisaic innocence, of primeval wisdom and integrity, such as that which Jewish Rabbis, and after them doctors of the Primitive Church, medieval schoolmen, Puritan divines, have imagined. Independently, however, of all scientific conjectures as to the origin of the human race, as to the condition of prehistoric man, as to the progress of mankind through successive stages of intellectual and moral growth, the old theological doctrine of the fall of Adam, and the consequent death in sin of all his posterity, seems, in these days, to many men and women of cultivated intelligence, untenable. The spread of democratic ideas has rendered impossible for them the belief in hereditary demerit any more than in hereditary merit. They admit of course the hereditary transmission, from generation to generation, of habits, aptitudes for good or evil, qualities intellectual and moral no less than physical. They deny, on the other hand, the hereditary transmission of guilt or blameworthiness, the imputation to the son of the sin of the father. They refuse to believe that the Infinite Being, of whom we speak as the Moral Governor of the universe, has dealt with the successive generations of men as earthly sovereigns have with the children of rebels, whom, in obedience to a political exigency, real or imaginary, they have condemned to perpetual poverty and disgrace. They reject the proposition that the non-elect will, because of Adam's transgression, be punished with "the everlasting punishment of eternal fire." They hold with the old Hebrew prophet, as against the scholastic divine, that under his government whose "ways are equal," "the son shall not bear the iniquity of the father." Their deepening conviction as to the perfect goodness of the Almighty, as well as their belief in the independent, personal, non-hereditary relation of each human spirit to the Father of Spirits, compels persons of minds devout as well as cultivated, to reject the scholastic doctrine of the imputation of the sin of Adam to all his posterity. The Divine Spirit, such persons hold, has abandoned no human spirit to endless and hopeless depravity, has not suffered the human race, or any portion of it, to enter on a career that is ceaselessly and inevitably downwards. The Maker of men, they believe, has implanted in all men the consciousness of imperfection and shortcoming, the sense of sin, which impels them to long and strive for better things. He has thus been securing for the race, as a whole, moral progress from age to age. He thus gives to us, concerning those individuals of the race even whose lives here have seemed to end in failure, the hope of improvement hereafter.

The prevalent scientific beliefs, it thus appears, in regard to the antiquity of man, and the moral and intellectual development of the race, combined with the growth of the democratic spirit, and the spread of what may be named humaner conceptions in regard to the Divine character and the method of the Divine government of the world, have rendered the dogmas of scholastic theology concerning the nature and the origin of human sin, incredible to many minds.

Those who thus feel themselves constrained to reject the scholastic dogmas in regard to sin, cannot, it is plain, accept those corollaries from them, which together make up the scholastic doctrine in regard to salvation. They recognise the truth which is in these doctrines, in so far as they assert the unconditional freedom of the Divine grace, or, in other words, the Divine readiness to forgive and restore the sinner. They believe in what has been called the omnipotence of repentance. They hold, that while the evil consequences of a man's evil deeds dog his footsteps to his dying day, there are yet ever open to the greatest sinner the possibilities of entrance on a new and nobler life. They assert, with Paul, that "the goodness of God is leading the sinner to repentance." They use language of his, still more evangelical in its ring, and maintain, "that God is in Christ reconciling the world unto himself, not imputing unto men their trespasses," not making, that is, the sins that are past, obstacles to his mercy, but causing his grace to superabound over our many offences.

But while the modern theologians whose views I am endeavouring to expound, thus use evangelical language, and recognise a certain amount of truth in those scholastic dogmas concerning redemption which are popularly known as the Gospel, they reject these dogmas when they are presented to them in scientific form and systematic completeness, as constituting what is called "the scheme of salvation." They decline to believe that there is unveracity in the Divine dealings with man, or that God can count men righteous on any other ground than that of the sincerity of their repentance, and the reality of their endeavours after new obedience. Christ, they hold, has died that men might thus die with him, and live again. The scholastic notion, however, that his sufferings constitute the exact arithmetical equivalent of the penalties incurred by the elect for their sins, they reject as formal, unreal, unverifiable. The whole of that latest development of theological scholasticism, the Dutch covenant theology, with its solemn bargainings between God and Adam, between God the Father and God the Son, they regard as a fashion as quaint and artificial as the Dutch landscape-gardening which along with it came into vogue in the British Islands.

It is in vain to insist with those who, while they retain, they believe, a genuine Christian faith, are yet not unsensitive to the influences of the modern scientific spirit, that those doctrines which they are willing to abandon are derived from the teachings of Paul. They admit that Paul does seem to countenance those doctrines of substitution and imputation which they reject. But from Paul rabbinising, they appeal to Paul speaking out of the depths of his profound spiritual insight. Does Paul speak of the redemption which there is in Christ? He there uses a figure, which, they assert, is derived from the Levitical legislation in regard to bondmen. This simile, however, they insist must not be made to run upon all-fours. Even where Paul's simile is most elaborately developed by him, the systematic divine is scarcely warranted, his opponents maintain, in asserting that the Pauline doctrine of redemption implies persons bought back—sinners; a person buying back—God the Son; a person to whom a price is paid—God the Father; the price paid—the penal sufferings of Christ in the room of the elect. Does Paul again speak of Christ's sufferings as sacrificial? Again he uses a figure derived from Levitical legislation; but his use of it, the modern theologian asserts, does not entitle the systematic divine to formulate that doctrine of an arithmetical atonement which he rejects. Paul's central and vital doctrines, the modern theologian maintains, were not those of substitution and imputation, however easy it may be to find for them a plausible support in isolated sayings of his. His central and vital doctrine was: Die, that you may live indeed. Christ died for you, but only that you might die with him, to your lower and worser selves, only that you might find joy in mortifying your members that are upon the earth. By his cross your affections and lusts are to be crucified. By his cross you yourselves are to be crucified to all that is low and evil. Through entering into the fellowship of his suffering, you are to learn that in dying to self and living for others you find truest blessedness.

This doctrine, that righteousness is blessedness, which Paul is fond of stating in a somewhat paradoxical form, insisting chiefly on the blessedness of righteousness on that which may be named its negative side—repentance and self-renunciation, the dying to our worser selves—is the statement of a fact verifiable in human experience. It embodies a truth which has been recognised by religious minds in all ages. That truth had dimly dawned on the first son of Israel's race who perceived that the power working in the world without him was the same with that power within, whose voice he heard bidding him do right. It was more clearly realised by the higher minds of Israel in each succeeding generation, as Israel's religious life grew in purity and in intensity. It was a conviction which inspired and stimulated the later prophets of Israel, strengthening them for their work, finding expression in their noblest utterances. It was, we may say, the central truth in the teaching of Jesus. Any expressions which were given to it previous to Christ's day were, it may be affirmed, anticipations of his teaching comparatively hesitating. The kingdom of which the earliest discourses of Jesus were the annunciation was the kingdom which is within each heart that is swayed and influenced by those conceptions of the pure, the just, the honourable, the lovely in character, which by him were introduced into the world. In so far as the divine kingdom was an outward thing at all, it was the society of those who were striving after the realisation of that ideal righteousness which Christ set before men as the mark of the prize of their high calling. In his parables He describes the nature of that kingdom which is peace and joy in the spirit, because it is righteousness of the spirit; and points out the conditions of entrance into it, the helps and the hindrances to its development in individual souls and in society. He begins his Sermon on the Mount by an express proclamation, we may say, of the truth that righteousness is blessedness, which, it is my endeavour at present to prove to you, is one of the things which cannot be shaken. On each of the dispositions which go to make up righteousness in the largest sense of the term He pronounces a special benediction. Meekness, mercifulness, purity of heart —each has its attendant beatitude. The very desire to possess these and kindred virtues insures blessedness, nay, is blessedness: for those who hunger and thirst after righteousness are blessed in the satisfaction of their spiritual cravings. And this manifold blessedness, promised to righteousness, in its multiform manifestations is independent of the outward circumstances in which men's lives are spent. Poverty does not deprive them of it. On the poor, indeed, a special benediction is pronounced. Sorrow does not exclude it from the heart, for sorrow has its divine compensations and brings its special blessings. The persecutor cannot steal it from his victims by his calumnies. No tortures which his malignity can invent will rob them of it. It is theirs in the most loathsome dungeon in which he can confine them. Through the flames of the stake, or the prolonged agonies of the cross, on its ampler enjoyment they enter. Throughout the whole of the sermon which thus begins, the truth that righteousness is blessedness of the inward sort runs like a thread of gold. Those who are forgiving, it teaches, are blessed in the sense of the Divine forgiveness. On the life which is that of unostentatious self-restraint, devoutness, charity, the Divine approval rests. Those who live such lives in secret, their Father, which seeth in secret, rewards openly, blessing them not merely with his peace, which passeth all understanding, but giving them also a hold on the affections and an influence over the characters of others, which become fully apparent, perhaps, only when they have passed into the silent land, and can hear no more the voices that praise or blame. All again, Christ teaches in his Divine discourse, who come to him unharassed by the carking cares of earth, are blessed in the consciousness that their Father in heaven, who feeds the ravens, and clothes the lilies with beauty, cares for them and provides for all their wants. Those, once more, He teaches elsewhere, who rise superior to the ambition which sets great store by the petty distinctions of earth, make themselves greatest of all by being servants of all, and realise that they are in his fellowship who came not to be ministered unto, but to minister.

This doctrine, that righteousness is blessedness, which the prophets taught in anticipation, and Paul in re-enforcement, of the teaching of Christ, is that by faith in which the just in all ages have lived. No misunderstandings of the teaching of Paul, into which the Catholic Church, and still more remarkably the Protestant Churches have fallen, have prevented devout souls from apprehending that truth, and feeding upon it in their hearts. They may not have avowedly rejected the doctrines by which Paul's teaching has been so strangely perverted; but those doctrines have not entered into their souls so as to poison their spiritual life. It is upon souls whose piety is of the formal and conventional type that the Solifidian doctrine, by which Paul is misrepresented, has had its most mischievous effect. Into the latter it has entered as the leaven of Antinomianism, which has been the bane of the Puritan sects. To the former it has proved almost innocuous. The belief to which their hearts cling, whatever may be the doctrine which their tongues confess, is that Christ died, not to save them from dying, but to enable them to die with him to everything that is evil. To this belief the gifted among them in all ages have given utterance in their spiritual songs and their books of devotion. Jesus in these utterances of saints, Catholic and Protestant, is not their substitute, doing a work for them, and outside of them; He is the source of that life within which is righteousness and peace and joy in the Holy Ghost. In the well-known Hymn of St. Bernard, He is addressed as the fount of life, the light of men, the imparter of that bliss which is beyond compare, who makes all our moments calm and bright by delivering us from sin's unrest and darkness. Of that great monument of medieval piety, the *Imitation of Christ*, we may say that the foundation and chief corner-stone is that saying of Paul's—Die with Christ, that you may live indeed. William Law, in a book whose singular charm of style makes it attractive even to those who have but little sympathy with its fervid piety, enforces the same truth. The teaching of his *Serious Call to a Devout and Holy Life* may be summed up in the sentence: Salvation is the abandonment of the worldly, self-indulgent, careless life which we are all so apt to live, and the entrance on a life which is animated by a sincere intention to attain to a Christ-like purity and devotedness, and the earnest effort to make that intention good.

All, I believe, whose lives have been characterised by moral earnestness, are prepared to indorse these utterances of the gifted. There have been in their lives, they admit, no hours more blessed than those in which they have fought and conquered some bosom sin,—than those even, in which, in the familiar language of the Catechism, they have turned from sins which had overmastered them "with grief and hatred of them, and full purpose of, and endeavour after, new obedience." Through that death to sin which repentance is, they have entered upon a new life; and all life which is fresh and vivid is full of joy. Again, when their existence has been stirred by no special conflict, when it has been that simply of patient continuance in well-doing, they have been possessors, they feel, of a peace all unknown to them while they lived a careless life, unsteadied by principle. They have taken then Christ's yoke, and borne his burden of pious conformity to the Divine will; and they have his rest to their souls.

That righteousness is blessedness is, it thus appears, a truth verifiable by what may be called a universal human experience. It is thus plainly one of the things that cannot be shaken. It does not, like those propositions of scholastic theology with which I have contrasted it, involve a belief in any opinions as to the age of the world, as to the antiquity of man, as to the origin of sin, which science may demonstrate to be false. Our acceptance of it does not depend upon our submission to the authority of any teacher or of any book. It is unaffected, therefore, by the discoveries of the Biblical critic as to the date or the authorship of the books which make up the Bible, or as to the manner in which they have been put in their present shape.

It is unaffected also by his refusal to concede to the Bible any other authority than that which he recognises in the truth of its utterances, and their power to awaken a response in the reason and conscience of man. Amidst the ruin of theological systems which the waves of inquiry, scientific and Biblical, engulf or dash to fragments, it rides secure like a sturdy barque which has its anchor surely fixed. Those who cling to it cannot finally make shipwreck of the faith, long tempest-tost though they may be.

From this simple verity, that righteousness is blessedness, others may be deduced which, too, are among the things that cannot be shaken. Foremost among these I place the truth that there is a Divine Being, and that this Being is seeking to make us sharers in his righteousness and in his blessedness. Many of the conceptions of the school divines in regard to the nature of God, like many of their conceptions in regard to his work in the salvation of the elect, have ceased to commend themselves to thoughtful and devout minds in these days. There are many amongst us who are unable any longer to think of the infinite Spirit as a mechanician divinity who overcomes difficulty by ingenious contrivance. They may see much of poetic beauty in the saying of Kepler, that, in making his astronomical discoveries, he was "thinking the thoughts of God after him." They may even admit that the argument from design, on which the divines of the eighteenth century laid so great stress, has its value. They may accept it, as helpful to them, in so far as it enables, as no other argument does, their finite intelligence to realise the presence in the universe of an infinite intelligence. They cannot accept it, however, as a scientific definition of the nature of Divine Being and the mode of Divine operation in the world. Space and time, they hold, are but forms of human thought. Of the Infinite and the Eternal, the substance of all things—the all-pervasive life of the universe, you can predicate, they assert, neither after nor before, but an eternal now, —neither presence in this portion of space nor in that, but omnipresence. The conception of this Infinite Being, therefore, as a kind of modern Vulcan fertile in resource, presented to us in the argument from design, is of no scientific validity. It may have its use as an expedient of thought. But when men deduce from it, and formulate as a scientific proposition, the statement that God made the world as the mechanist makes the machine, "they dwarf their conceptions of the Divine Infinitude." But not only do many of the thoughtful and the devout among us refuse to look upon the Divine Being as the kind of *opifex deus* or Workman-God given us in the argument from design, they reject, in like manner, the old conceptions in regard to creation. They cannot think of that which men call the material universe as a positive something produced by the fiat of Omnipotence out of absolute nothingness. Such a conception, they hold, is incapable of realisation in thought. The supposition "that matter and spirit are equally substantial and ultimately different" seems to them an untenable hypothesis. They are driven, therefore, to the conclusion that the material universe is the phenomenal manifestation of the only true substance

—of " Him in whom all things consist," to quote the language of the Epistle to the Colossians. Forasmuch as they can only understand the material universe, in so far as they do understand it, in virtue of the intelligence with which they are endowed, they regard it as the expression of an Everlasting Intelligence—the embodiment of the Eternal Reason, ever shifting in its form, but eternal as itself. They look upon it, in fact, as God's ceaseless conversation with his creatures, as Bishop Berkeley grandly said. Is this not Pantheism? they are asked. Be it so, they reply. To some such pantheistic conception of the universe, intellects at once speculative and devout will be driven, they believe, as the only refuge which will afford them secure shelter from the assaults of materialistic atheism. This Pantheism, they further urge, which seems to afford the best solution of " the Mystery of Matter," is by no means, as its opponents allege, destructive of moral distinctions. The One Being " of whom, and to whom, and through whom, are all things" is, it must be remembered, in the view of the Christian pantheist, the ground of our moral as well as of our intellectual and physical life. Christian Pantheism does not, therefore, like some of the cruder forms of pantheistic speculation, attribute a moral indifference to the Being who is " all in all." It holds, on the contrary, that this Being presents himself to man as the moral ideal—that He is in man as that mysterious energy which convinces him of sin, and urges him on to higher moral attainments. It does not attempt to solve the problem of the origin of evil; but in presenting to us the hope that " on the scale of infinity all is well," it gives men the hint of a solution of it which has more of help and comfort than they find in the dogmatic replies which the adherents of traditionalism make to the objections which the pessimist brings forward against the doctrine of the Divine Benevolence.

The proposition that God is thus the eternal goodness—the Being who is seeking to make his creatures sharers in his blessedness, by making them sharers in his righteousness, may not be, like the simpler proposition—Righteousness is blessedness—the expression of a truth verifiable in human experience. The former proposition, however, is deducible from the latter by processes of reasoning which I believe are legitimate. The law of righteousness to which men are constrained to conform their lives, by conforming their lives to which they find blessedness, implies a lawgiver who loves righteousness. Men have not created the ideal of the just and the merciful, which a mysterious energy within impels them to realise. They have not found that ideal for themselves any more than they have formed it for themselves. It has found them and implanted itself within them, growing with their growth, and strengthening with their strength. The Perfect Love has found them, and it works with them and in them, that it may transform them into its likeness. Apart from the belief, that a Being higher than man presents himself to him as moral ideal, and works in him as moral impulse, the moral life of the race, its moral growth, and that of the individuals who compose it, are inexplicable. We may therefore hold, that the statement, that the Eternal

Goodness is seeking to make the finite creatures, which it has brought into being, righteous, and blessed because righteous, is a legitimate deduction from the proposition, verifiable we have seen in human experience, that righteousness is blessedness. This statement is simply an assertion in other words of the doctrine known as that of the Fatherhood of God. The doctrine consequently of the Divine Fatherhood is one of those things which cannot be shaken. Whatever opinions and systems of opinion may perish, the truth which Jesus, by his personality even more than by his teaching, first brought fully to light, that the Infinite Being, the source and substance of all things, is best known to men by the name of Father, must abide for ever sure.

As belief in that God who was specially revealed in the grace of our Lord Jesus Christ may thus be deduced from belief in duty, so, I go on to remark, may belief in immortality be deduced from belief in God. Thus the proposition, that man is the heir of a personal immortality, may also be regarded as one of the things that cannot be shaken.

Many of the conceptions entertained by the theologians of the past in regard to the nature of human immortality may seem, to theologians of the present, untenable. They may find it, in the light of modern science, impossible to believe in the resuscitation of the material framework of the body. The belief in a material heaven, into which the resuscitated bodies of the righteous shall pass, has perished with the belief in the crystalline spheres. So likewise has the belief in a subterranean limbo in which the bodies of the wicked shall be grievously tormented. Discussions as to the nature of the general resurrection and the final judgment, as to an intermediate state, and the condition of disembodied spirits during the period which intervenes between death and the end of the world, are grown somewhat out of date. The whole of the eschatology of the schoolmen, in fact, like their soteriology and their ontology, seems to the modern theologian to be in its details untenable.

The modern theologian, cleaves, however, to the old belief of Christendom in the personal immortality of each human spirit. There is, he maintains, nothing inconceivable in the continued personal life of the human spirit. The soul he defines as the true self in each of us, as that in which " our sense of personal identity inheres amidst various impressions and continued disintegration of organic matter. It cannot therefore be, as the materialist asserts, a substratum of brain tissue. It seems to be, on the contrary, a portion of the true spiritual substance of the universe, so conditioned by those forces which present themselves to the physiologist in the phenomena of brain, as that it is largely dependent upon them for the form it takes as a personal life with an individual character." The soul being thus a true spiritual substance, which survives the gradual conversion of the portion of living protoplasm, through which it first came to have the sense of personal identity, into dead protoplasm, which is slowly going on through life, may outlive also the more sudden change which passes upon it at death. Thus a continued personal life of the soul is at least conceivable. Among the infinite possibilities of being, there may well be the bodies celestial of which Paul speaks. With such new organisms wherewith to express themselves to other intelligences, wherewith also to define themselves to themselves, and thus to retain self-consciousness, "we, the living agents that we call ourselves," may be clothed upon at death, the modern theologian is prepared to believe.

The survival of the soul after the death of the body, its retention of its consciousness of continuous identity in a new or in several new states of existence, being thus by no means incredible in the light of modern science, all the old arguments for immortality are still available to those who are influenced by the scientific spirit.

These arguments may be briefly described as—*first*, That derived from the prevalence of the belief in all lands and ages, and among men at every stage of civilisation and culture ; *second*, That derived from the affections—that which results from the conviction that the attachments we have formed on earth must be renewed in some other form in the better world beyond for which we hope ; *third*, That derived from our sense of justice, which demands that the inequalities of the present life shall be redressed in a better life to come ; *fourth*, That derived from the incompleteness of the present life, viewed as a state of education ; *fifth*, That which is derived from the mind of man itself, with its intuitions of the Infinite, and its craving for a knowledge of God, which shall ever grow fuller and clearer.

The two latter of these arguments seem to the

theologian who is influenced by the modern spirit the best and the strongest. They appear to him to be necessarily involved in those theistic conceptions of the universe which, in their turn, are legitimate deductions from the belief in and the recognition of the truth that righteousness is blessedness. If man be, as he is constrained to believe that he is, the subject of a Divine education here, the work of his spiritual education must surely be carried on in other states of existence hereafter.

Those in whom culture, in the highest sense of the term, seems to have produced its highest results, realise but imperfectly, it is plain, the Divine ideal of humanity. Dare any one dogmatically assert that the progress such persons feel possible for themselves in knowledge and wisdom and goodness, is for ever arrested by death? It is possible in thought, we have seen, to conceive that the souls of the good, their true selves, with all their capabilities for intellectual and moral growth, may survive the dissolution of the body. Must not that possibility of thought become an actuality if only thus man's ideal of man can be realised? But if the incompleteness of their moral development constrains the theologians for whom I speak at present, to cherish even for those whose moral growth has been the happiest the hope of a continued existence, what shall they say, they ask, of those who are their opposites? What shall they say of the vast multitude who die in the immaturity of their powers —of the many whose lives are so circumstanced as that their latent capacities never get a chance of development—of those in whose characters, to the end of life, good and evil are strangely mixed—of those who seem to have made deliberate choice of evil? They find that "of fifty seeds" nature "often brings but one to bear." But shall they affirm of the Father of spirits that He deals thus with the human children whom He has fashioned into separate souls and endowed with the capacity of growth in knowledge and wisdom and goodness? They may have their cynical moods, in which they are tempted to regard the mass of mankind as mere moral rubbish, fitted only for destruction from the presence of the Lord. They may be tempted to think with Spinoza that immortality is a boon conferred only on those whose souls have been conversant with ideas that are immortal; or they may be induced to assert, with some modern theologians, that immortality is a gift purchased by Christ for those who are called to faith in him. Such conceptions, however, cannot be permanently cherished by any who have embraced the higher forms of theistic belief.

These thinkers observe, even in those members of the race whose moral growth has been most stunted, the germs at all events of that which they regard as a Divine life. They cannot believe that the souls, in which such germs exist, are destined to extinction like wasted seeds. Believing in God as wise and good, they cherish the hope at least, that under more favourable conditions (among these favourable conditions may be included, of course, the sharp discipline of pain) the capabilities of moral and spiritual excellence, which remain almost wholly undeveloped in the present life of some human beings, will be developed in the life that is to come.

In the fact then that man is the subject of a Divine education which is unperfected here, there is a very strong argument, they hold, for the continuance of his life hereafter.

That argument becomes even more conclusive, they think, when it is presented in the slightly altered form noted above, as that which is derived from the mind of man itself.

The mind of man in its normal state is animated by a ceaseless craving for the knowledge of divine and eternal truth. It is for ever making inquiries as to the origin of all things and the nature of the power which shapes its destiny. It is for ever engaged in attempts to solve the problem of existence. Now in man's desire for such knowledge as this, there is the best proof of his immortality. Here he may know in part; and the knowledge of God which, even in the present state of existence, the devout soul possesses, is, in the language of the New Testament, eternal life—*i.e.* constitutes it a life full of the consciousness of its own endurance. But the knowledge of God is capable of endless increase; and the creature who puts to himself the question—What is God? is surely destined to have it more and more completely answered as the ages of an endless life roll on. "In God we live, and move, and have our being." These words are as true in one sense of the worm, as of the genius, or of the saint. In another sense, however, they have a fuller meaning for the devout and thoughtful soul than for any others of the creatures of earth. That soul (and all souls in a measure) is conscious of a moral and spiritual as well as of a sentient life. Its higher life, it knows, is derived from God and sustained by him. It longs after a communion with the source of its being, which shall grow fuller and fuller. Is there not, in that longing, the pledge of its immortality?

The three propositions therefore : *first*, that righteousness is blessedness ; *second*, that there is a Divine Being who is seeking to make men sharers in his blessedness, by making them sharers in his righteousness ; *third*, that in the cravings of the human soul for communion with that power without it, which is the source of its being and the ground of its moral life, there is the pledge of its immortality—are, the modern theologian, whose position I have endeavoured to define, holds, things which cannot be shaken. The two latter of these propositions he knows are questioned. They cannot however, he maintains, be legitimately denied except by those who are willing to abandon themselves to an absolute scepticism. It is of course open to the stringent sceptic to deny that there is a voice speaking in his conscience, bidding him do right, which is not his own voice, speaking to himself. But the scepticism which would constrain the atheist to refuse to the theist his assumption—a command outside of his moral nature—would compel him also to deny to the physical philosopher his assumption—a physical world apart from his thought of it. He would thus be driven into that dreariest scepticism, which paralyses our intellectual as well as our moral powers, which leads us to doubt whether we have any real existence or no, whether we think, or only think that we think—which consequently turns our whole life into a dream within a dream. Thus then, the modern theologian holds that the conceptions which may be expressed in the three words, Duty, God, Immortality, are truths which no discoveries of science, no investigations of the biblical critic, no wind of modern doctrine, can really endanger.

Those, whose views I have undertaken to expound, welcome accordingly the attacks which are made by the students of science, natural and biblical, upon the dogmatic theology of the past. They believe that painful though these attacks may be to many devout Christians, they must ultimately be beneficial to the religion of Christ. They will result, they perceive, in the demolition of those doctrines, artificial and unverifiable, which have wellnigh concealed Christ's simple gospel, that man has a Father in heaven, who is seeking to make him "perfect as he is perfect." They are confident, that when the dust-clouds, raised by the pulling down of those unsightly structures of scholastic dogma, which have been piled up around the doctrine of Christ, clear away, that doctrine itself will reappear again before the eyes of men in all its stately simplicity.

XIII.

THE SUCCESSORS OF THE GREAT PHYSICIAN.

BY THE REV. ALLAN MENZIES, B.D., ABERNYTE, PERTHSHIRE.

As ye go, preach, saying, The kingdom of heaven is at hand. Heal the sick, cleanse the lepers, raise the dead, cast out devils.
—MATT. x. 7, 8.

IN several passages of the later prophets of the Old Testament, we find it predicted, that in the great restoration to which these seers looked forward, there would be an end of various kinds of physical evil. "In that day," we read, "shall the deaf hear the words of the book, and the eyes of the blind shall see out of obscurity." "Then the eyes of the blind shall be opened, and the ears of the deaf shall be unstopped. Then shall the lame man leap as an hart, and the tongue of the dumb sing." In such vivid language did they describe the happiness of that epoch which was the subject of their faithful longings, when God should renew the heart of his people, or when the exiles should return to Jerusalem, and the kingdom of God be established there. It was not enough to say that Israel would at last be true to its high calling, that the divisions of the people would be healed, and all nations flock to the worship of the true

God. In that happy time every possible good would descend into the world; every deliverance which the poor and needy could desire would be accomplished; all tears would be wiped away. Even physical evil would disappear, even the life of nature would partake in the universal blessedness.

Are these expressions of the prophets to be understood literally? Was it really their expectation, that the time would come when not only those evils which spring from man's sinfulness—injustice and unbelief and warfare,—but those evils also, which lie beyond man's control—pain and disease and physical infirmity,—would cease to afflict him? It may be doubted whether they actually expected this to come to pass: these expressions were probably intended simply as powerful figures or metaphors for the great deliverance which they saw in the future.

But when we come to New Testament times, we find new life given to this class of sayings, in a way which we could scarcely have expected. Our Lord repeats them, and seems to find in them a true description of the events which accompanied his preaching. When John the Baptist sends from the prison to ask Jesus for some declaration as to his Messiahship, Jesus replies that those things are actually taking place, which the Jews believed on the strength of prophecy that the Messiah would do. The blind receive their sight, and the lame walk, the dead are raised up, and the lepers are cleansed, just as the prophets predicted; thus it is proved that this is the time of which the prophets spoke. From these things John may draw his own conclusion.

Is Jesus to be understood literally, when He uses the expressions of the prophets in this way? Is He speaking of real outward cures, and founding upon them an argument for his own Messiahship? That also has been doubted, and in support of such a doubt attention has been called to the fact that He on one occasion speaks of "the dead" in a metaphorical way, as those who do not care about the kingdom of God. With regard to the rest of these phrases, it is remarked, that He refused to work a miracle when He was asked to do so, to prove that He was the Messiah; that He spoke disparagingly of miracles, and generally tried, when He had cured any one, to keep the matter quiet. It is thus quite possible to assign to these phrases, as used by Jesus, the same figurative significance, in which they had been used at first. Jesus may have meant nothing more than to state in a vivid way the impression which his preaching was producing on the mind of the country. If new ideas were set afloat, which made a new world rise upon the mental vision of those who received them—if the indifferent or the despairing awoke to the glad tidings—if natures sunk in the death of sin arose to a new life—if those whose conduct had been stumbling and irregular were set upon their feet to do right steadily and consistently—then the metaphors of the prophets were not too strong to describe so happy a revival.

For a religious use of the Gospels no more profitable view of these phrases need be desired. As poetry, they are full of instruction and of spiritual suggestion, and speak to the heart of every age. Even in quarters where there is no sympathy for any attempt to explain away the miracles of Jesus, there is often a strong tendency to use them as symbols and parables of the spiritual infirmities of humanity, and of the cure of such infirmities by the gospel. In the preaching which dwells most upon the Saviour and the sinner's need of him, the leper symbolises the sin-polluted soul, which no waters of earth's culture can cleanse; the blind man at the gate of Jericho is a figure of those whose eyes have never opened to the gospel; the dead whom Christ raised up stands for the worldling, in whom the true life has never been suffered to awake; the demoniac is the man whose passions no restraint can overcome. Most beautiful, most richly fraught with deep and tender wisdom, is this symbolical view of the healings of Christ, which finds in the words and actions accompanying these cures indications of the character and of the modes of operation of the great Physician of the soul.

But Christ cured the bodily ailments of his countrymen as well as the sicknesses of their spirits, and it is to this fact with the lessons to be gathered from it that we now wish to direct attention. It is a very imperfect view of him, which regards him merely as a teacher, or merely as a spiritual deliverer. As a pure matter of history, it is impossible to understand his life or his character, if we remove from the gospel narrative the cures which He is recorded to have wrought. When his first disciples looked back, after his death, on what He was, and sought to give a compendious account of his activity, they spoke not only of his preaching but also of the power which He exercised; they said that He went about doing good, and healing all that were oppressed of the devil (Acts x. 38). They recorded that when He sent them out on their first missionary tour, He commissioned them not only to preach the gospel, but also to do works of healing, as He did himself. And we know from various sources, that the gift of healing was believed to survive in the early Church for a considerable period after the death of Jesus.

What are we to think of this feature of the life of Jesus? If we do not spiritualise this part of the history, what lessons are we to deduce from it? The great interest of this part of the gospel story has often been thought to consist in its value as evidence to the truth of Christianity. The miracles have been considered as one of the chief supports of the divine nature of the Christian revelation. We need not now discuss how much force there is in such evidence to establish such conclusions: that is a point on which very different opinions have been and still are held. But there is another conclusion to be drawn from this element of the narrative, the legitimacy of which is open to less question. Whatever the miracles may prove about the authority of those who put forth such a power, they certainly prove something as to the conception of the kingdom of God which was held by Christ and his disciples. If it was a characteristic sign of the Messianic era, that works like these should accompany its progress, and that men should be relieved in it from physical distresses and infirmities, then clearly the kingdom of God, which was believed to be impending, had deliverance in store for the bodies of men as well as for their souls, and disease and pain were to come to an end, as well as unbelief and discord and social injustice. And when we consider the character of Christ, and ask with what eyes He must have looked on the sicknesses and misfortunes of his countrymen, we are strengthened in the conclusion, that He must have sought to set them free from more than one kind of infirmity, and that his hope for the future included the triumph of good over evil, not in one particular only, but in all. When He saw the multitudes and had compassion on them, He sought to set them right not only by preaching, but by his works as well. When He felt the Spirit of God resting upon him, He was impelled not only to preach the gospel to the poor, but also to heal the broken-hearted, to preach deliverance to the captives, and recovering of sight to the blind, and to set at liberty them that were bound. He knew that He was sent to overthrow the enemy of mankind in every province in which that potentate had exercised his tyranny. He was not deaf to any cry that was addressed to him for help. He knew human life too well to look upon the problem of man's deliverance in any partial or one-sided way. If the miracles were the premonitory signs of the period when God's Spirit should take full possession of society, they showed that in that happy state, which Jesus believed to be at hand, mankind should be set at liberty from every evil power, that every burden would be removed and all tears wiped away, and the blessedness of the beginning restored to the world once more.

So broad and generous is the conception of the benefits it was to confer, which lies at the root of Christianity. Urged by a faith in a loving Father of men, with whose will all pain and sickness must be inconsistent, Christianity began a bold attack upon the hostile powers which had carried on such an oppressive reign. Looking for a kingdom in which the loving will of God should be realised, it refused to believe that any kind of distress could be perpetual, and looked boldly for the time when the ancient rule of evil should be dissolved, and the creature delivered from the bondage of corruption into a glorious liberty. As it existed in the mind of Christ—and to what other quarter can we turn to recognise the true genius of our faith?—Christianity was much more than a doctrine, much more than a scheme for propagating truth; that was only half its mission: it was an impulse to deliverance, a power to deliver, which must work its way in every part of human life, till the deliverance became absolute and universal. It aimed at the reduction of every tyranny, at the liberation of all who were any way oppressed, and it could not cease to operate, until God's loving will was done on earth as it was done in heaven, and God's kingdom had come in a saved and regenerated world. And therefore Christ not only preached the gospel, but He also cured the sick, and gave sight to the blind, and cast out devils.

In the preaching of the gospel Christ has not wanted successors. To carry on this, the first and noblest portion of his work, great institutions have arisen and have flourished; thousands of churches have been reared in every land; thousands upon thousands of devout and able men in every age have devoted their lives. And claiming to stand in his place, and to speak in his name, the churches have been accepted by the world as his representatives. But it may be worth while to ask, Who are the successors of the Lord in the other and not less essential part of his activity? Where are they to be found, what are they called, what recognition do they receive from those who represent Christ in the preaching of the gospel?

They also are legion, but as their tasks are many and various, and not specially connected with the outward part of religion, they are not combined into an organism, and put forward no united claim; many of them are but loosely connected with the associations which claim to represent Christianity; many of them make no religious profession at all, and look with suspicion on the churches. Yet whether we regard the impulse by which their labours are inspired, or the object to which they tend, they are one among themselves, and one with the Church of Christ.

Every age has its own conception of that kingdom of God in the hope of which Christians live and labour. In our age the growing organisation of society, the rise of new sciences, the division of knowledge into a multiplicity of provinces, have brought with them very large conceptions of the benefits of which men stand in need, and of the end towards which the world advances. To raise men out of the various evils which afflict them, and to procure for them a healthy, and free, and rational existence: this, we are coming more and more to see, is a very wide and complex problem, and requires the cooperation of many labourers in many fields. It would lead far beyond the limits of a sermon, were we to specify the various lines on which contributions are being made by men of public spirit, and by the stately sisterhood of the sciences, towards the emancipation of mankind from the various influences which hinder its growth. But where any labour is unselfishly engaged in, which tends even remotely to further this emancipation, there we need not hesitate to say that part of the task is being done which the love and the enthusiasm of Christ imposed upon his followers, and this irrespective of the consideration, whether the name of Christ is named or not. Christianity is broader than the creeds, wider than the churches. The impulse which prompts any man to deny himself in order to do good to others, and to win for them what they cannot achieve for themselves, is essentially a Christian impulse, and connects the man who lives in its power in a real and historical bond with him who claimed for his kindred all those who did the will of his Father.

It is a commonplace of religious teaching that a man is serving Christianity not only when he is engaged in directly religious affairs, but also when he is rendering practical service to his neighbours, perhaps without thinking of religion at all. Indeed the requirement of good works stands in the very front of the Gospel: faith only makes a man half a Christian, and good works are needed to make up his full title to that name. Every Christian, even the humblest and weakest, is called not only to believe in Christ, but also to do what he can for his neighbours. These are very obvious truths, and they will scarcely be controverted when we apply them on a larger scale, to the life, not of the individual, but of the society. Something more than faith is needed to make up a Christian society or State. Taken by herself, the Church does not represent the Christianity of a country. A State is Christian not only in virtue of her Church or Churches; these denote only one element of her religious life, and though they were to gain all the ascendency they crave, the religious life of the State might still be extremely defective. Another and not less essential element of national religion is contributed by those who are labouring in any way for the improvement of society. Those who execute the behests of the Christian spirit by seeking to do for society what miracles sought in isolated cases to do for the individual—to heal its sick, to cleanse its lepers, to cast out its devils,—are as real servants of Christianity as those who preach its doctrines. The labours of the former are to the full as indispensable as those of the latter to the realising of a kingdom of righteousness and peace and joy upon this earth.

If, then, we count the preacher peculiarly the servant of Christ, who seeks to open men's minds to the thought of the relations which they bear to God and man, and to the loftiest view of the meaning and purpose of their lives, and if God's blessing be thought to rest on the Sunday-school teacher, and on the district visitor who seeks to serve our Master by little acts of kindness to his poor, must we not hold worthy of the same honour those who are labouring in other and not less arduous ways to bring to human life the blessings of light and peace and freedom? Are not the doctor and the physiologist and the sanitary reformer engaged in works which Christ directly enjoins?

Are not the political economist, the legislator, the administrator, aiming at the removal of those evils from the root, with which the physician deals when they arise? Are not the teacher and the student of educational science labouring for such an elevation of the people, that they will save themselves from many of the evils under which at present they are so helpless? And who can tell in how many ways the progress of science will prove to be the emancipation of mankind? It would be possible to take a much wider sweep, and to maintain the essential alliance of all those whose efforts spring from a higher source than their own private ends—scholar, philosopher, man of science, poet or artist—in the great work of satisfying the growing needs and advancing the welfare of mankind. For our present purpose we may rest content with saying that all those who are engaged in labours by which they seek to serve their fellow-creatures; who are saving the distressed, or instructing the ignorant, or thinking thoughts by which man's life shall be guided or illuminated, that they are all engaged in the same work which Christianity began, and has for so many centuries, with varying success, carried forward.

And here, it will more and more be found, lies one most obvious reconciliation of science with religion. That all truth is one, is a doctrine which, in an age filled with such conflicting tendencies of thought as this, all cannot be expected to grasp, except perhaps by faith. That all honest effort, that all striving to do good, is one: this is a doctrine, the prevalence of which is perhaps nearer at hand. It may be, that the time is not far distant, when it will be recognised that all who are seeking to render any service to mankind are labouring in the same cause. And when the Church can bring herself to acknowledge this great fact, she will have done much to disarm the hostility with which she is frequently regarded, and to regain her rightful position as the conscience and the great inspiring force of the country. The battle of beliefs may not be destined soon to issue in a general consent, but a speedier victory than any she can gain by argument and insisting on her evidences awaits the Church, when she takes thoroughly to heart her Master's words, "He who is not against us is for us," and rises to the thought that the cause of Christ is not to be identified with the interests of religious bodies, but with the interests of mankind. If there are many good works to be done for mankind, which the Church as such has no call to undertake, if the growing complexity of civilisation and the increase of learning have made the progress of society a wider problem, and divided it into a multitude of parts, each calling for hard and disinterested labour, the Church, if she is wise, will claim as her fellow-labourers those who are discharging other functions than her own of the great public service. While holding that her own function is the highest and most central of all, she will not think of detracting from the value of what is done in different fields, and with a different method from her own. As the early apologists showed the heathens who derided their faith, so she will show to them, that they are Christians though they know it not, and that in proportion to their love of truth and their unselfishness they are serving Christianity.

We have spoken of the division of the work which is done for society into an increasing number of parts, and of the rise of new provinces of learning, and of new departments of the public service. In connection with this tendency towards specialisation and elaborate organisation, which is characteristic of modern times, we cannot forget how frequently the rise of new departments has taken the aspect of a restriction of the activity of the Church, and of a curtailment of her power. The great institution which formerly controlled every province of human life, and claimed a right of dictation in nearly all the world's affairs, is thrust back from one province after another, and made to surrender one after another of her offices to secular hands. It is long since the Church ceased to regard the healing of the sick as a function pertaining to herself; it is long since the whole of the learning of the world pertained to her, though not so long since she, in part, relaxed her hold upon our universities. The period which has elapsed since she gave up seeking to control the civil government in this country is now to be reckoned by centuries. It is not half a century since the relief of the poor was removed from her management, and placed under an authority created for that purpose; and the change is quite recent which has withdrawn the schools of the country from her jurisdiction, and intrusted them to School Boards, over the election of which she has no control. Other tendencies are at work which may possibly issue in similar changes.

But in being committed to the hands of the general population of the country, these activities have not ceased to be Christian, nor is this tendency one which need occasion dismay to a church conscious of the true foundation of her influence. Marking these changes and meditating on the true relation of the Church to the various bodies which exist at her side, we are led to a very large conception of the place and duty of the Church in a highly organised community. What she loses in direct power she ought to gain in influence. While she recognises the usefulness of what is done for society by the various secular agencies, she is herself the only meeting-point at which a unity can be established between all those labourers in different fields. Apart from her they are divided, but in her they are one; and she can infuse into them the spirit which they shall carry into their various operations. While she does not seek to dictate to them as to those matters which society has intrusted to their hands, while she does not seek to force herself into provinces which belong to other bodies, she yet claims to declare the motives and the principles of conduct which in every department ought to be respected and acted on. Leaving the scholar and the legislator and the teacher—shall we not say the theologian also?—free to form their own convictions, and not seeking to coerce them to her own belief, or her own policy in matters of which they are the best judges, she yet unites them in her worship, and fuses them together in the pure enthusiasm of self-devotion and religion. Recognising them all as brethren, as servants of the one Lord, as fellow-workers in the same great cause, she sends them forth to work in his spirit, and by their different efforts to win the world to him. And thus she not only fulfils his command to preach the gospel, but by the influence which she exerts on all true-hearted and public-spirited men she fulfils his other commands also, to heal the sick, to cleanse the lepers, to cast out devils.

May the Lord grant to his Church to be of this mind! Amen.

XIV.

THE CHRISTIAN PRIESTHOOD.

BY THE REV. ALLAN MENZIES, B.D., ABERNYTE.

Who hath made us . . . priests to God and his Father.—REV. I. 6.

WORDS similar to these are reported to have been spoken to the Jews at the outset of their national history. When they were assembled at the foot of Mount Sinai to receive their legislation, we read that Moses addressed them in words which were meant to give them a high conception of the position they were called to occupy in the world. God, he said, had commanded him to say to them that if they were true to the covenant then being formed, they would be a kingdom of priests and a holy nation.

These phrases were re-echoed at the outset of Christianity by several of the sacred writers, and applied to the community of believers in Christ. Christians were bidden to believe that what Christ had done for them was to make them kings and priests to God, a royal priesthood, a holy nation.

It is not difficult to understand what is meant when the adherents of these young religions are exhorted to think that they are kings to God. The words point to the fact, so soon forgotten in each case, that the full consciousness of being under God's authority emancipates the worshipper from all human dictation. He who is fully aware of his responsibility to God escapes in his spirit from the control of every other ruler, whatever his outward lot may be. His ruler dwells within him; he is his own king; he sees no one above him; the sense of the allegiance which he owes to God enables him to govern his life consistently, without feeling the control of outward magistrates and laws.

What does it mean when we find it said to the Jews at the outset of their history, and repeated to the Christians at the beginning of theirs, that they are to be priests to God?

First of all, we cannot fail to see that the expression marks a great difference in each case between the new religion and the religions which had gone before. In the older religions, it is suggested, only some of the worshippers were priests; there was a priestly caste or class, which stood between the people and the object of their worship; the people had to transact their religious affairs through the medium of a priesthood. The priesthood and the laity were marked off from each other as two distinct and separate classes.

But in Judaism, Moses said, and in Christianity, the apostles John and Peter said (and the apostle Paul asserts the same, not in these words, but in others quite as strong), that is not to be the case. Here there is to be no distinction between persons who are sacred and persons who are secular, no line is to be drawn between priesthood and laity. What the priests did in these older religions, it is implied, you Jews and you Christians are to do for yourselves. Where the priest stood in these imperfect and elementary faiths, you, if you are true to your calling, are all to stand. You are all priests: you are not to get your religious affairs done for you by proxy, you are to transact with God by and for yourselves.

This, it will generally be agreed, is the notion which the words of our text expressed at first, both in the Old Testament and in the New. They marked the passage from a mechanical and superstitious religion to one direct and spiritual; from a worship which it required priests to carry on, to a worship which was to be carried on in the individual soul.

And it is a very obvious remark that neither in Judaism nor in Christianity has the ideal thus set up at the beginning been at all generally realised. In Judaism an elaborate system of washings, sacrifices, and offerings came to be instituted, for the proper observance of which the services of the priesthood were essential. It was found impossible to carry on the national religion without all this machinery. The people soon fell back from being priests, and the functions which every individual ought to have discharged were delegated to a class, who, standing between God and the worshippers, gained a great and not always a salutary power over the conscience and the belief and the whole life of the people.

In Christianity better things might have been expected, but here also the old notion soon crept in of having a class set apart to transact the religious affairs of the rest. It soon came to be believed, a belief of which we find no trace in the New Testament, that a man could not stand on good terms with God except by the mediation of the priesthood. The priesthood was thought to be in possession of the bread of life and of the keys of heaven. There have always been, and there are still, forms of Christianity which practically deny that the human spirit stands in any immediate relation with God. Great systems of Church polity and of doctrine are founded on the assumption, that there is a great gulf fixed between God and man, and that that gulf is not to be bridged except by great and well-contrived appliances, administered by those who are properly initiated into their modes of working. In the most unlikely quarters it might perhaps be found that the old heathen notion of a religious aristocracy still survives, by whose favourable offices men may advance themselves with God.

But the great interest of our text lies less in what it suggests with regard to a particular class than in the standard it sets up for the religion of all. It does away with the priestly class, not by dragging it down, but by lifting up the lives of those who do not belong to it. There is no function of priesthood which the Christian who is alive to his relations with the spiritual world may not find represented in his own personal experience and actions. And the end of sacerdotalism will have arrived when men in general come to realise the sacredness and dignity of their own lives as spiritual beings. There will always be priests in the world. Of that the spiritual instincts and needs of mankind will certainly take care. And there will be priestly assumptions and attempts at domination, as long as men remain too worldly or too indolent to claim this office for themselves individually, as a part of their natural birthright.

Let us then consider what is meant when we find it said in the New Testament that Christians as such are priests to God. What are priests? and in what way is that title applied to Christians in general?

We may mention three points in the priestly character which we may appropriately, and in full sympathy with the teaching of the New Testament, consider to be transferred to ourselves. Firstly, the priest is set apart to his holy office: he is consecrated or ordained. Secondly, the priest stands in communication with God: he stands in God's presence. Thirdly, the priest offers a sacrifice.

I. *Consecration.* If the priesthood has generally been marked off in various ways from the laity, if they have lived in separate dwellings, if they have generally worn a professional dress, if they have absented themselves from certain entertainments, and have not shared in certain pleasures in themselves innocent, this is a happy symbol of that self-denial and separation from the world which ought to have a place in every life. Of course, when we speak of separation from the world, we do not mean going away from mankind, and ceasing to take an interest or a part in its concerns. But to every man some object presents itself, some purpose is revealed, which he feels that he ought to follow, even though he has to turn away from many other things he might desire. We speak of a man having an inward call to the ministry when he feels it in him to speak to his fellow-men of the counsel of God and of their duty. It is a limited number who experience this call. But every man has a call, more or less clear, to the work there is for him to do, and to the character into which he ought to grow up. There is an infinite variety of calls, as there are infinite diversities of gifts and operations, all of which are needed by the world, to help its many-sided growth. But each of us has his call, and it is well for him if he recognises and obeys it. It points him to the work which for him is sacred work, and for which he ought to give up all besides, to buy this goodly pearl. And there is a secret ordination or consecration, though at the hands of no presbytery or bishop, by which those whose ears are open to the call addressed to them by their higher selves or the world's needs are set apart in their appointed sphere for the service of God. The call may come in a very homely fashion, but to the obedient spirit it cannot be other than sacred and religious. A man may feel it a duty to support his aged parents, and give up for them his savings or his leisure. A man may see it to be needful for the health of his spirit to withdraw from society. The student is called on to give up his ease; the practical worker among men may be obliged to sacrifice learning: these are but symbols of the great self-consecration which in one form or another all are called to make. To all of us there presents itself in one shape or another the ideal with its beauty and its crown of thorns. The world is full of priests unrecognised, who have taken on themselves vows of faithfulness and poverty, and turned away from what they too were fitted to enjoy.

In this sense, then, it is in the power of all of us to

take upon ourselves the priestly character. Although he wears no special dress, and does not live in any separate abode, nor in any way give himself out to be holier than other people, yet he who has heard God's call to duty and has arisen to follow it, turning away from other pursuits and pleasures, is in the highest and the best sense a priest to God, separated from the world, and consecrated to the service of the Highest.

II. *Worship.* In Judaism, as in other old religions, the priest was thought to possess means of approaching the Deity which ordinary men did not enjoy. The people remained in the outer court, and could only see the priest pass inwards to the Holy Place, in which God was thought to dwell between the cherubim, and which none of them could hope ever to enter. In Christianity this is all changed. We do not believe that any man or any set of men is in possession of a special privilege which admits them to God's presence, while others are excluded. And the reason why we do not believe this is, that Christianity has given us a new conception of where God dwells, and of the means to be used to approach him. Where does God dwell? Where shall we say that the Most High is to be found? Not in any local shrine, not in any church with doors that men may shut or open. We cannot go to him upon our feet. We cannot send a message to him through another. No one can go to him instead of us, if we do not go ourselves. No one can debar us from his presence, if we wish to meet with him. God is a Spirit, and He dwells in our spirits: that is where we have to seek him. Our spirits are the temples of the living God: in our spirits only can we meet with God or Christ. Our worship, therefore, must take place where no one but ourselves can come to be our priest. Of that only true and real service of God which is offered in the heart, all outward services, be they never so grand and beautiful, and conducted by whatsoever dignitaries, are but types and shadows. Our solemn march along the aisle up to the altar where He dwells, our music and the burning of our incense, our bowing down to the Most Holy, and the offering of our prayer; the absolution we receive, the sacramental grace, the benediction with which we are sent forth again into the world, all, all are inward and unseen. The outward act of worship does but faintly symbolise this inward and most solemn and only real contact with Divinity. If we have not met with God in our own spirits, we cannot have met with him anywhere; and this is a service from which no one can exclude us, in which no one can take our place or represent us.

Shall we not say then, that we are priests, and dwell each one of us, would we but know it, in the precincts of the tabernacle of the Most High? Each of us has his own sacred place of which he is the guardian, and which he is charged to keep pure and bright for the sake of God who loves to dwell in it. If we keep alive the worship belonging to this sanctuary, that will be our best security against forfeiting our liberty to a superstitious priesthood or an outworn creed. How can we let any one stand between God and our conscience, when we know that He is with us in the hidden shrine to which we can at any time repair? How can we allow the conclusions of men long dead to be the standard of our faith, when those relations which they interpreted in the way suited to their age are present and living in ourselves?

III. *Sacrifice.* The third point in regard to which it may well be said that Christ has made us all priests, is that we do not look to a professional priesthood to offer sacrifices for us, but offer sacrifice to God ourselves. In the Jewish religion this was different. There was a particular way in which the thing had to be done: a number of minute formalities had to be observed, and the priest was acquainted with all these, so that the worshipper had to bring his sacrifice to the priest, and get him to offer it up to God upon the altar.

But if God dwells in our spirits, then that must be the place where our sacrifice has to be offered. And there no one can offer it except ourselves. And besides, when we consider what is the nature of the sacrifice which Christians are called on to present to God, we see that in such a matter no one can possibly take our place. What is the sacrifice God asks from us? It is nothing outward, nothing that can be transferred from one individual to another. It is nothing different from ourselves. It is just ourselves. It is our bodies, the apostle says; that is to say, our whole personality, not a dead but a living sacrifice, not a careless but a holy sacrifice, not a material or mechanical but a reasonable sacrifice. And if we are to offer ourselves to God, then it is not an occasional or formal act that we are to bring him, but all we are, all the seasons and all the departments of our life—a sacrifice lasting all the week and growing all the year.

This is the true sacrifice, of which all others are but types and suggestions. The cross of Christ does not supersede it, but enables and encourages us to offer it more simply and heartily. It need not express itself in any special phrase or outward act; it may be unseen by all the world. When we intrust the direction of our life to the highest that is in us, when we yield to the Spirit of God the guidance of our whole activity, and take up duty with the cross that is bound to it, then we are offering this sacrifice, and are the true successors of the priesthoods of old times.

Let it not be said that, if each man is to be his own priest, we shall part company from each other, and cease to find in religion a bond of union. It is not the case that the purest and most spiritual faith opens the door to unbounded individualism or makes a Church impossible. It would be a poor compliment to pay to the Church, to imagine it to be a condition of her existence that her members should not give full heed to the voice of the Spirit that utters itself within them. It is said, and historical examples are cited to support the statement, that when men cast themselves upon their inner consciousness of God, each man comes to have a religion of his own, and common action becomes impossible. It would be well if each man had a religion of his own, and not merely a copy of his neighbour's; but that should lead to no disintegration. If disintegration has at any time taken place, it was not because men listened too much, but because they did not listen wisely and in humility, to the voice of God in their hearts. For one of the first words that we hear when we listen reverently to that voice is one which bids us strive after unity with our fellow-creatures. In retiring to the secret place of our personal religion we are not fleeing from our kind, we are seeking that which most truly unites us with them. The unity to which we shall contribute by being true to our best inspirations may not be identical with any of the organisations now existing around us; but it will be something greater. While tolerant to those symbols and institutions which at present afford in their degree the connection with each other for which all religious hearts must yearn, we shall look forward to a nobler fellowship, a fellowship based not on the shifting sands of intellectual assent or the needs of to-day's policy, but on the simple recognition that in their thirst for God and in their wish to serve him all men in proportion to their sincerity are one.

XV.

THE ASSEMBLING OF OURSELVES TOGETHER.

BY THE REV. JAMES NICOLL, MURROES, FORFARSHIRE.

The assembling of ourselves together.—HEB. x. 25.

MAN is eminently a social being. He craves for and needs the company and co-operation of his fellow-men. However rude may be his condition, he is at least capable of associating with others. Of men in their savage as well as in their most civilised state, it may always be said with truth that their nature prompts and enables them to "assemble themselves together."

No doubt the kinds of association that we see amongst men are extremely varied. As men advance out of ignorance into civilisation they become divided into different sections. At first the members of a savage community are equally familiar, each with all the rest, for practically there is but one class; but, as the community develops, various classes arise; various trades and interests arise; and then we find that men begin to form amongst themselves, as it were, sub-associations. Different grades are evolved. The poor come to sympathise and associate with each other, and form a society by themselves; and, in like manner, the rich form their society, based, too, on mutual acquaintance and sympathy. And so it comes about that this very instinct of union which at first leagued men together, at length, in effect, works disunion. Whole classes bind themselves together in opposition to other classes. Do we not sometimes see something of this at the present day? The members of one class will toil for each other, will make sacrifices for each other, but, then, in so doing, they do not hesitate to avow that the interest of their particular class is paramount, and opposed to that of other classes. And so the instinct of association, which at first bound a community together, begins by and by to split it up and to subdivide it. Each man seeks to associate, not with his local neighbours, but with those who are like-minded or like-interested with himself. The learned seek to associate with the learned. They read the same books; they discuss the same questions; they converse through the same periodicals; and with them the multitude outside holds but little or no communication. The ignorant are most at home with the ignorant. They yield to the same prejudices; harbour the same superstition; are devoured by the same indifference; and they too become a class apart. It is the same with the rich; the same with the poor; the same with every well-marked difference of character and circumstance. All are seeking to obey a social impulse. All are seeking to "assemble themselves together:" only, whereas at first they formed together but one compact mass, they come latterly to be cut up into separate and even hostile sections; and the danger which threatens every community which has reached a certain stage of development is, that that very power of association, which at first impelled men to union, may latterly impel them to separation and ruin.

Now, were this all that were to be said of man's social capacity, the result would be unsatisfactory beyond description. We should see only one invariable law of nature dominating all human action, namely, the law of, first union, and then dissolution. We should see nations and communities first slowly building themselves up, and reaching a certain height of prosperity and strength, and then gradually, by natural necessity, becoming the prey to internal struggle and discord. We should see, first of all, a nation bound together by a vigorous sentiment of patriotism inspiring its different members, and then, ultimately, becoming the scene of dissensions and jealousies amongst its various classes, till at length, either by internal weakness or external violence, its place was taken from it on the earth. And, in point of fact, this is what, not once or twice, but repeatedly, has been witnessed in the course of history. A rude tribe of warriors, hardy and self-denying, has "assembled itself together," and so laid the foundation of a future nation. It has advanced, and conquered, and become civilised, and formed a vast empire. It has subjugated every enemy, fulfilled every ambition, left no stone unturned to secure and perpetuate its greatness. And yet, why has it disappeared like a dream from the world? Why has it collapsed in the moment of its triumph, and, with steps swifter or slower, passed into oblivion? Because of the play of that very instinct of association which at first built up its fortunes and its strength. The various classes into which it had become divided came to think of themselves exclusively, and to forget the common weal. The soldier thought of himself only; the merchant of himself; the rich cared only for his pleasures and his privileges; the poor, no longer proud of simple independence, envied the wealth that was not theirs. And so each class "assembling itself together" with itself only, and becoming alienated from all other classes, the community became broken up into contending fragments. This is what has been seen in the past, and may possibly be repeated in the future. The social power, therefore,—the capacity that enables men to "assemble themselves together"— would not of itself do great things for mankind. It would first build up indeed, but then, in course of time, it would as infallibly pull down again. It would first bind men together into one community, and then, splitting them up in due course into various sections and hostile classes, it would impel them to work out each other's ruin, and procure their common downfall.

But this is not all that is to be said. The social instinct in human nature has been laid hold of by a mightier power than itself, viz. the power of religion. Religion addresses us not as members of an outward society, but simply as human beings. It bids us unite with each other, not as members of any particular community, or of one particular class, but as partakers of the same common nature. It speaks to us, not as rich men or poor men, or learned or ignorant, but simply as men having the same hopes and fears, the same human hearts, the same human sympathies. It discounts all the outward distinctions that separate to the eye one man from another man, and stripping them both bare, as beneath the gaze of God, says the same thing to each. It deals with a region of experience, where all men are on a level, and where all men understand each other. It speaks of such things as conscience, guilt, pardon, the hope of future bliss, peace and rest within. And it bids men as beings equally interested in these things, as beings having an equal stake in them, band themselves together and form a union on that ground. As human beings it tells them they have common woes; common joys; common aspirations; common points of contact each with all the rest. And hence religion, because it takes up this position, is the true bond that permanently binds together men as such. No other bond within the ken of human knowledge is there that can long hold men together. As we have seen, the mere social instinct in man, if it unites men at first, ultimately breaks up society into sections, and separates man from man. Take religion out of human affairs, and leave man to the ordinary play of natural forces, and then, however closely men may adhere to each other for a time, their disunion comes sooner or later, and their unsubstantial brotherhood is broken up and dissolved. The poor will rise against the rich; the rich will hate the poor; the many will tyrannise over the few; class will conspire against class; and universal disintegration and discord will be the issue. But the voice of religion comes to us, and, bidding us turn from those outer things that excite by turns our ambitions and our jealousies, speaks to us as the inheritors and partakers of one common nature. It opens up to us a sphere of union where disintegration and alienation need have no place. It appeals from the outer accidents of life to the inner essentials of being. That we have to deal with a just God, unto whom all secrets are open, all desires known; that we are hastening onwards to the certain grave; that we bear within us the sense of responsibility for an earthly stewardship—with vague hopes that we cannot always justify, and vague fears that we cannot always still; that, in other words, we are more, far more, than the traders, and the merchants, and the scholars, the rich men or the poor men of outward appearance—*this* does religion seek to make the ground of a new and inexhaustible association. It seeks to bind us, to make us "assemble ourselves together" on the basis of our common humanity. It discloses to us a bond of union which can never be dissolved. If men, yielding to the social necessity implanted in their natures, associate on any narrower basis, in due time the association breaks up of its own accord, and disintegrates. But if they associate on the broad ground of their common human nature disclosed by religion—seeking to understand each other; seeking to sympathise with each other; seeking to correct and stimulate, and encourage and exhort each other—then, and then only, is their union a stable union, with no seeds of future disruption lying latent in its bosom. And this precisely is the union among men which religion seeks to form and to foster. The Church is the associating of men together simply as men. Alone of all the organisations to which you can point, it is this. Its members are not united to it by reason of any sympathy based on similarity of calling, or similarity of knowledge, or similarity of external position. They are united to it—not as rich or poor, or learned or ignorant, but simply as the possessors of a common human nature, of common human feelings, of common human sorrows, and joys, and hopes. Once within its pale, his riches drop from the rich man, his poverty from the poor, and each beholds the other as a brother soul, with common griefs and common aspirations. This is the kind of union which religion aspires to effect. It underlies and guarantees all the other associations which men can form and develop amongst themselves. It brings them all face to face with each other and with God, and proclaims that, despite minor differences and surface distinctions, all men are, at heart, brethren, in virtue of possessing a common nature, and awaiting a like destiny.

Now, this being so, religion, as the name itself implies, is the supremely binding force in human affairs. The word *religion* simply means that which binds or ties together. Other bonds are temporary, other unions are sure to be broken up. But this bond, because it seizes on that in us which is common to us all, and is built upon our essential brotherhood, is the perpetual sweetener of human life, the perpetual restraint on human passions, the perpetual enlightener of human conscience, the perpetual encourager of human hope. Look, my friends, upon the most gigantic achievements which men have attained to by co-operation as workers, or statesmen, or conquerors, and you have no guarantee that these achievements, splendid as they seem, will long endure. The nation which, to-day, seems strongest and most united, may, a century hence, be hastening to dissolution. The community which, to-day, seems harmonious by reason of its industry and plenty, may, ere long, be in the throes of civil war—man flying at the throat of his brother man. We know that such things have happened, and what has happened once can occur again. But let men be united together—not by mere statecraft; not by peace and plenty only; not by industry only; but by that knowledge of each other's real and deepest wants, by genuine sympathy, by genuine participation in each other's interest and beneficence; not as citizens merely, but as human beings—in one word, by *religion*—let this be the union that cements and unifies a nation or a people; and then, be the trials and difficulties and social struggles of that people what they may, there is a force amongst them that guarantees their stability; that will clear away misunderstandings; that will discredit violence and injustice, and stimulate mercy and helpfulness, as between individual and individual, and class and class. But, on the other hand, let the binding force of religion be absent from a community; let men forget to "assemble themselves together" as brethren; or let religion become a mere hollow form, without power, or love, or sympathy; let it be a thing of phrases and unintelligible dogmas, pretending to describe that which cannot be known, and forgetting to look into the human heart which lies close at hand,—forgetting to be simply truthful, and to deal with the soul's life as it actually exists,—then, I say, let a nation's prosperity be what it may, the seeds of dissolution are there notwithstanding, slowly germinating, and destined to bring forth in due time their terrible fruits. Men will not cease to "assemble themselves together,"— to associate together in obedience to their social instinct—no, that is a law of their nature and cannot be reversed!—but, failing to unite in the bonds of religion, they will unite merely in those of class-selfishness, in those of reckless faction, in those of mutual antipathy, in those of estrangement and lawless greed. There are countries in Europe which at this moment are threatening to illustrate these words. They have abandoned, wholly or in part, the bond of sympathy as between man and man implied in the practice of a real religion, and, having thus parted with that power which alone can restrain men's passions, and incline them to justice, and mercy, and truth, they are falling back on grim force, the stronger holding the weaker against its will; the weaker waiting in silent hope that its turn will come next. That is the union imposed by external force, and not the unity of inner life; and the whole teaching of past history is false, if such a state of matters be one that can long continue.

Such, then, is the bond which religion seeks to form between us. Such, in its widest sense, is the "assembling of ourselves together," which it contemplates. And it is that wide bond of sympathy, making each seek to understand the other, which is typified, and made in a sense visible, by our weekly assembling for public worship. The outer and visible thing which we do here does not end with itself; it is meant to symbolise a far wider and deeper, even if unseen, union subsisting between us as fellow-creatures accountable to the same Creator. And it is only when we remember what is behind, that we rightly understand the symbol. It is not real religion, merely coming together outwardly, and participating in the stated rites of worship. Such observances have no power of themselves to bind and consolidate the life of a community or a congregation. It is only when they are allied with heart-service—with the desire of learning truth and duty, of yielding obedience to the will of God, of being just, and true, and merciful to our neighbour—that they express a reality and become a badge of brotherhood between man and man. Nothing less than this can adequately fill up the sense of the apostle's words—"the assembling of ourselves together."

And, yet, let us not disparage the outward symbol. Of all beautiful customs in this world, what more beautiful than that which brings together once a week the inhabitants of a district, without respect of outward distinctions, and makes them blend in a common fellowship of praise and worship before the shrine of duty, and faith, and God? Here at least, if anywhere on earth, should men forget the mere accidents of station and external circumstance, and strive to think only of those things that belong to them in common as the children of one Father, as the sharers of common cares and burdens, as all equal before the throne of grace and mercy. As we come together, not to know those things that separate us, but rather those that unite us, does it not oftentimes happen that the sorrow which is bred of isolation is dispelled before the larger view we get of life beside our fellow-creatures? The grief that fed on solitude, the care and disappointment which, in the loneliness of our private dwellings, may have assumed exaggerated proportions, we bring them here, and, lo! we are gently rebuked by the very presence of our neighbours, and we overcome our selfishness or self-love. Here—if elsewhere we might perhaps forget it—we are reminded that others have their trials as well as we. Here—if elsewhere faith has drooped within us, and life has seemed poor and unworthy, and we have asked who will show us any good—a simple word has recalled us to our better thoughts, and bid us take heart anew, and fight once more the fight of principle and faith. Those things which, as individuals, we are shy and backward to commune about with one another; those sins we dare not confess; those weaknesses and trials we cannot tell, but can only brood upon, we here give utterance to; and the language of public prayer, and the voice of exhortation, and the song of gratitude give expression to our pent-up feelings, and we have relief. Yes, there is a dignity in our assembled gatherings that does not belong to us as isolated individuals. There is a blessing where two or three are met together, that hides itself from only one. The petty things that belong to us as units drop from us in the larger atmosphere of fellowship with one another, and, by simple contact with our fellow-Christians, we are elevated out of the commonness and depression of our solitary lives. Week by week the muster-roll seems read as we assemble ourselves together, and ever and again some well-known form disappears, while others come and take the vacant place. There seems to be ever a twofold congregation at the spot where we meet: the one we see, the other that we cannot any longer see, but can only recall. Flashes of memory will anon people pews with faces now no more,—and yet we remember that even where the living meet to cement their solemn league, the departed rest in the silent expectant majesty of the grave. Death does not wholly sunder us from "the assembling of ourselves together," for when our appointed day is done, and the spirit goes to Him who gave it, it is here, beside the place which religion has made its own, that we hope to lay our ashes, and to await the future call. What more beautiful custom can there be than that which links in life and death generation to generation, and testifies to the underlying unity that, beneath all diversities, unites the souls of men before the eye of the almighty God?

Let us, then, as we repair to our accustomed place of worship, remember, in the light of what I have been saying, the great object of our weekly gatherings. Here we meet for ends only peaceful; here we meet to renew and strengthen the bonds of brotherly sympathy; to symbolise our community of faith and hope and joy before our Maker. May that which by its very design points us to the widest and deepest aspects of our common nature never be perverted by our thoughtlessness or obstinacy into a badge of separateness or aloofness from our fellow-men! For of all perversions of the sacred symbol of public worship, that surely is the blindest and the most mischievous which degrades the high token of human brotherhood into the occasion of earthly jealousy and dissension. When such perversions are suffered, not only do the outward rites of religion lose, as it were, their very soul : they become active sources of alienation and mutual misunderstanding ; and religion herself, so far as affected by her visible representatives, forfeits her unique rank amongst the binding elements of humanity, to take a lower place amongst those partial and unstable associations, whose duration, however long, is never more than temporary and accidental. Here, then, we meet not to separate ourselves from others, but to remember our essential fellowship with them. Here we meet to worship One who is the Father of all, and, in the recognition of his relationship to us, to recognise also our mutual bonds to one another ; that so we may promote that great fellowship of justice and love and mercy, which to exhibit in our daily lives is both our greatest homage to God and his best reward to us. We meet here to cultivate this spirit ; to meet each other on common universal ground ; to share each other's fears, and hopes, and faith ; to correct each other's waywardness if need be ; to provoke and encourage each other to love and good works ; and so help each other along " the trivial round, the common task," that mark out for most of us the actual sphere of duty and service. May this idea of true religion never forsake us, nor we it ; and may this sacred edifice long stand to witness to the reality of the human soul's fellowship with God through Christ !

XVI.

INDIVIDUALISM AND THE CHURCH.

BY THE REV. THOMAS RAIN, M.A., HUTTON, DUMFRIESSHIRE.

In this place is one greater than the temple.—MATT. XII. 6.
The Sabbath was made for man, and not man for the Sabbath.
—MARK II. 27.

THESE two sayings of our Lord belong to one another, and we may call the latter the complement of the former. In the verse taken from Matthew He claims an extraordinary position for himself, and in that from Mark He makes the same claim on behalf of mankind. The claim made is this: that the individual soul possesses rights superior to ecclesiastical organisations, and by implication to all other organisations that may be set up. For the principle enunciated is so great and deep that it may be universally applied. The living soul, He seems to tell us, is Lord of all earthly powers, and particularly of all institutions and mechanisms which as vehicles of its thought it may choose to frame. It is the creator of these. But for it, the vital principle, they, the body, had not been; and when through ignorance or sluggishness it forgets this fact and lets its own creature rule over it, it, Esau-like, sells its birthright.

Such a doctrine must have come with startling

effect upon the Pharisees who heard it uttered: though they would hardly apprehend all it meant, and may have regarded it as the wild utterance of an egoistical enthusiast. That it contained a spiritual principle which is eternally at war with all like them in the world would hardly enter their thoughts, and possibly some of them deemed it so visionary as to be harmless. But others would at least note that the enthusiast had threatened the Temple, which was the palladium of their system, and the Sabbath-day, which was an important outwork of it. I doubt if the most ecclesiastically-minded among us can realise the obstinacy with which a latter-day Pharisee would revere the Temple at Jerusalem. For even orthodoxy in our day is less rigid than it was then, and we are constitutionally of a less stubborn temperament than the Jews. Besides, at that time in Palestine the recovery of political freedom was thought dependent on the continuance of the national religion; and to threaten or disparage the Temple was like damping patriotic aspirations. It, and the ordinances gathered round it, were expected to form a rallying principle for the nation, and the Jew who spoke against it was marked down for a traitor, no less than a heretic.

Therefore I hardly know another saying of our Lord's that, from the priestly point of view, looks so revolutionary as these. For they cut away the very ground on which priesthoods take their stand, and were their principle universally recognised, there would be no room for sacerdotalism anywhere. Like Noah's dove, it would find no rest for the sole of its foot, but would be driven back to the place whence it came out, the uncivilised or half-civilised understanding. But unhappily the world is ruled to a very small extent by spiritual principles, and to a very large extent by expediency and the imitative instinct; one consequence of which is that priesthoods have abounded and do abound. Further, we need not expect them to be extinguished in our time, or our children's time, and it is probably better that they should exist yet awhile. Had they never been necessary to the world's development they had never been in it, and were they altogether useless to-day they would speedily disappear. It is because there is still a certain co-adaptation between the spirit of man and the overgrown Romish hierarchy, as well as other hierarchies, which, though disclaiming Rome, are yet its satellites—that Popery so successfully holds its ground. But as man advances, sacerdotalism must retrograde; as he comes to a clearer consciousness of the powers within himself he will give less heed to external guides to truth, though they be never so venerable.

Our subject then is Individualism and the Church. That is to say, we have to show in what relationship Christianity would have the soul stand to ecclesiastical institutions: how under one form of the relationship such institutions are of great value, while under another form of it they are turned into a curse. It is a large subject, and exhaustive treatment of it cannot be pretended to; but some consideration of its more important aspects may have its uses.

Institutions are to be the servant of man, says Christ: liable to modification, to increase or diminution, to total annihilation, as the needs of his spirit may determine. He is to have entire power over them as the potter has power over the clay, and may mould them to his several purposes, or, if it suit him better, may break them under his foot. Like the ancient slave, relatively to his master, they are to be wholly in his hands for life or death. The world in which he lives is a place of ceaseless transformation, and as other conditions of his life change, Christianity gives him the power of changing also the institutions in which his faith is enshrined. Creeds and ordinances conformable to one age may not be conformable to the next, and man is to judge how far and in what direction they need modification. The right of adding to or taking from them is given by God into his hand. This is the doctrine of our Lord.

But the doctrine of all priesthoods is the opposite of this; for they make man the servant of ecclesiastical institutions, which they hedge about with theories of divine right that bristle with clever logic. With arguments which may be drawn from grounds of expediency or from the sentiment of reverence, in favour of retaining old institutions, there need be no quarrel. It is a different thing when it is argued that they stand above man, and that his part is simply to bow down to them. When, according to this theory, the divine afflatus comes into the world, it is through a corporate body—a huge piece of mechanism—that it comes, and not, as in old prophetic times, through the individual soul,—some lonely soul that thought had driven into the desert. The Roman Pontiff may be described as the axis of this mechanism, and his cardinals, bishops, fathers and councils, with all their picturesque symbolisms, as well as sacerdotally-minded Protestants, as machinery revolving round him. These form the elaborate body which God out of his mere good pleasure has elected to frame for the truth, and apart from this body satisfactory knowledge of the truth need not be hoped for. Ordinary mortals, who may not be bishops or fathers, must yet adhere to this mechanism as unimportant atoms of it, or they "will without doubt be damned everlastingly"! So declares priestcraft.

Time was, of course, when human nature needed such representations of God and spiritual things to excite its reverence, and had the Word not been made flesh in the sacerdotal form, it had probably gained fewer votaries. The fact may hold good to some extent yet, and we need have no quarrel with it; but with those who say that in its nature it is divine, that it is unchanging and indestructible, as Protestants we are forced to quarrel. Such a state of things we hold is necessarily provisional, and useful and admirable when recognised as such; but when endowed with infallibility, called sacred and eternal, and all the rest of it, a great mischief. That it should ever have been so regarded is not altogether strange, but that amid modern enlightenment such a view should be persisted in, and by men of genius and virtue, seems to me passing strange.

How it came that purely human ordinances were first invested with divine qualities, said to be inspired, and deemed of supernatural authority, appears, when we think of it, plainer than many things. It is closely connected with the deep reverence all ages feel towards a great man, and the faculty they lack for rightly comprehending him. A few of course have clear enough spiritual perception to distinguish between his essential truths and the outward covering of them, but this is not a gift that in its integrity falls to many. What the people fix their minds upon are the material forms which their revered hero laid hold of as vehicles of expression, and through which his moral nature flowed into action. They perceive that, working through these, he achieved magnificent results, and then infer, innocently enough, that some special virtue must belong to them. It will depend on the bent of the man's genius, the accident of his social position, the age and country he lives in, what these forms shall be. They may be this or that theological theory, a political institution, an educational system, some special mode of exercising self-restraint, of gaining moral stimulus, and always that for which, in the circumstances, his nature has affinity. They are called up by his mind spontaneously, almost unconsciously, and are always found, when tried, to help him to his object. But his time comes and death takes him away. The forms, however, are left behind him, all shining with a wondrous radiance; and it is not usually considered that it is a reflected and not an inherent radiance which gilds them. Whether it came out of their originator's spirit or is native to the forms is a question not patiently examined; and hence, in a generation or two, we have the forms irrationally exalted, while the mind that throbbed behind them is forgotten. It is not consciously or designedly forgotten, but to cling to the letter and neglect the spirit seems a failing inseparable from popular thought. In the most of us, by nature, the senses are more active than the intellect, so that the external details of a life, its outward vesture, are more readily apprehended than its soul or principle. Only to a thoughtful individual here and there does it occur that the forms through which the great man worked were accidental, and more the product of the time he lived in than of himself. Had the general circumstances been different, their character would have been different too. It was the living spirit of the thinker, and not his machinery, that worked the signs and wonders. Were not this the case, no age need ever perish through lack of power; for always the symbols of dead prophets are lying about like fossils in the rocks to help it. But alas, they do not help it, and, apart from the soul that gave them being, cannot help it, any more than the magician's rod can conjure without the magician. To fancy they can is like fancying you could paint sublimely if you had Raphael's brush, or become a great violinist with Paganini's violin. The fallacy of such a fancy is patent, and we know that the musician's and painter's art comes by a less ready method. Yet it is on a strictly analogous mistake that sacerdotalism is founded, and the mistake has quite as absurd an aspect in the latter case as in the former. It is fully as irrational to expect that by such legerdemain you can cultivate the religious life, as to think you can gain by it artistic dexterity.

Such considerations, I think, if properly used, form a

key that lays open to us the mental process by which church organisations have been raised above the individual soul; and explain how, long ago, the Sabbath was made more than man, and the Temple more than Christ. It is an error incident to a period of civilisation when the senses are yet regnant, and the deep powers of thought undeveloped.

The Saviour's principle, on the other hand, is the outcome of a look into life with the clear eye of the spirit. What he perceived was this: that there is always the believing man, God-created and God-inspired, and after him this, that, and the other institution. Given the devout soul, and churches become possible; without this they are wholly impossible. For as the web comes out of the spider, creeds, ordinances, and polities come forth from the inner life of man; and their character is in strict harmony with the character of that inner life. When the thinking soul conceives its idea comprehensively, and in a form corresponding to the general convictions of the age, the institution reared upon it is sure to be influential. The superficial, eccentric idea, on the other hand, does not become a principle of organisation so readily, and when it does succeed its influence is limited. Some insignificant sect may be formed out of it—for every age has its proportion of minds that love the fantastic —but no wide-spreading Church.

Another circumstance to be observed is this: that every idea which is congruous with the age it appears in, every idea that marks a new epoch in culture, spontaneously weaves a body for itself; and there is little need of distinct conscious effort being made to give it fitting organisation. I suspect it is rather ill than well with man when he says deliberately to himself: "Now we have got a great, fresh thought among us, let us found an institution to preserve it." For it belongs specially to the nature of such thoughts to build a habitation for themselves, and to do so by a noiseless, almost unconscious process. The idea takes the mechanical faculties into its service, and these weave for it a material vesture, but so completely are they subject to the idea that they know not precisely what they are about. Their aim is not to produce this or that well-proportioned institution of which they knew the plan beforehand, but they act as though they were inspired, and simply to satisfy the feeling of the hour. And this process, time after time repeated, and carried on sometimes for ages, will generally result in an organisation of great strength and adaptability. For, as we have often been reminded in our time, "institutions are not made but grow;" which is a most correct observation, and is admirably illustrated in the case of the Church visible. That grew up gradually out of the needs and aspirations in which the spiritual consciousness from time to time expressed itself; and all that is best in it is the product of the understanding incited by the spirit, not working mechanically by itself. There must always be the living soul ere there can be a well-proportioned body, as Spenser in his Hymn to Beauty teaches—

> "For of the soul the body form doth take,
> For soul is form, and doth the body make."

But how the soul passes into material substance,

building itself a temple and filling the earth with firm and beautiful structures—beautiful for a time at least—I profess not to understand. It is a mystery which I cannot fathom. One thing, however, is probable: that no great historical organisation ever was created by other agency than I have here named, viz., an impassioned life, often a religious faith, subsisting in the heart of man. Patient contriving of the understanding, knowing adaptation of means to ends, never of itself created such an institution. These have generally been a valuable auxiliary in the work; but the moving, masterly power is always an illuminating thought, a burning conviction in the mind of some individual. The Saviour understood all this, and in conformity with it enthroned the living soul,—the divine soul and the human we may say, his own and that of man, above the venerablest institutions: "I say unto you, that in this place is one greater than the temple;" "The Sabbath was made for man, and not man for the Sabbath."

Let us look in a general way at the conceptions of truth that are involved in these several principles. What is truth? is a very ancient question, and has been answered in a thousand varieties of ways. It has also been declared incapable of any answer that is trustworthy. I would not add one more to the endless definitions of it that have been framed. My object is to show what idea Ecclesiasticism and Individualism have each got about its relation to the understanding. Do they represent it as that with which the understanding has a necessary connection, or as a thing of foreign texture, which only makes the mind its temporal habitat, and which, like the ancient eremite relative to the world, lodges in it without being of it? Has it a subjective or objective origin? is it indigenous to consciousness, or something imported into it? The view which a particular system or institution takes of such a question will have a strong influence on its practical line of action, and we cannot appreciate rightly the practical value of Ecclesiasticism and Individualism till we ascertain the way in which they answer it. It is their speculative conceptions of truth, their theory as to where it comes from, and how it comes, that determines their character, and gives motive to their policy.

Now it is the doctrine of Ecclesiasticism in its integrity, and as represented by Rome, that the human soul possesses no natural faculty for apprehending the absolutely true. A certain power of thought is admitted to it, but it is of that mechanical kind which gives rise to industrial life, and not of the spiritual order whence come the doctrines of religion. These doctrines originate without, and are conveyed by an external authority into the mind, which forms a fitting nidus for their reception, but between them and the nidus there is no vital union possible. The fostering care of the Church is needed to keep them active, and guard them against corruption, and when that is withdrawn, or if it be discarded, they instantly disappear. At all events, their charm ceases to work, and the spiritual principle is taken out of man's life. For that is the gift of the Church, and is only given to those who put themselves in connection with her holy ordinances.

By the light shed from this doctrine, we readily perceive why Ecclesiasticism should have been so fierce an opponent to the free exercise of reason in judging of truth. Its opposition has been based on a conviction that reason and truth were two things essentially different, and that the former could not tell anything reliable about the latter. It might, no doubt, try its powers, and frame theories; but because between it and what it theorised about there was no community of nature, its deductions could only lead astray. The proper place for reason, therefore, was to be chained under the feet of ecclesiastical authority. And no right-minded Christian would expose his faith to its lawless criticism, any more than he would put his watch for adjustment into the hands of a ploughboy or a savage. In both cases the operator would be in total ignorance of what he operated upon, and the result would be pernicious. Hence Ecclesiasticism has regarded every new encroachment of the rationalistic principle as so much territory won from the realm of light and order, and put under the dominion of anarchy. Hence its jealousy of philosophy and science, of democratic movements, of all sorts of innovation, and its exaltation of the past at the expense of the present. That inspiration of the Almighty which giveth man— all men—understanding, finds no acknowledgment in its creed; and the so-called inner light is viewed by it as a dangerous Will-o'-the-wisp, to be guarded against continually.

It is the doctrine of Individualism, on the other hand, that truth in its nature is subjective, a part of the spiritual consciousness, and necessarily involved in it. This doctrine is scattered all through the prophetic writings of the Bible, and is sometimes stated there with antique Hebraic vehemence. We meet with it under a very beautiful form in Deuteronomy, and if the modern theory of that book's origin be correct, it is a strange place to find it: "For this commandment, which I command thee this day, it is not hidden from thee, neither is it far off: it is not in heaven, that thou shouldest say, Who shall go up for us to heaven, and bring it unto us, that we may hear it, and do it? Neither is it beyond the sea, that thou shouldest say, Who shall go over the sea for us, and bring it unto us, that we may hear it, and do it? But the word is very nigh unto thee, in thy mouth, and in thy heart, that thou mayest do it."

Here is the profoundest spiritual truth stated in quaint picturesque fashion, but so simply that he who runs may read. To form a correct philosophy of religion I do not think we need add much to what this passage gives us. If we bring to explicit consciousness the ideas that are latent in it, and give them an orderly setting, it will be enough. I would be satisfied with emphasising the general fact, that religious truth is by this passage placed on an internal and personal basis. It is represented as that which springs up in the hidden depth of man's soul, and for which God has prepared no other place than this hidden depth. This is the Christian view ages before the coming of Christ: and we can fearlessly admit that there is a real sense—more real than is known to dogmatic exegesis—in which the Saviour may be found in the Old Testament books. Neither shalt thou say, Lo here it is in this church! nor, Lo there it is in that ceremony! for "the kingdom of God is within you" is a word that was sounded by the ancient prophets long before He sounded it who is the Light of the World. The kingdom of God is within us, but of its times and ways of coming unto us no man knoweth. In all ages there have been thousands who imagined they could know—there are thousands among ourselves. But the grandest treatise ever given to the world on this subject is the half-dozen words of Jesus to Nicodemus, which say in effect that there can be no treatise. "The wind bloweth where it listeth, and thou hearest the sound thereof, but canst not tell whence it cometh, and whither it goeth: so is every one that is born of the Spirit." The Holy Spirit's work is as mysterious as the wind, says the Lord; and, in this winged sentence the whole race of theological triflers and pedants have their trifling and pedantry rebuked.

It is desirable to say something about the way in which Ecclesiasticism and Individualism stand related to the question of evidence. Probably there never was an age when the question was surrounded by so much interest as it is at present. Persons, who by every circumstance of their life are outside the learned and controversial classes, are pondering it with anxiety; and new books relating to it find their way not only into the scholar's study, but into the homes of public men and men of business. Women, and youths too, read that the dear faith which illumines and strengthens them may be preserved. "Refute materialism for us or we die" is what thousands are calling out to their theological masters, and with a passionate earnestness, almost a vehemence, never known before; sometimes with a fear, alas! that their prayer may prove futile.

There is something deeply touching, perhaps tragical, in this expectation which the multitude have of getting evidence for religious truth from their spiritual teachers. Evidence of a sort they doubtless do get, which may serve them well enough if they keep in sheltered places away from the currents of scientific criticism; but which proves very vulnerable when unreservedly exposed to these: and perhaps the best advice that could be given to simple souls just now—if they are at all susceptible—is to remain in these sheltered places where there is no danger. Better that their faith should rest on an insecure basis—not felt to be so by them—than that they should have no faith at all. Anything rather than that they should sink permanently into that night of scepticism whence have been emitted some of the dreariest cries in literature. Better even the shriek of the "revivalist" than the "vanity of vanities" of Ecclesiastes.

Now, we learn on reflection that evidence divides itself into two great classes, one of which naturally connects itself with the sacerdotal principle of religion, the other with the individualistic. That which is homogeneous with sacerdotalism refers as a rule to historical testimony, calls in the aid of empirical logic, and generally adopts the method of verification employed in science. Where the thing to be proved is conceived as wholly outside the mind and of a different nature from it, it is hard to imagine any other method that would work; and the speculative position taken up by ecclesiasticism leaves it almost no choice as to its mode of proof. It has to demonstrate its doctrines after the same manner as physical science does. Leaving out of view all philosophical objections to this mode, there is a practical one of very great force which it is worth our while to consider. The objection is the want of success which this sort of evidence for religious truth has hitherto had in combating scientific scepticism. That it has been unsuccessful will probably not be admitted by the Christian controversialist. But the whole life both of nature and man will soon be the recognised domain of physical science, and then there will be seen more clearly than now the inability of religion to defend itself by the old empirical method. People will have to relinquish it altogether or discover a new basis for it, and uphold it by a more enlightened method. Let Christian apologists be ever so clever or so laborious, they will have to change their principles ere they can make much way among the educated classes. I believe they will have to make trial of that form of evidence which connects itself with Individualism, whereof the principle is this: that religious truth is its own evidence, and the ultimate court of appeal the spiritual consciousness.

This is a position that hitherto has served the materialists much as Samson served the Philistines—it has made sport for them. "Intuition," "necessary truth," the "subjective method," are things that they have laughed at, and battered with their keen logic alternately. Scepticism has sneered, and bigotry has raged, and between these two fires the spiritual philosophy has sometimes had a hard time of it. But the deep-minded men of the world have been on its side. That this universe has a supra-sensuous basis, and is far more than it seems to be, is a conception round which, in all ages, genius and intellect have ranged themselves; and though they have often erred in systematising their thought, and may err again, something in them has kept them true to its principle. But we are only concerned here with the spiritualistic or transcendental principles of evidence, and these tell us, as I say, that the criterion of truth in religious matters lies in the soul itself. According to these, it is not by a logical arrangement of facts, nor by the cleverness of empirical philosophers, that religion is to be defended, but by the witness of the Spirit to what is true, which is part of the nature of the regenerate man. And the popular apologist ought to consider whether, fighting the battle of Christianity on an objective basis, he is not rather harming his cause than helping it. For, the moment you bring the reasons for your belief from the depths of inner consciousness, and state them logically on paper, a thousand to one but they seem feeble to yourself. There are processes in human nature that very few of us have as yet found a phraseology for giving clear expression to, and I am afraid if the spiritual ideas of the Bible, and of later teaching, do not commend themselves as true to the consciousness of those who read them, there is no method at present by which they can be proved. At all events, in the present state of popular culture, philosophical proof of them could not be made widely intelligible. And perhaps the best "Evidences of Christianity" which in the meantime can be had are those inarticulate intuitions and feelings which dwell deep down in believing souls; that intense, unaccountable life which has inspired men from the beginning, and which the wisest of them have ever looked on as a mystery. That the day shall never come when this life shall find a voice, and be able to give intelligible account of itself, I by no means suggest. Meanwhile it is to the great majority of us as good as dumb, and only gives us vague hints which one cannot communicate to another. Each one must possess it for himself to understand its secret. And this is why I described the spectacle of the multitude looking to theology for evidence to support its faith as pathetic and even tragical. The evidence that theology is able or willing to provide is not in this age particularly valuable, and people should be taught, though with caution, to seek refuge from unbelief in their spiritual instincts. These, at all events, possess a much greater value than argumentative divinity. The state of religious belief is not a state into which an individual ever can be reasoned: for faith is an organic growth of the soul, caused, we may say, by the wonder-working of God's Spirit, and about which the common logic knows nothing.

Some weight might also be given to the circumstance that no great religious teacher ever troubled himself about the evidences, in the common sense of that term. Where are the subtle argumentations of the ancient prophets, or of our Lord, and where their testimonies from history? It seems ridiculous to propose such a question. In them the individualistic principle dwelt strongly, and hence they appealed for proof to the hearts and consciences of men, the witness that was within their hearers. And there is nothing grander in their lives than the way they bore themselves amid the race of ecclesiastical reasoners, themselves reasoning not. It was not for them to mingle their great voices with the vulgar polemics of the time.

But in setting forth a view of the more prominent aspects of Ecclesiasticism and Individualism, something should be said about their relation to the established opposition of secular and sacred. Such opposition is a necessary expression of Ecclesiasticism, and in ancient times when that principle was everywhere dominant it was more distinctly seen than now. There were secular and sacred times, secular and sacred places, secular and sacred actions, secular and sacred doctrines, and of each of these a considerable variety. But now among most Protestant communities, the opposition exists actively in the sphere of doctrine only; while of the large number of sacred days there is but one, the Sabbath-day, remaining. This is owing to the action of the individualistic principle, out of which Protestantism took its rise, and the tendency of which is to extinguish the opposition altogether. For it leads necessarily to the Pauline position that there is nothing clean or unclean of itself, but that everything becomes one or the other according as we conceive it. It is the way in which we think of things, and the uses to which we put them, that determine whether or not their character is religious; and all places, times, and ideas are holy to the holy-minded man. Such a thought probably does not fill, as an inspiring faith, the mind of the great Protestant multitude, for in the unthinking masses the echoes of a bygone creed survive for ages; but there are, I fancy, few among them who would not acquiesce in it were it brought intelligently before them. This acquiescence would be the outcome of that Individualism which is working unconsciously in the atmosphere of the age. Once it has established itself, and taken conscious possession of the age, it will, if it be a true and not a false Individualism, extinguish the division between the Church and the world entirely, substituting for it that grand idea of St. Paul: "To the pure all things are pure." With this idea pervading and filling our souls, we shall come to perceive that the whole universe of consciousness is at our service for spiritual culture. The earth, says the Positivist, exists for the economical good of man; and science is the thrifty handmaiden that finds where its treasures lie, and applies them to his uses. This is a sound enough doctrine, but as Christians we must go beyond it. We must say in addition that the earth is given us for the culture of our souls, and that Christian philosophy is the instrument that explains to us its complex symbols. Christian philosophy must take up the discoveries of science and give to them a spiritual interpretation. Earth's seas and skies, its rocks and animals, the foliage and the flower, the flux and reflux of its life, its iron, relentless laws and the marvellous history of man, are all facts through which God would teach and discipline us. They are a portion of his revelation, and not one of them but shadows forth his being and his thought. I believe there is none of them which has not got a moral counterpart that may become interfused with our being. We may find them not only givers of the bread that perishes, but in some sense givers also of the bread of life.

It might be said further, that if Individualism were to extinguish the opposition between secular and sacred, and Paul's conception were to lay hold of us, preaching would then become practical. That is to say, it would no longer confine itself to one set of ideas, and these of a bygone age, but, studying the world that lies around it, would address itself to the problems, moral and intellectual, that are pressing on the present. With open and sympathetic mind it would turn towards the highways of every-day life, and would gather from its scenes and incidents the materials of a finer eloquence than the study of books can give. The love and sorrow that are in poor men's dwellings, the labour that fills the day, and the rest that comes with evening, the laughter of children, and the brow laden with care, earth's sunlight and starlight, the noisy stir of life, and the mystery of death, —these are the things that, passed through the fire of Christian thought, have power to move mankind. And the true office of the preacher in modern society is to be a revealer of the beauty and the deep meaning which lies in such common phenomena, but which the world, engrossed with its business, has neither time nor faculty to discover. He should strive so to speak, that when people hear him they will feel that their own life—which they had deemed so stale and unprofitable—is coming back to them, in his words, an august and venerable thing, because ennobled by having every fact of it construed as in relation to Christianity. Then our religious life, fed from fresher and more numerous springs than hitherto, would become robust and manly, not a thing to shun the noontide struggle of the world and walk in shady places, but that which stands forth to hallow toil, and make business pure, and all intercourse sweet, and give the state an ennobling policy.

There is one most pernicious growth of the sacerdotal principle that should not be left unnoticed. I refer to the ecclesiastical self-consciousness which exhibits itself so strongly in many of our Protestant Churches, and which is a real hindrance to their spiritual usefulness. It fosters a party spirit in them and makes them very active in the matter of statistics. It gives them a sharp eye for denominational differences. It gives them also a wonderful knowledge of the scriptural theory of Church-government, and such matters. But of the soul's spiritual quickening, and evolution out of ignorance and earthliness into divine wisdom, it teaches them little. Mechanism is its God, and consequently it has little faith. It believes only in what the outward eye can see, and the logic of the understanding can trace. The evidence of things not seen—of the powers of spiritual thought, whose working is silent—has no place in its composition.

I would say, in closing, that the struggle between

the two principles of Ecclesiasticism and Individualism is destined to be one of the great struggles of the future. It has been going on since the Protestant Reformation began, and in every later age on a wider scale, pushing itself into new departments of thought and life; and it cannot cease until one of the combatants is driven from the field, and unity has been brought back to the spiritual sphere of man's life. I think the heretical outbreakings of our time must possess an importance even to thinking minds when seen to connect themselves with this struggle.

Lastly, let it be understood that the Individualism which I advocate is not a lawless or profane Individualism, but one which the mind only can develop when quickened by God's Spirit. And let no one imagine that I ignore the value of ecclesiastical organisations, or would have those existing destroyed. The inward life necessarily embodies itself in visible institutions, and though spiritual thought may have ebbed low in many of our churches it has not wholly left any of them, and they are performing a useful work. Their doctrines are the bread of life to thousands, and they form a real holy of holies, in which devout souls all over Christendom worship. I would only warn you against entering into a false relation to them, calling them your master and lord, and forgetting they are your servant; raising them to the position of an end, and forgetting they are but a means. And I would say, especially, that not a single doctrine of which they are the official guardians—the most essential or the most accidental doctrine, the earliest framed or the latest added—can be of moral value to anybody when taken into the mind at the bidding of authority.

Let the simple-minded Christian, who hears of progress and dreads the havoc it may work upon his creed, gather comfort from the thought that the spirit of true religion is eternal. The visible body of it may wax old like a garment, and as a vesture God —or man under God—may change it, and it shall be changed. But this shall only be that Religion may weave for itself a simpler and more fitting covering; and when the churches of the present break up and go their way, they will make room for something that is higher.

XVII.

THE PHARISEE AND THE PUBLICAN.

BY THE REV. THOMAS RAIN, M.A., HUTTON.

Two men went up into the temple to pray; the one a Pharisee, and the other a publican. The Pharisee stood and prayed thus with himself: God, I thank thee that I am not as other men are, extortioners, unjust, adulterers, or even as this publican. I fast twice in the week, I give tithes of all that I possess. And the publican, standing afar off, would not lift up so much as his eyes unto heaven, but smote upon his breast, saying, God be merciful to me a sinner. I tell you, this man went down to his house justified rather than the other: for every one that exalteth himself shall be abased; and he that humbleth himself shall be exalted.— LUKE xviii. 10-14.

HOWEVER much the numerous sects of Christendom are divided as to their ideas of Christ's nature, they are all agreed in looking on him as a great religious teacher. That He made it his mission to put mankind right on the greatest subject that can occupy their thoughts is what no school of Christians will deny. It is when we come to consider the way He took of doing this, that our sectarian differences appear; and possibly these differences are more owing to our mode of studying his life, than to inherent difficulties in the life itself. Were we to become more historical in our method, and less theological, the religious unity of Christendom might attain to other than it is at present—a pious wish.

But leaving this question aside, I want you to start with me from the idea that is common to us all, Christ a religious teacher, and to observe the remarkable attitude—the startling and original attitude—which, as such, He took up. He set himself in deadly antagonism to the official religion of the age in which He lived. From a religious point of view, and speaking broadly, the community in Palestine was at that time divisible into two well-marked sections: the Scribes and Pharisees—the church-goers; the publicans and sinners—the lapsed masses. It was pretty much then as now: the respectable classes were surrounded by a seething mass of people whose lawless lives, or whose alien blood or faith, had outlawed them from society. There was the traditional party, and the party in rebellion against tradition; the former in a state of death-like rigidity, the latter in a state of moral chaos —for their rebellion had been dictated less by principle than by wild and lawless appetite. The Saviour had to choose which of these great sections, the conventional or the lawless, He would most sympathise with, and the instincts of his nature led him towards the latter. It is not among the robed gentlemen about the temple that He goes to seek his coadjutors, and it is not in his talks with Pharisees that He becomes sweet and tender; but when He would surround himself with friends, He calls to him labouring men, and when his nature warms and softens, it is among simple-minded villagers. Simon Peter and Andrew the fishermen, not Caiaphas the High Priest, are chosen to be his helpers. It is for these poor ones that He feels affinity, and not for the venerable dignitary.

The stains of labour would be upon their rough garments, and labour's narrow thoughts would be in their souls; they would be homely-mannered people as well as obtuse-minded and hard-handed. For manual toil is a poor inspirer of intellectual life, and the craft of fishing reacts in this respect no better than its neighbours. Our fishing villages at home are not distinguished among labouring communities for mental brightness. Yet Peter, with his mind in a state of nature, and clothed in his rusty garment, was deemed a preferable companion to the pompously-robed Priest. So thought the Lord.

Therefore when the Saviour would draw a religious hero, it is the ecclesiastically outcast class from which He takes him. He has given us a model of humble piety in the person of a Publican, and a model of true neighbourliness in that of a Samaritan, while he who got from him the credit of greatest faith was a Roman soldier. More than this, the infamous person whom, with the instinct of an artist, He introduces to bring into relief his hero's virtues, is taken from the ecclesiastics; so that beside the good Samaritan there stands the pitiless priest, and the canting Pharisee stands over against the Publican. What means the like of this but a pointed rebuke of priestcraft, and a clear announcement that ingenuous paganism is better? It is honour shown to whom the world had deemed dishonourable, and reproach poured on those it had exalted; and once we have observed it we cease to wonder at the twenty-third chapter of Matthew, or at the tragedy on Calvary. It comes home to us that the Lord had chosen traditionalism to be his special enemy; of all the evils in the world He would put down it first, and there could be no bandying of soft words between them.

Now the attitude assumed by Jesus towards the ecclesiastics on the one hand, and the ecclesiastically outcast on the other, colours his outward career more deeply than any other fact of it. It never wholly disappears, and is constantly coming into prominence. It determines the evolution of the most important scenes and incidents; so that to study Christ apart from it would be like studying Luther apart from Indulgences, or writing a life of Wilberforce with the Slavery Question left out. Our Lord's hatred of Pharisaism is about the notablest fact in his history, and we may assure ourselves that the feeling was no accident, but a necessary outcome of the nature He possessed. That which exhibits itself again and again in a man's life is not the creature of circumstances, but corresponds to some truth of his moral being. The explanation of it has to be sought for within, and, intelligently regarded, it becomes a valuable clew to character. Do you want to find out how this or that individual is inwardly constituted?—note carefully the facts that come up oftenest in his life, and the sayings that are oftenest on his tongue. The principle of these deeds and sayings is at one with the individual's deepest nature. Hence if we would gain a right understanding of Christianity, we should fix our minds on the events that are most prominent in its Founder's history, for through perception of the moral character of these our first real insight into Christian truth is gained. On the threshold of our religious studies there is nothing we should give more heed to than that antagonism between our Lord and the priesthood of which the evangelists say so much. We should lend our minds thoroughly to it, and look searchingly at it in all its aspects, should question and cross-question it, pray over it, Jacob-like wrestle with it, and refuse to let it go till we win from it its secret. And it will be well if we see so clearly into the great principles underlying it, that we shall be able to transfer these to our own time, and apply them as a test to the religious phenomena around us. How would the present ecclesiastical life of Scotland, nay, of Christendom at large, look in our eyes if we had in our hearts the same hatred of the merely outward, the formal and traditional, as dwelt in Jesus? There are few questions we can ask ourselves that are so worthy of consideration.

Then, having noticed our Lord's attitude relative to the Pharisees, it would be a great gain if we could find out what instinct prompted him to assume it. How came it that He turned angrily away from the law-revering, ordinance-keeping people, and joined himself to the God-forgetting multitude—called God-forgetting by the churches? I think it was owing to an instinct which we find animating all who in this world have shown themselves truly great; and as an ingredient in Christ's character we must not value it less, that it is found among ordinary men. I allude to the attractiveness, the irresistible charm which things vital and real possess for deep souls, and the corresponding aversion they feel towards the artificial. Give us life, breathing reality, is their sincere and constant cry. That a thing be in the order of nature and throbbing with nature's wondrous vitality is to them the first condition of its loveliness. No matter that it look outwardly insignificant, or lie low in the scale of being—if it be joined in living relationship to the mighty whole, it touches the chords of their sympathy and they are interested. But the arbitrary and conventional is a hideous spectre they cannot away with; and the impulsive bad man is less intolerable than the ceremonially just one. They can look with more calmness on the errors of genius than on the excellencies of the soulless imitator. Again and again this sort of men has appeared in worn-out degenerate ages, and then it has been their privilege to lead the world back to truthfulness of life. We find the pages of history full of them, and they are particularly prominent at the great turning-points of progress. When there was nothing but devotion to the outward, and all art and literature, as well as religious worship, were a mere imitation of what had once been, it has been the glory of these men to appeal to the inward voices. What their souls told them they would believe and do. The thoughts and feelings that had grown up in the depth of their being were dearer to them than traditions, and they would put these into their poems and pictures, and into their sacrifices to God. For guiding rule they trusted absolutely to the law within, and did their work with a joyous strength, heedless of the outcry raised against them that "use and wont" was outraged. Through their lives and teaching society has again and again been brought back to sincerity of view, and to a perception of the unending worth that lies in reality. Among all peoples where the human mind has left a lasting trace of itself, these Luther-like souls are to be found, and all are alike in their scorn of the conventional, and their craving for God and nature's truth. That an individual be wholly himself, speaking and acting out the life that is within him, whether it be of base passion or of spiritual reason, is what they constantly demand. Better a loving, erring Magdalen, than ninety-and-nine faultless formalists. Such is their animating principle, and further analysis of them cannot be offered here. There are depths in their natures to which analysis cannot reach. Instead of explaining them, it will be wise for us to realise how thoroughly their principle bears rule over their minds, the scorn it wakens in them for every kind of waxwork, and the leaping up of heart it causes towards all ebullient life. So realising, we shall get to understand them in the only real way in which it is given to one man to understand another, by participation in a common feeling through the law of sympathy. Then from their words and ways a glory will flash out upon us which we never saw before; and such a key to our Lord's history will be put into our hands as no theology, new or old, critical or apologetic, could supply. Why He hated priests and formalists, and why the human nature that was cast out and tossed about, and that was stained with foul passion, and knew want and loneliness, was dear to him, as He was dear to it—shall all be made plain. His love for the compassionate Samaritan, and the broken-hearted harlot's love for him, shall have their mystery solved.

The parable chosen for treatment affords a striking illustration of the principle I have described, and there can be no doubt that the principle was, consciously or unconsciously, in the mind of Christ at the time He spoke it. But it was not purposely to illustrate this principle that the parable was framed; but rather, I think, to expose a special error into which Pharisaism is ever prone to fall. That conception of religious duty which represents it as something outward and finite is here held up to scorn.

Two men went up into the temple to pray, the one a Pharisee and the other a Publican. It was to the same place they went to worship, but we can hardly imagine them urged thither by the same motive; for the one is pictured to us as professionally a pious man, the other as outwardly a sinner. So that in the one case the impelling agent would be a deliberately framed rule or custom, some shred of sacerdotalism, while probably in the other it would be a devotional thought that had risen in the soul. The Publican did not presumably recognise those outward laws which ecclesiasticism had framed to regulate the religious life, and he had no particular hour or number of times a day for paying vows, but when the prayerful mood came, then he prayed. In this respect he stood further from the church than the Pharisee did, but nearer to nature, and nearer probably to God. For the devout exercise of the spirit is a too delicate operation to be successfully regulated by laws coming from without; and in giving utterance to its piety we will do well to let the soul be a law unto itself, employing devout words and attitudes only when there is the devout feeling.

Sometimes of course, nay many a time, the outward form of worship, when decorously observed, may wake to life the inner spirit, and what began a mere sounding brass and tinkling cymbal may end a great reality. But the deep soul that feels sure of itself, in which devout impulses spring up naturally, like flowers in a sunny place, contemns the binding of its piety to priestly times and seasons. It is its own lawgiver, and makes times and seasons for itself.

We usually regard this parable as the authoritative commendation of humility and warning against self-righteousness, and pass on satisfied with our interpretation. But this superficial exegesis does not tell us what it is needful we should know : where lies the root of the two feelings here set in opposition. Whence cometh self-righteousness ? and Whence cometh humility ? are most important questions in the psychology of religion, and the right answer to them forms a centre of light by which cognate problems can be better viewed. Let us analyse then the spiritual condition of the two men here depicted in the attitude of prayer, and find out if possible the essential difference between them. What made the one feel satisfied with himself, and what bowed the other to the earth with shame and self-reproach ? To say the reason lies in this : that they were both sinners by nature, inheritors of Adam's guilt, but while the one remembered this circumstance and was sorry for it, the other quite forgot it and felt no sorrow—is to adopt an explanation which is no explanation. For the vital truth of the parable is not hereby brought to view. And we must get off this ground altogether if we would learn the great lesson which Christ would teach us by his simple story. A consciousness of original guilt in the one man, and the absence of this consciousness in the other, had nothing to do with the marked contrast that is in their prayers. Rather this contrast was occasioned by the different standards of duty by which they had been measuring themselves, and towards which in their conduct they had been striving. That employed by the Pharisee had been provided by his church, was an ecclesiastical measuring-rod, so to speak, and had been in use for centuries. The ideal it raised before his mind was this: to give away a tenth of his income, to keep appointed fasts, to pray so many times a week, and do other like formalities. I would observe regarding these ceremonies that they awaken no thought of the infinite, and there is nothing about them that a person of methodical temper could not easily accomplish. They are very clearly defined, and have a distinct beginning—and end; so that he who trusted to their covering the whole field of duty would not have his soul vexed by the sense of aught unattained. Where there is a compact little theory of right conduct, you do not meet with vague aspiration. Righteousness is something fixed and external, and needs only for its practice such orderly habits as we see exemplified by successful men of business. And if this Pharisee, as is likely, was an unimpassioned man, and possessed a talent for living by rule, what should hinder him from keeping the ordinances perfectly? For they could all be observed without any spiritual movement taking place within him. And once they were observed, when the several attitudes had been gone through, there was nothing left him but to thank God that he was not as other men. He had no intuition of any other obligation than those included in his church's directory, so that no feeling of misgiving, no sense of unattainment, would raise bitterness in his heart. The field of duty was measurable, finite, well fenced in, and it lay clear before him, not a hollow or corner in it but he could see; he cultivated the whole of it every day, and bore thankfulness in his heart for his ceremonial virtue.

I must say this was a fearful idea to have had of duty, the most real and unfathomable thing that mankind can be conscious of, and which by the spiritually-minded has been constantly set forth as an object for deepest reverence. And it was held not by this or that private individual, but by a powerful institution which controlled the religion of a whole people. Such religious instruction as is shadowed forth by the Pharisee's prayer was that given to orthodox Jews in the age of the Saviour; and when we reflect on the nature of it, we cease to wonder at the end its professors have come to. We cease to wonder that Judaism should have failed as a principle of national existence, and that its bigoted adherents to-day are wanderers without a country. For here is that sublime verity called duty, which in its integrity eludes our subtlest analysis, whose form is ever changing, and which in its essence is infinite as God himself, briskly identified with half a dozen ceremonies, and lying on men's minds as lightly as the taking of their meals. Truly traditionalism brings human nature to strange passes of imbecility, and colours history with a grim unconscious humour. No wonder that Christ could not away with Pharisaism.

On the other hand the standard used by the Publican for measuring his conduct was no object that we can define. Duty to him, so far as it had been consciously conceived at all, meant infinite attainment, and, laid in the balance against it, his holiest actions seemed less than nothing. What could he do but feel sad over his little life when comparing it with the high thought of what life should be that dwelt within him? For sadness steals into all our hearts when the infinite in any of its forms rises visibly before us, and we measure against it our finite strivings; and I fancy this remorseful publican was in the same moral state as Kant was in, when he contemplated the starry heavens and the sense of right and wrong in man; as the writer of the eighth Psalm well knew—of all the Psalms; as is expressed in the third chapter of Philippians, and as comes out in the spiritual conceptions of all deep-hearted men. To them duty is not this or that finite obligation which can be put into a handy formula and mechanically performed, like the digging of a garden or the making of a spade, but is an immeasurable, indefinable ideal of good that overshadows and enchants them. Moreover it is a changeable ideal, and in every new age the intellect under the inspiration of conscience has to create it afresh. To the earnest-minded savage it is one thing, and to the half-civilised man it is another. It should not be the same thing to us as it was to our forefathers, and to those who come after us it should be different still; for it takes this and the other form according to the historical position, and to the culture, of the individual who conceived it. And this ceaseless transformation of its outward vesture hinders it from ever becoming the actual, and is the secret of its beauty and its power. Once it ceases to change, and men get familiar with it, and can see, as the Pharisee did, every nook and corner of its nature, it is a sign that moral progress has stopped. The spirit has given place to the letter, and there is an age of formalism. Instead of poets and thinkers, we have commentators and learned men. But when spiritual life is in the soul, that infinite ideal we call duty must necessarily change; for spiritual life means progress, and when one form of the ideal has been realised a more splendid form must instantly appear. It means death to man in his heavenward career if he overtake the vision he is pursuing. That must ever fly before him as the mirage before the traveller in the desert. As the quality of his virtue grows more refined it must grow more splendid in its beauty, and, as the sunlight puts out the stars, must put out by its pure shining the glory of his deeds. For fate has decreed that to the Christian-minded the ideal shall never become real; and it is the kindly decree of a stern mother—stern, *but* a mother. There is to be constant following after, but never perfect attainment. And the reward promised is one with which all noble souls shall be well pleased,—the inward strength and loveliness that are bred of such following. This is how we must account for these sad confessions of unrest that so often have come out of earnest hearts, and for the deep religious idea, old as man himself, that likens life to a pilgrimage.

A pilgrimage it truly is, and in a moral sense as well as a material; for we change and progress not only from one bodily state to another—from weakness to vigour, and then back to weakness again,—but if I am a living soul as well as healthy body I move forward through endless stages of spiritual being. There is a time when I believe and hope as a child, and a time again when I put away—when God calls me to put away—all childish things. Step after step we have to rise "on stepping-stones of our dead selves to higher things;" and must valiantly co-operate with the stern, beautiful law which raises the world, and by which the faith of to-day becomes the superstition of to-morrow. There is a sense in which we must die daily to the past that we may inherit fully the riches of the present; for he only lives deeply and truly who lives in the spirit of his time, and moves forward as it moves. But hard is it to do this; hard is it to have every organ of the soul awake and in a state of struggle, hard is it to be ever leaving behind the old, some part of ourselves that has grown effete, and to be constantly assimilating fresh elements of being.

They are few who are equal to these things, and therefore, in the spiritual sense of the term there are few that be saved. "Strive to enter in at the strait gate, for wide is the gate and broad is the way that leadeth to destruction, and many there be which go in thereat: because strait is the gate, and narrow is the way, which leadeth unto life, and few there be that find it." Sad and true are these words, and it must have raised sadness in the soul of Christ to have had to speak them.

Now it is among the progressive sort of people—the ever-following, never-attaining sort—that we must class this Publican of the parable. For he stands before us as one in whose soul the principle of spiritual growth is visibly at work, and who, wanting in a precise theory of duty, has yet a pervading sense of its infinitude. And it is this sense that fills him with feelings of remorse when, turning his mind inward, he looks upon himself and asks what he is and what he has accomplished. It is a living sense of the infinite nature of religious duty, and of finite man's inability ever to realise it, that is the inspirer of his prayer. Technically he knew less about that duty than the Pharisee did, had no smart theory of its nature, and could not reduce it to a precise number of ceremonies, but yet had God put an instinct into his soul which told him of its awful nature. That instinct did far more for him than theological knowledge could do for his self-righteous neighbour, for it kept his piety fresh and living, and made it in the sight of God a sweet-smelling savour. He had no logically arranged scheme of religious doctrine, but the great principles of religious life were within him, and worked within him no less effectually that he could not have explained them. It is not necessary that we understand the powers of the Spirit to make them potent, for the deepest processes of nature and human life are long in action ere they appear in reflective consciousness. Holy men lived ages before there were theologians, and there was the lovely garniture of earth when there was no botany or physics.

Let us see the explanation of the parable to which

we have attained. It is simply this: That two opposite views of life and duty are put forward by it, and that one of them is a principle of incessant aspiration, what we call life eternal, while the other is a stationary principle, producing self-satisfaction and moral death. According to the one view, the things we ought to believe and the things we ought to do can be brought to the clearest consciousness and embodied in unchanging formularies. So literally finite are they that human logic can circumscribe them by a precise definition, and human practical endeavour fulfil their utmost demands. We can see the beginning and the end of them, know their exact number, separate them from things secular, and observe who performs them and who performs them not. They are such things as these: The adhering to a dogma, the keeping of a Sabbath, the paying of a tithe, the mumbling over the altar of a set style of ritual,—this is the Pharisaic conception of religion.

A very different one is suggested by reflection on the Publican and his prayer. It is a conception which presents truth and goodness as an ideal that is the same in no two stages of our spiritual development or growth in grace. As we change and ascend it changes and ascends too, and we can as little overtake it as the steed racing westward at morning can overtake his shadow. But it charms us after it with a power that is irresistible. We cannot choose but follow on its radiant track. The sight of its splendour sickens us with ourselves and prompts us to the bitter cry, "Lord, be merciful to me a sinner," yet we cannot help gazing after it with longing heart. Though to behold its shadowy form take away from us all hope of that mental settling down which is so pleasant,—which is the heaven of many churches and whose opposite is their hell,—and turn us into the Paul-like state of not having already attained, we will not cease from our dream of duty. For such a dream is native to the Christian soul. It is what the living soul always sees when, looking upward, it asks that ancient question, "What must I do to be saved?" It sees not finite doctrines which it must believe, and finite ordinances which it must perform, but an unspeakable image of the ideally true and fair lifted far above it, as the heavens are above the earth. This is what the praying publican saw; hence his self-reproach, and hence too his greater nearness to God than the Pharisee's. But of course if it be not the eternal soul that looks upward, but only some theologically trained understanding, the image seen is of a very different order.

XVIII.

ETERNAL LIFE.

BY THE REV. ADAM SEMPLE, B.D., HUNTLY.

And this is life eternal, that they might know thee, the only true God, and Jesus Christ, whom thou hast sent.—JOHN XVII. 3.

THE phrase "eternal life" conveys to many minds the idea of unlimited duration of existence. It strikes them first and chiefly as a life that will never end, but will continue unbroken, after all that they have been accustomed to regard as most stable and enduring has ceased to exist. The element of duration is not unfrequently regarded as the most prominent element of eternal life. And this prominence may be due to the contrast which the phrase "eternal life" presents to the period of man's visible life, and the answer it furnishes to the wail that has been echoed in all ages, that human life is too short for human work—that it is but as a shadow, a span, a tale that is told. The trees whose blossoms delighted our infant eyes remain unchanged when our eyes are dimmed by years; the sea, which ripples its music in our ears, has sung the same notes in the ears of a thousand generations; men come and men go, but the world seems to remain for ever the same. When, therefore, we hear of an "eternal life," we naturally think of one in which all this is changed—where it is the duration of the world that is short and transient, the life of man that is enduring and perpetual. We think of man, as the possessor of eternal life, surviving when the trees have withered and the sea is silent, even when—if that shall ever be—the whole material creation has been blotted out of existence.

But that this is not the meaning of eternal life, that infinite duration is not its most important element, Scripture makes plain to us. For it is there described as a state of unmingled bliss, of unalloyed joy—as that which is of all things most desirable by man. Now, the mere prolongation of life is not by itself a thing to be desired. Bare life is not necessarily a blessing. We can easily imagine cases in which death is better than life; circumstances which cause a man to pray for death as earnestly as ever captive sighed for liberty. There, for instance, is a soldier who has fallen into the hands of his enemies, and men high in office whisper to him that great rewards will be his, and picture the brilliant career that will be opened to him, if only he betray his country; but indignantly he turns from them with the words, "Death rather than dishonour." Or, again, ask him on whom hopeless disease has fastened if he would have this life of his made everlasting, and he will cry out in his agony, "Nay, rather let me die." No, life is not necessarily a boon, and an eternity of life might be the bitterest curse that ever lighted on man. Give to one, whose heart has become so dulled to the influence of virtue that goodness is seen by him but as a fading shadow, and felt by him as the perfume of flowers which he can never pluck—give to such a man a lease of life which will never end, and you have given him *eternal* life indeed, but an eternity that might gladly be exchanged for annihilation. An eternity of pain and woe is equally enduring with that of perfect happiness, and each is an eternal " life." If, then, Scripture represents eternal life as that which is of all things most desirable, and if, as we have seen, the simple duration of life may be of all things the most undesirable, it follows that mere duration is by no means the main element—nor in any sense a characteristic element—of eternal life. The phrase can have reference only to a state or condition of the soul. That this state lasts for ever is true; but that is also true of many other things, and cannot therefore enter into our consideration of the true nature of eternal life. The question we have to answer is not, How long does this state last? but, *What* is the state which is thus perpetuated?

The answer is furnished by the words of our text, which makes no reference to duration. When we speak of eternal life, we mean simply the knowledge of the only true God, and of Jesus Christ whom He has sent. What, then, is meant by such knowledge?

Now, of all knowledge, whether of things sacred or profane, there are two kinds—a false and a true. The false is that in which the facts which are known remain always apart from the knowing mind, as things which we can look at and reason about, but which no more form part of ourselves than the stone we hold in our hand. We possess such knowledge in the same sense as a casket contains its jewels: the jewels are valuable no doubt, but the casket is none the better for them. We may admire the stores of knowledge which some learned man displays, but if he identifies himself in no way with his knowledge—if it remains, as it were, something foreign to him—we feel that the man is little the better for all he knows; that, indeed, he no more truly possesses knowledge than the book does from which he drew his stores. But there is another kind of knowledge, where what we know enters into the soul, incorporates itself with our nature, and breathes its influence through our whole life. The facts remain no longer cold and dead, but become living principles, vivifying and transforming the soul which possesses them. The jewel-box becomes itself a jewel. Such knowledge is to the soul what the sap is to the tree. The juices which the roots draw from the earth are very different from the tree; but by some wonderful transmuting power, and through mysterious processes, those juices, so different at first, finally become wood and blossom and fruit, so that we may truly say the sap and the tree are one. So, too, the soul draws from many sources the knowledge by which it grows; but before that can be said to be truly known, it must be so worked up and transmuted—so assimilated to the nature of mind—that the soul which knows and the facts which are known become in a sense one and the same. If, then, what we truly know becomes part of ourselves, our knowledge will be best tested by the extent to which we act and live it. True knowledge and life can never be separated.

This relation might be traced in all spheres of knowledge, though there are some in which it is mor patent than in others. A man may know, for instance, all that geology teaches, and yet be little the better for it, but it might be shown that even here true knowledge has an influence on life. Let us take, however, a more obvious example. A great revolution has occurred in the history of a nation, and you are able to recount the acts which roused the indignation of the people, you can name the leaders of the movement, give the dates of the battles which were fought, and recite the terms of the treaty that closed the movement; but in all this you may be no better than the book which taught you these details. You may be only a handbook of history that has somehow found a tongue. To know the movement truly, you must be able to go back in thought to the buried past and touch it again into life, you must feel the great heart of the nation throbbing in your own, must realise the ferment of wrath which roused the slumbering energies of the people, and follow them in their career of struggle, as if you too were living and acting with them—in a word, you must *live* in thought what you *know*. But there are other cases where this must be done and is done in actual life; perhaps the most striking of which—and one which throws considerable light on the meaning of our text—is furnished by the poetic mind. When the sense of beauty, for instance, steals over the sculptor's soul, it becomes to him the very breath of life; it takes possession of him and rules his whole nature, and forces him to give it outward expression in the living marble. When fair thoughts, again, kindle the poet's imagination, it is no longer he but they who live; they dominate every faculty, they rule his soul like a new will, and he too must utter them forth in burning words. As the lyre, through which the wind is sweeping, cannot but breathe out melodious sounds, so the poet or the painter, over whose soul pass thoughts of beauty, must body them forth in visible form. Now, it seems to me that moral and spiritual truths act in the same way as the creations of genius. A man may, indeed, know the moral law in the same way as he knows the constitution of the earth or the distance of the fixed stars, and it may have as little effect on his heart as on the tables of stone on which it first was graven; but let him truly know that law, and he will, with the same necessity as the poet writes or the sculptor carves, give it outward visible expression in the form of a beautiful life. The true knowledge of the moral law can never remain dead and inert; it must transmute the soul into its own likeness, become, as it were, a new will, expressing itself in holy desires and loving words and tender acts.

These illustrations may serve to explain what is meant by "knowing" God. There is a false knowledge by which God is known as the dread and infinite Being, dwelling in mysterious glory far away in the clouds, possessed of marvellous attributes, which we discuss and analyse and arrange in logical order, but having no more vital connection with our hearts and souls than the lifeless corpse with the anatomist who dissects it. Such knowledge is but ignorance of God. What the knowledge of the moral law is to the spiritual man, what the forms of beauty are to the genius, that the knowledge of God is to the devout mind.

As we truly know the evil of lying only when we refuse to lie, as we know the moral law when we act the moral law, so we know God only when we live the Divine life, when we reproduce on earth in our dim human way the glorious perfections which constitute heaven. So, too, like the inspiration of the poet, the knowledge of God breathes into the soul new energies, becomes the very life and will of the man who possesses it, and compels him to express his knowledge in living act, and body forth in his own life the human likeness of the life of God. God is love; and when we learn to know that love in all its depth and intensity, when we recognise its massive proportions in the guidance of the world's history, and feel its all-embracing tenderness in every episode of our own lives, we cannot but render back to God the love He has lavished on us. The knowledge of God's love begets the Divine love in the human heart. God, again, is perfect holiness; and when we learn to know that holiness in Christ, attracted as we gaze by the faultless beauty of the picture, pervaded by the subtle influence it breathes forth, "we are changed into the same image from glory to glory." What God is in love, in purity, in holiness, man in a measure also becomes. When the knowledge of these infinite qualities enters into the human mind, and so becomes part of man's nature, they cannot remain dead and barren, for they are living principles, and exist only so far as they are carried into action. Just as the sunlight which the plant absorbs is not for ever lost, but comes forth again in the tender-tinted flowers, so the perfections of God, which through knowledge penetrate the soul, appear again in action, and lend a Divine beauty and sweetness to human life.

This is also the idea contained in the second part of the verse. Eternal life consists not only in the knowledge of the only true God, but also of Jesus Christ whom He has sent. What, we have to ask, is meant by "knowing" Christ? Is it enough that we are able to tell all the marvels that attended his birth, to go through all the incidents of his strange life, to recount his miracles, and repeat his parables? No, truly: these are not Christ, but the vestments which may even conceal him from us. The mere facts of Christ's life may be known as facts by the atheist and the hypocrite as accurately as by the most spiritually-minded of men, but the life of Christ—the Man himself—lies deeper than his words and acts. We must penetrate beneath the surface to the moving spirit, and come into living contact with the heart and mind, which prompted the actions. What avails our knowledge of Christ's miracles, if we feel not the tenderness and love which speak in them and prompted them? Are we the better or wiser for our ability to detail all the mysterious agonies of Calvary, and yet be untouched by the spirit of self-sacrifice which breathes through them? What to us are Christ's kindly acts and tender words, if our hearts be cold to the human sympathy which lies beneath them? Not by familiarity with the record of Christ's outward life, not by the knowledge of what is patent to the eye, but by communion with the inward life—that communion which imbues us with the living Spirit—does Christ become known to men. The mind which was in

Christ must be in us—we must be able in some measure to make our own that tenderness and love, that purity and self-sacrifice, which distinguished him. If we cannot die as He did for our fellow-men; if we cannot by a word make suffering cease; if we cannot bid the guilt of sin depart, there are still many ways in which we can be Christ-like. We can at least *live* for our fellow-men, and so doing breathe that spirit of self-sacrifice which produced its noblest fruit in the death of Christ; we can at least make suffering less, and soften the pains of disease; we can at least show the sinner the vileness of his folly, and lead him to that Love which will say, "Thy sins are forgiven thee." The coming of Christ did not make the sin and sorrow and suffering of the world vanish—his work will still be carried on by those in whom He lives, when each in his sphere labours, by active work or patient example, to leave the world better than he found it. And only when we thus are "labourers together with God," when we take up in our feeble way and according to our opportunities the work which Christ himself began—when our hearts throb, though faintly, with the same feelings as stirred the breast of Jesus, and we are re-living (but yet, how far off!) the life which long ago He led on earth—only then have we attained that state of purity, of love, of self-sacrifice, which is implied in the knowledge of him whom God has sent. To *know* Christ is, if we dare say it, to *be* Christ.

From the language of the text, thus explained, two consequences seem to follow.

In the first place, eternal life—or, as it is sometimes

called, the Kingdom of God, or the Kingdom of Heaven—is a state of the soul, and not any outward glory. Our ideas of the eternal kingdom are drawn chiefly from the brilliant descriptions of the Apocalypse. But when once we understand that eternal life is knowledge—a property only of the soul—these splendid descriptions cease to be literal, as incompatible with the nature of a truly spiritual religion. Not in crowns and palms and snowy robes, not in golden streets and thrones, does the truest heaven of the Christian consist, but in the knowledge of God and Christ, in the possession by the human spirit of the qualities that distinguished our Redeemer. "The kingdom of God," says St. Paul, "is righteousness and peace and joy in the Holy Ghost." When the Spirit of God meets the spirit of man, and from the contact the light of God leaps up in the human heart, softening it into sympathy with all distress, purifying it into the love of holiness and the horror of sin, and leading it into the path of the perfect life, then has that soul become the possessor of eternal life, an inhabitant of the kingdom of heaven.

In the second place, it seems to follow that eternal life is a *present* as well as a *future* state. Too often is it regarded as the reward of a life of active virtue, as the far-off hope which stimulates the fainting heart to "patient continuance in well-doing;" too often is it supposed that only when the battle is over and the victory won, shall we pass beneath the dark gateway of death into the bright peace of the heavenly kingdom. But, on the other hand, the herald of Christ came with the cry, "The kingdom of heaven is at hand," a cry which Christ himself confirmed by proclaiming to his hearers, "The kingdom of God is come unto you." Eternal life, then, is not set before the world as the prize of patient purity, the reward of long-continued well-doing, or the stimulus to incite men to a life of holiness. It is not a glory which only after death will crown the successful endeavours of the faithful; but it is the purity, the well-doing, the holiness itself. It is the knowledge of God and Christ, with all the spiritual virtues which attend it—knowledge which, if the rational nature of man be no delusion, may be ours now—virtues which, if the life of Christ have any significance, if his blessed example and exhortations have any meaning for us, may adorn our present earthly life. Doubtless as the years roll on, that knowledge will become fuller and clearer, the purity deeper and stronger, and the holiness more perfect; but not even in the most distant age of eternity can these graces be different in kind from what they are now. The tree may spread abroad its increasing branches, may clothe itself in thicker foliage and bring forth sweeter fruit, but it does not thereby become a different tree; and so, to whatever perfection we may in the future attain, the life which will blossom there is a life which has its roots here, and has already borne its fruit on this side the grave. We weary ourselves with vainly wondering *where* the kingdom of heaven is—whether in this world of ours or in some fair realm beyond the skies; while the important question for us, and the one that settles all minor matters for us is, *what* the kingdom of heaven really is. If it be a spiritual kingdom, then where-ever and whenever a soul is found which is leal and loyal to Christ, which in loving humility has given up its petty wilful freedom for the higher freedom of the light of God, which seeks for purity and righteousness as the only atmosphere in which it can truly live, and goes forth in deeds of love and self-sacrifice, there and then—whether in this life or the life to come—the kingdom of heaven is.

XIX.

RELIGION—THEOLOGY—ECCLESIASTICISM.

BY THE REV. JOHN STEVENSON, GLAMIS, FORFARSHIRE.

Then said Jesus unto his disciples, If any man will come after me, let him deny himself, and take up his cross, and follow me.—MATT. XVI. 24.

And no man putteth new wine into old bottles ; else the new wine will burst the bottles, and be spilled, and the bottles shall perish. But new wine must be put into new bottles ; and both are preserved.—LUKE V. 37, 38.

And when he was demanded of the Pharisees when the kingdom of God should come, he answered them, and said, The kingdom of God cometh not with observation : neither shall they say, Lo here ! or, lo there ! for, behold, the kingdom of God is within you. —LUKE XVII. 20, 21.

"IF any man will come after me, let him deny himself, and take up his cross, and follow me." These words were spoken by our Lord, when He first began definitely to prepare the minds of his disciples for the humiliation, and suffering, and death, which lay before him. The conception of a suffering Messiah was so alien to the thought of his time, that it became needful to prepare the minds of his immediate followers for receiving the Divine idea of self-sacrifice, which He was to reveal in his sufferings and death. " From that time forth began Jesus to show unto his disciples, how that He must go unto Jerusalem, and suffer many things of the elders and chief priests and scribes, and be killed, and be raised again the third day." One of them, with characteristic impulsiveness, repudiated the idea; and Jesus, reading at once the earthly thoughts which prompted the remonstrance of Peter, laid down the indispensable condition of spiritual life, the Divine law of self-sacrifice: "If any man will come after me, let him deny himself, and take up his cross, and follow me. For whosoever will save his life, shall lose it; and whosoever will lose his life for my sake, shall find it."

"No man putteth new wine into old bottles; else the new wine will burst the bottles, and be spilled, and the bottles shall perish. But new wine must be put into new bottles; and both are preserved."

No open conflict had as yet taken place between Christ and the Jewish Rabbis; but it must have been becoming more apparent how impossible it was that there could be any alliance between his teaching and theirs. Questions had arisen about the disciples of John fasting, and about prayer. Our Lord had silently ignored the one, and had prescribed no formal rules for the other, and his disciples were perplexed. In answer to their inquiries, He pointed out to them that spiritual teaching such as his could never be limited by the rigid forms and mechanical rules to which they were accustomed. With all his grand enthusiasm, and noble sense of the spiritual reform which was needed for the coming of Christ, John had tried the hopeless task of patching up the old garment of Judaism. But it was worn out, and the attempt to repair it only made the rent worse. Our Lord, therefore, at once took up the ground that the old system of the Jewish theocracy was useless for him—that it could no more preserve the Divine revelation of Christianity, than old and worn-out skins could preserve new and fermenting wine. "New wine must be put into new bottles." New and higher forms were needed for the doctrine which He came to teach.

"When He was demanded of the Pharisees when the kingdom of God should come, He answered them, and said, The kingdom of God cometh not with observation: neither shall they say, Lo here! or, lo there! for, behold, the kingdom of God is within you."

The hostility of the Jewish Rabbis had become more pronounced, and their attacks more virulent. With the desire of ensnaring and convicting him, some of the Pharisees put a question to our Lord about the coming of the kingdom of God. These Pharisees were the ecclesiastics of their time. They busied themselves with the externals of religion—with external institutions, and forms, and ceremonies. Many of them, like all men in error, were better than their creed; but the essential nature of the Pharisaism with which our Lord had to deal was a formal and dead ecclesiasticism. He knew that this lay at the root of their question, and therefore He told them that the kingdom of God would never come, as they expected, "with observation," with outward pomp and ceremony. They were looking for political revolution, and, as part of a restored Jewish empire, the establishment of a great visible church, in which they should be advanced to pre-eminence and power. Jesus told them that such a kingdom would never come, that it was a dream and a delusion of their own. He told them further that his spiritual kingdom, which was to hold its sway in the hearts of men, was already in the midst of them—that, as it was to come without observation, they could not point to any outward signs of its approach, either in the political or ecclesiastical worlds, so as to say, Lo, here it is! or, Lo there! for, behold, at the very time you are looking for such signs of its coming, it is already silently making its way in the midst of you.

These sayings of our Lord involve principles which are peculiarly applicable to Christian thought, and to the development of Christian life, in our own day. The growth of religious education, from age to age, implies an ever-increasing demand for a clear apprehension of the vital principles which underlie it, and for the intelligent application of these principles to the circumstances which must, in greater or less degree, hinder or advance it. But especially is this the case in every age of well-marked transition like the present. When the historian of the future seeks to trace the development of religious life in the nineteenth century, he will find it no easy task to discover its vital elements amid the antagonisms of doctrinal belief, and the conflicts of ecclesiastical power. Old theological beliefs are crumbling around us. Old ecclesiastical systems are falling into pieces. And the religion of Christianity has, unfortunately, been so identified with creeds and churches, that it will be a hard task to trace the process of their disintegration, and to separate the essential elements of its life from their ruins.

It becomes especially important in such circumstances to realise the truth, that religion is in no sense dependent upon any special phases of doctrinal belief, or upon any peculiar forms of ecclesiastical institutions. The distinct recognition of this position is necessary for the right apprehension of many of the questions which are trying the minds, and for a just estimate of many of the difficulties which are perplexing the hearts, of serious and earnest men. It is with the view of getting hold of this truth, and of keeping clearly in view the relations in which our Lord always placed religion, theology, and ecclesiasticism, that I have brought these passages together. Special applications are beyond my present purpose.

The sphere of religion is spiritual; the sphere of theology is intellectual; the sphere of ecclesiasticism is political; and however these spheres may run into each other in the way of influence—and in this sense it is neither desirable nor possible to separate them— we must keep clearly in view, that it is fatal to real life and progress in religion to identify with it, or to substitute for it, either the one or the other.

I. The sphere of religion is spiritual. There is a higher sphere investing alike the life of sense and of intellect, a sphere in which what we call our spiritual life alone can find quickening and energy. The capacity for this spiritual life, which consists in Divine righteousness, purity, and love, is indestructible.

However it has been marred and blighted by sin, it has never been extinguished. Its quickening comes from a Divine Spirit within us, and nothing outside of the spiritual sphere can originate it. To live in this higher sphere, and to be in sympathy with the Divine Spirit which pervades it, is to be religious.

From such a standpoint we advance to degrees of religious life. We become religious, in greater or less degree, as our spirits are quickened into higher life by contact with the Divine Spirit, as we intelligently realise this quickening, and as we intelligently put forth into action the energy, or vital force, which it imparts. Now, in whatever form the energy of this spiritual life may find its issue, it must operate for the Divine healing of a sinful life; and it does so through self-sacrifice. The distinctive feature of the Christian religion, on its practical side, is the redeeming power of self-sacrifice. The cross of Calvary, as the concentrated expression of that power, is the central principle of Christianity: " I, if I be lifted up, will draw all men unto me." To accept and to live in the spirit of self-sacrifice is to be Christian. " If any man will come after me, let him deny himself, and take up his cross, and follow me." This, we venture to think, will be conceded by most men, however they may differ when they come to deal with questions of Christian theology, which arise when they pass to the dogmatic treatment of the subject.

All our Lord's teaching gathered around this conception of the higher Divine life, which is quickened within us, going forth in the saving power of self-sacrifice; and, where all other religions have failed, the Christian religion has proved itself to be the power of God for salvation. It lifts human nature out of its vileness, and purifies it with the beauty of holiness. It lifts us above all the coarseness and selfishness of the worldly life, "crucifying the flesh with the affections and lusts." It overcomes every evil passion by which our hearts are debased, and ennobles us with every Divine virtue. It calls us forth out of darkness into light. In proportion as we live in the spirit of Christ's self-sacrifice, we grow into the life of God, which is no self-life, but a life of self-giving for the welfare of all his creatures. In proportion as self is crucified in us, and as our spiritual faculties are trained and disciplined by self-renunciation, light breaks in upon the mysteries of life, and we understand "the deep things of God." The true test of religion, therefore, is the vicarious love which the Divine Spirit awakens in us—the love which "seeketh not her own," but the good of others, the love which is ready always to sacrifice self for the well-being of others. It is Christ's own test. "By this shall all men know that ye are my disciples, if ye have love one to another." "He that loveth not his brother whom he hath seen, how can he love God whom he hath not seen?" But let the love of a brother be true, and the love of God is there. "If we love one another, God dwelleth in us, and his love is perfected in us."

The right recognition of the spiritual sphere of religion, as altogether independent of theological systems or ecclesiastical relations, and of the nature of the spiritual forces which are at work within us, lies at the root of the solution of many of the social problems, which have become so perplexing under the complications of modern civilisation. The self-sacrifice of Christianity is undoubtedly the most powerful weapon for social reform. Nothing, for instance, strikes a thoughtful observer of modern social life with deeper pain, or awakens greater apprehension of danger to our whole social fabric, than the antagonism between the different classes which compose it. The struggle between capital and labour, which has been going on for years among us, might be cited as an example of such antagonism. It is incident to a more complex civilisation, but it is one of those questions with which no principles of political economy alone can ever deal effectively. It is only when such commands as these—"Rejoice with them that do rejoice, and weep with them that weep;" and, "Bear ye one another's burdens, and so fulfil the law of Christ," have come to be understood in a deeper meaning than has yet been read in them, and practised with a wider application than has yet been given to them,—only, in short, when it is more deeply felt that true Christianity lies in self-sacrifice, that class antagonism can be effectually removed, and the problems which spring from it satisfactorily solved. In proportion as we live in the spirit of self-sacrifice, we become fellow-workers with Christ in redeeming the world to God.

II. The sphere of theology is intellectual. Theology is a science, and we must claim for it the same place in human reason, and the same rights of intellectual investigation, which any other science demands. It has no claim to Divine authority such as the revelation of truth which Christ has given has. It is, moreover, a progressive science. Creeds are but the reflection of the thought of the ages which give them birth. Take, for example, the doctrines of the universal Fatherhood of God, and Brotherhood of Christ. These are the ideas of Christ, universal as all his ideas were, but they were destined to be moulded into narrower forms by the imperialism of the age in which they were promulgated. For many centuries they have kept these forms. The conceptions of God, and of his relation to Christ, and of our relations to God through Christ, which have moulded the theological views of men for centuries, have been essentially imperial; and they are still ruling the minds of many who cannot look beyond the historical aspects of their creed. It is only during the last quarter of a century that the theological mind of Scotland has, to any great extent, risen above this conception of Divine imperialism; but it is shaking off the fetters by which imperial conceptions have sought to bind it, and it is no longer possible, in an age of searching inquiry and of wider aspiration like the present, to put the new wine of awakened thought about the universal ideas of Christ into the old bottles of the historical creeds.

We do not imply that the religion of Christianity, and the speculations of theology, are to be dissociated, as if religion could be dissociated from the highest intelligence and culture. In this sense they are inseparable. Theology, if it is reverent in its ideal, will awaken and foster religious feeling; and religion, if it is catholic, will lead up to a more enlightened theology.

But we must demand, in the interests of vital Christianity, that theology shall not be substituted for religion. It is here that confusion exists in many minds, and that anxiety is awakened in many hearts. The religion of Jesus Christ is identified with creeds, and when creeds are criticised, or sought to be modified, it is imagined the religion of Christianity is imperilled. But as creeds embody only the views of particular schools of theological thought, and not the religion of Christ, they can in no sense be regarded as tests of religious life, far less as commensurate with the Christianity of Christ.

For instance, the biologist holds that protoplasm is the physical basis of life; that "wherever there is life, from its lowest to its highest manifestations, there is protoplasm, and wherever there is protoplasm there too is life." The theologian, if he has an intelligent grasp of the fundamental facts of physical science, holds also that life is a property of protoplasm. When they pass from the purely scientific to the philosophical and theological aspects of the question, and seek to determine the connection between life and thought, and to account for their origin, they occupy wholly different ground.

The biologist, if a materialist, may connect the vital force of spiritual life, as he connects the vital force of intellectual life, with the protoplasm of certain cerebral cells; but he no more denies the existence of the one than of the other. He fails only in his explanation of its origin. It becomes a lesser matter, that he denies the possibility of its existence after the life of these cerebral cells has become extinct. His denial is only intellectual error, and no intellectual error can ever be fatal to spiritual life. He may not be a Theist in the sense in which you are a Theist. He may not accept, as you accept, the Christian doctrine of immortality, but does he thereby cease to be religious?

And within the limits of what is understood more strictly as Christian theology, the religion of Jesus Christ may be equally in the hearts of men who hold the most widely divergent views on the questions with which theology deals. The dogmas, alike of the Trinitarian and of the Unitarian, are not the test of whether these men are Christians, and have the vital energy of spiritual life within them. Are the spiritual wants of their nature dependent upon the solution of the intellectual questions which separate them? Is the satisfying of these spiritual wants to depend upon their accepting, or rejecting, each the intellectual conclusions of the other? Are the Divine Fatherhood of God, and the human Brotherhood of Jesus of Nazareth, to cease to be spiritual realities to our hungering souls, and are we, wandering prodigals and orphans of sin, to be kept away from the love and forgiveness of the Father of reconciliation, because we are divided in opinion about some question of dogma which we may never be able to comprehend in this life? This were indeed to give a stone for bread. And, unfortunately, this is what theologians too often do. We hear much about the increase of scepticism in our own day, and irreligion is spoken of as the natural result. They are in no sense necessarily connected. What is commonly called scepticism is simply a reaction in minds which have outgrown the conceptions of the older theologies,

—a reaction which is sometimes impatient, often profoundly sad,—and theologians, in their blindness, dread, and suspect, and condemn it. It is not thus that they can help it; not thus that they can satisfy the intellectual craving which excites it; not thus that they can meet the spiritual aspirations which are the deepest sources of its unrest. While scientific theology must necessarily be the study only of the few, there are the many who cannot be at peace till their intellects are satisfied; and it is the wisdom of the theologian to provide them with intellectual conclusions, which are as broad as the conceptions of Jesus Christ. Modern scepticism is in some aspects a healthy sign. While it is true that a creed of mere negations has not the same power to nourish spiritual life as belief which is positive, if, at the same time, it is reverent, and tolerant, and humble, there is often far more of living thought and of real progress in the divine life, in what theologians condemn as scepticism, than can possibly exist in belief which claims to have exhausted revelation, and to have attained the sum of all truth. Scepticism in belief is hostile to religion, alone when it degenerates into indifference, or becomes the ally of immorality. We are living, as I have said, in an age of well-marked transition, when it is of vital importance to keep this in view: that whatever intellectual antagonisms in the sphere of theology may arise to darken our path, and whatever intellectual conclusions we may reach in regard to questions of dogma, the fruits of the Spirit are these,—"love, joy, peace, long-suffering, gentleness, goodness, faith, meekness, temperance."

III. The sphere of ecclesiasticism is political. Religion is not to be identified with any ecclesiastical institutions, or limited by any ecclesiastical forms. "The kingdom of God cometh not with observation." It has no external constitution, or organisation of forms. We cannot therefore identify it with Churches, or with any ecclesiastical machinery, so as to say, Lo, here it is! or Lo, there! When men talk of the ideal of the Church, they speak of a state of spiritual perfection which we are reaching after, but can never attain in this world. The Church, in the common acceptation of the term, is an external institution, made up of a multiplicity of imperfect organisations; and no ecclesiastical form, or multiplicity of forms, can embody the kingdom of God, any more than a creed, or combination of creeds, can embody Divine truth. At the very moment when men are identifying vital Christianity with individual churches, the kingdom of God is silently and surely asserting its supremacy independently of all forms of ecclesiastical life.

In saying this we do not undervalue churches as societies of Christian men. They are necessary, in some form, as the exponents of Christian action, just as creeds are the necessary result of Christian thought; but to substitute the one for the other, in either case, is to mistake the form for the substance, and to accept the letter which killeth for the spirit which giveth life.

In all the vexed ecclesiastical questions which are trying men's minds at the present day,—such, for example, as the connection between Church and State, a question prominent, and destined to become more prominent, in Scotland; or the limits of Ritualism, a question of the deepest gravity in the Church of England,—it is of vital importance to keep in view that these are questions of mere polity. Whether we regard the connection between Church and State as essential, or non-essential, to the health and vigour of national religious life, we should remember that the kingdom of God is not to be limited by connection with any Church. Then, a great visible Church, a Church great in ecclesiastical machinery and means of worldly power, grand in ceremonial and gorgeous in ritual, may, nay does, do a great deal of good in its own way; but vital religion is in no sense dependent upon these things. Churches serve to advance the kingdom of God in proportion as they are living and growing in the spirit of Jesus Christ, but they may be only hindrances to the progress of that kingdom. Indeed, the Church, no less than the world, has often hindered the coming of the kingdom of God, by setting up some little kingdom of her own in its place; and the more surely the true kingdom comes, the more surely the influence of eternal righteousness and purity and love is felt among us, the more surely will all the little kingdoms of the Church, as she now exists, be swept away. We are no nearer to the solution of the question, "What is the Church of the future?"—a question to which each section of the Church is too often blinded by the nearer and narrower one, "What is the future of our Church?"—I say, we are no nearer to the solution of the question, "What is the Church of the future?" in any sense in which a solution of it is desirable, till we come to realise it, that the kingdom of God is a far vaster kingdom than any Church, or any multiplicity of Churches, can embrace. What wonder that amid all the ecclesiastical battles of Churches, reformed and unreformed, orthodox and heterodox, high and low, evangelical and non-evangelical, men of earnest thought and life grow wearied at heart, and become more and more disposed to cast all Churches aside, and to say, "The kingdom of God is a far more living thing to me than I can find it to be in any of your Churches." Nor should it be forgotten, that there is no more deadly enemy to the progress of vital religion than the spirit of mere ecclesiasticism. It cannot see beyond its own sect, and the dogmas of its own creed. Bigotry, intolerance, and the worst spirit of controversy, seem to be inherent in it. All history teaches us the same lesson: that there are no views more contracted, no hatreds more intense, no disputes more bitter, no controversies more uncompromising, than those which have been cherished and carried on by ecclesiastics, in the name of religion and of Christianity.

With such views of our Lord's teaching in regard to the relations of religion, theology, and ecclesiasticism, we would plead for greater catholicity of spirit.

If a man claims to be catholic, he is too often pronounced "broad church," "latitudinarian," "a freethinker," or characterised by some similar term, meant to be a bad name. It is profoundly saddening often to find men, who seem to be large-hearted, manifesting a spirit of narrowness, and exclusiveness, and intolerance, whenever creeds or churches come into question. Nothing can be further removed from the mind of

Christ than such a spirit. He had tolerance for all types of religious character and thought, of religious belief and worship:—all types of religious character: the "Israelite indeed in whom there is no guile," and the young ruler who "went away sorrowful because he had great possessions;"—all types of religious thought: the calm contemplative mind of Mary, sitting at his feet in rapt confidence, and the intellectual scepticism of Thomas, because, deep below his refusal to believe without a sign, there was honest doubt and perplexity; —all types of religious belief: the Sadducee with his unspiritual creed, as well as the earnest believer in himself as the Son of God;—all types of religious worship: the true worshipper, whether at Jerusalem or Gerizim,—the worship of the heart, however feeble its light, or fantastic its form.

We would, therefore, plead for greater catholicity in theology. As creeds are only the reflection of the thought of the ages which give them birth, we should be ready to modify and change them with the growth of theological thought, and with the advancement of scientific discovery. Christianity has nothing to fear, but much to gain, from free historical criticism, and from the light of scientific research. If, therefore, men who are dealing with the deepest problems of human life and destiny, and are searching for Divine truth with an earnestness and reverence befitting the profound questions which perplex them,—if scientific men, who are devoting their lives to fathom the mysteries of creation, and to elucidate the eternal and immutable laws which govern the universe,—if philanthropists, who are labouring with self-sacrificing devotion for the amelioration of the evils which burden humanity, cannot accept the special forms of Christian theology which you present to them, refrain from stamping them as sceptics and unbelievers. And if men who have received the same creed cannot regard some of its special dogmas in the same light in which you regard them, refrain from suspicion, and intolerance, and persecution. Let us believe that catholicity of spirit is a greater virtue than orthodoxy of belief, and that tolerance for all human differences is more precious than zeal for personal convictions. Let us believe that in views and systems of truth, which differ most widely from our own, there may be the same divine life and hope; and let us acknowledge and rejoice, that the outer form is nothing if it breathes the spirit and the life.

We would plead, also, for greater catholicity of spirit in the Churches. The spirit of sectarianism has eaten deep into the heart of religion in Scotland. Nowhere else perhaps can we find, at least to the same extent, the melancholy spectacle of such a multiplicity of Churches, professing to be animated by the love of God, yet so deeply estranged from each other, professing to desire the common good, yet undermining each other so systematically in their efforts to promote it. It is inevitable that sects shall exist. The union of which many good men dream, which would seek to obliterate sects, would produce, not Christian unity, but only a dead uniformity. It is the spirit of ecclesiasticism, not of difference, that we have to strive against in the Churches. It is the spirit which can see what is right only in what is its own that we have to deprecate and deplore. In proportion, and only in proportion, as the Churches realise the religion of Christianity in self-sacrifice, will intolerance, division, persecution, and strife, give place to large-heartedness, unity, concord, and peace.

XX.

UNITY.

BY THE REV. PATRICK STEVENSON, INVERARITY.

That they may be one; as thou, Father, art in me, and I in thee.—JOHN XVII. 21.

Ye are all the children of God by faith in Christ Jesus.—GAL. III. 26.

CHRISTIAN Unity is a subject about which it is much easier to feel than to speak. It is so highly spiritual a thing that it is difficult to convey ideas about it through the coarse medium of words. It is so broad and comprehensive a thing that it is impossible to avoid those seeming contradictions which arise when we turn to look first at one side of it and then at another. Yet in its essence Christian Unity is a very simple thing,—a thing which, however alien to the atmosphere of theological and ecclesiastical debate, is known, in its nature at least, by every meek and childlike spirit.

In the broadest sense it may be said that every discovery of truth, whether in physical science, philosophy, or religion, is a contribution to an ever-growing knowledge of the nature of that Unity which God is—a revelation of the nature of Unity as that exists perfectly in God. In the full sense God is One—rounded

—whole—complete. It is therefore as men grow in knowledge of what God is, that their ·knowledge increases of what unity is; and it is as they become liker God that unity is realised in them, whether as individuals or as a race.

On its spiritual side, this is the definition of unity in the motto from the fourth Gospel which is prefixed to this sermon. The prayer there ascribed to Jesus is a prayer for *Unity*. But it is more than that. It is a definition of the nature of the Oneness asked for. In whatever ways God was in Christ, in whatever ways Christ was in God, these are the ways in which men can be truly one—one with each other, with Christ, and with God. That we fall short as yet of this Oneness in degree need not and does not prevent our having it in part; and if we would have more of it, we will attain it as we have in us more of the mind that is in him.

St. Paul's central thought about the Christian Church was the personal relation of each believer to Christ, brought about by the exercise of what he calls "Faith." Whatever the apostle's views may have been as to the bearing of Christ's work upon God's relations to men—and this point we are not now called upon to discuss—he always meant by the term Faith that in the exercise of which each soul enters for itself into spiritual fellowship with Jesus—partakes of the Holy Spirit as the principle of a new life— realises itself as a spiritual child of God, and as already in part a sharer of God's nature. It is true that St. Paul limits the idea of the Christian Church to those in whom this fellowship with Christ was found. But on the other hand, that fellowship being found, the member of the Christian Church may have been Jew or Gentile, bond or free. He teaches that, irrespective of nationality, previous religious connection, social condition, or preferences of form, all in whom this fellowship of spirit exists are, in virtue thereof, one with Christ and one with each other. He teaches that the Christian Church is necessarily and inherently, up to the measure of this fellowship, a unity. He teaches that only in so far as the Church ceases to be Christian can it cease to be One. In the being made to drink into the "one spirit" of Jesus consisted the unity of the Church of his day. Therein lay the unity, and that not as a thing future but as a thing present,—not as an ornament to be added, at some indefinitely future period, to an otherwise finished temple of God, but as the first and most immediate consequence of the founding of that temple in Christ, —not as a blossom or flower destined to be only the last and crowning beauty of the tree which God had planted, but as the very first leaf which the life, quickened in the seed, had produced—as a thing therefore to be realised as having come—as essential indeed to the existence of the Christian Church at all —as a thing inherent in the nature of Christianity— apart from which it must cease to be Christianity. St. Paul teaches that in virtue of the common faith in Christ—because of the reference within each Christian's soul of the self-same spirit of holiness—all her members are in this sense sons and daughters of one God, brethren and sisters of one Saviour and of each other; the Christian Church is in all her members, and throughout all her branches, essentially, inherently, from the very nature of her central and animating principle, a unity.

Why then, it may be asked, do we hear so much in our own time, and among those who profess to agree with the sentiments of Christ and of St. Paul, about the necessity for bringing about unity in the Christian Church—and why are so many schemes propounded for the purpose of attaining it?

Chiefly, I believe, because members of the several branches of the Christian Church have largely forgotten three simple truths:—

1. That unity is a thing which comes with the indwelling of the Spirit of God—with spiritual fellowship with Jesus Christ,—so that, wherever that spiritual indwelling and fellowship is not, no schemes which have theological and ecclesiastical sameness as their end can do aught to bring it about;—so that, on the other hand, where that spiritual indwelling and fellowship exists, such schemes can do little other than endanger men's estimate of its importance.

2. That the authority upon which spiritual truth must ultimately rest is its own intrinsic light.

3. That in consequence, not of the instability or changeableness of that truth, but of its vastness, unity must be accompanied by, or rather must comprehend within itself, almost endless doctrinal and æsthetical variety.

We live in days when it is worse than vain to imagine that sameness, whether in thought or in government or in worship, even supposing it attainable, can be any longer mistaken for Christian unity.

Intellectual power and spiritual insight are being every day brought to bear with startling force upon the sacred books, not only of Christianity, but of the other religions of the world. Their historical value is being again estimated, their internal truthfulness is being again appraised, and their contents are being compared, with a view to a relative measure of the value of each as a moral guide of mankind. No power can stop this process. Its results are as yet only very partially wrought out. They have not yet been widely spread in any popular religious literature. We have passed through a religious revolution, and men are only beginning to know it. As however that knowledge spreads, we must be prepared to find more differences of opinion than exist at present, as to what is fundamental in religion—as to how much of it is common to at least the higher faiths of the world— as to what the sacred books are in themselves and in their relations to each other—as to their whole place and bearing, whether in regard to doctrine, government, or ritual. These are questions which cannot be answered by any one age for the ages that are to follow. They are asked afresh, and afresh they must be answered, from time to time. Our own is such a time, and, being so, the problem arises: "Is it possible to preserve and to increase Christian unity throughout the changes that are sure to come?"

To any one who has formed large and comprehensive ideas of the nature of unity the answer must be Yes. It is Renan who has said that Christianity, "to renew itself, has but to return to the Gospel." This is very specially true of our time. What we need is to go back to the "simplicity" that was in Christ. We have got spiritually choked by a thick and murky atmosphere of creeds and catechisms, and of ecclesiastical laws and forms. What we need is to breathe again the air He breathed who was no maker of dogma or of ritual,—whose work was to call up in humanity the spirit of the child, and to teach that the true worship of God is that "in spirit and in truth." What we need is to think of the Christian Church as St. Paul thought of it—a corporation as far as possible removed from all bondage to sameness, whether of thought or of form.

The body is not the less, it is all the more, a unity, that its different members work in different ways for the maintenance of the common life and the doing of the common work. "The whole complex organism," as it has been recently put, "is a society of cells, in which every individual cell possesses an independence—an autonomy. With this autonomy of each element there is at the same time a subordination of each to the whole, thus establishing a unity in the entire organism, and a concert and harmony between all the phenomena of its life. . . . Then there devolves on each cell, or group of cells, some special work which contributes to the well-being of all, and their combined labours secure the necessary conditions of life for every cell in the community, and result in those complex and wonderful phenomena which constitute the life of the higher organisms." Thus does science, pursued in a reverent spirit, revenge herself upon her accusers—repeating to us, in modern scientific phrase, the teaching of St. Paul, —enforcing upon us by the revelation of nature the teaching of our Lord himself. One would think that he who runs might read the lesson. It is passing strange and very sad to think how few, even at this time of day, are able to do so.

Three great enemies to the realisation of the truth that wheresoever the spirit of Christ is there is unity are easily detected. These are—the abuse of theology, —the existence of sacerdotalism or priestcraft,— and the exaggeration of ceremonial or ritual. To these we may add two others, as being somewhat specially developed in our day—the one a tendency, found in such as are wearied of the first and last of these, to seek refuge in what of the past has proved most permanent,—and the other a tendency, in such as are sick of all three, to find what they think a haven of rest in one form or another of scientific materialism or in agnosticism.

By the strongest class of minds all these dangers are avoided. Agnosticism is dismissed as not only contrary to experience, but as a contradiction in terms. We know,—if it be only in knowing that we do not know. Science is adjudged her proper sphere and function. Within it she is left free play. All of truth that she is competent to learn,—nay, all of truth that belongs to the matter and to the energy which she investigates,—is gladly welcomed, so far as known, and will be gladly welcomed when further known, welcomed as a revelation of a side of God. The test of comparative value in what claims to be spiritual truth is seen to be the intrinsic light that shines from what is put forth as such. Its ultimate value is seen to be independent, absolutely and relatively, of consensus, whether of few or of many, and of the duration, short or long, of that consensus. Ceremonial is seen to be valuable, but only as language or symbol,—a vehicle to convey or express religious opinion or feeling. Sacerdotalism, whether Roman, Anglican, Protestant, or Scientific, is simply sunk, ignored, passed by and refused. And theology has her place and importance justly defined. She is seen to be the ever-shifting outcome of attempts to compass the Infinite by the feeble powers of reason. Each and every one of these attempts is seen to be more or less valuable. It is held to be more or less historically interesting. It is noticed that each contains more or less truth. It is marked that no one of them, nor all of them together, contains it all. By such minds it is seen that Christianity, as taught by Christ, is an attitude of the human spirit towards God and towards man; an attitude the existence of which no sameness of theological and scientific opinion will necessarily bring about; an attitude which may exist along with almost any amount of scientific and theological divergence; an attitude which may be, and very frequently is, present apart from theological and scientific knowledge altogether. In Christ's own day Christianity consisted simply in attachment to his person. In our day it may be said to consist simply in attachment to his teaching. The idea of a child and of a brother, as realised in the picture which the Gospels present: that is Christianity; and unity is wherever that spirit is, and the extent of its existence is the extent of the oneness; and schism, the opposite of Christian unity, is seen to begin, not where difference of opinion begins, or where preference in feeling begins, but where badness and bigotry begin, where uncharitableness begins, where distrust and selfishness begin. As the human body ceases to be a unity, not when the hand works in one way and the eye in another, not when the feet are used for movement and the head for the very different function of thought, but when the eye says to the hand, "I have no need of thee," and the hand to the feet, "I have no need of you;" so is the unity of Christianity broken, not when theological creeds diverge, and ecclesiastical laws and observances differ, and forms of worship vary, but when individuals or sections of the Christian community make their personal and sectional aims independent of the good of the community as a whole, or cut themselves off in any way from the fellowship of search after truth, and the helpfulness of mutual sympathy and succour.

If now we turn for a moment to contemplate the actual state of feeling around us about this matter, two closing remarks may be made:—

1. That unity, consisting, on its religious side, in the presence of the spirit of Christ, wherever found, —free play being allowed for the intellect on questions of science, philosophy, criticism of sacred books and theology,—this ideal is actually much more seen and aimed at than is apparent to the superficial observer.

This country is sick at heart of doctrinal and ecclesiastical warfare, and of unreasoning abuse of biblical, philosophical, and scientific research. Laymen have practically ceased—with exceptions, of course—

to persecute because of difference of opinion. And when the mass of an army thus steps aside from the battle, no noise nor spurring on the part of the officers can long carry on the fight, though it may blind many to the fact that the combat is really over. In Scotland at least the victory is now on the side of freedom. Many contemporary circumstances conclusively demonstrate this. The questions for the future are these : How is that freedom to be used with least risk of abuse ? and, How is it to help the quickening of the religion and morality of society ?

2. Since it is already vain, and will become increasingly so, for Churches to seek to force thought and worship into any fixed grooves,—since, in fact, uniformity, so long mistaken for unity, has been amply shown to be both shallow and impossible,—it would seem that unity may be best promoted by endeavouring to bring the principles of the life of Christ to bear upon the education everywhere of the Christian conscience. That the community should be a family, saturated with family feelings, and practising a family life, is infinitely more of consequence than that all should think precisely alike about the Father's character, ways, and purposes, or help only such of the brothers and sisters as belong to the same class, or work at the same work. The old grounds of social relationship are being broken up. The old ways of expressing this relationship are being changed. This is inevitable as the family enlarges, and as the demands of a complex mechanism increase the difficulties of the social bond. Still, the relationship remains. Men, as men, are brothers. Whatever

their source, it is a common source. Whatever their destiny, it is a common destiny. That the family is large, and that more rooms of earth are being filled, does not abolish mutual duty, or open any path to freedom other than that of discharging mutual responsibility. To quicken everywhere the filial and fraternal feelings—to stimulate to that trust which steadies, and to that bearing of one another's burdens which is the fulfilling of the law of Christ—to promote the cultivation of reverence for that which transcends us, the deepening and broadening of sympathy for many-sided humanity, and the quickening of active helpfulness :—these have been always, it is true, the aims of Christianity, wherever its nature has been rightly understood; but that they are its proper aims still is just what society needs now to be retold. As this conviction regains its hold, as the central law of the divine life, that of self-giving, is seen, welcomed, and followed, each, as he loseth his life, will practically find that he has therein found it, and that he is contributing, in his place, to the growth of that only Oneness which is large enough to satisfy the cravings of the human soul.

XXI.

ETERNAL LIFE.

BY THE REV. PATRICK STEVENSON, INVERARITY.

This is life eternal, that they might know thee, the only true God, and Jesus Christ, whom thou hast sent.—JOHN XVII. 3.

THE notion of Eternal Life, it is here asserted, involves more than the idea of eternal existence. Merely to exist, either here or hereafter, is not necessarily a blessing in itself. What kind of existence then is for man's spirit—and that whether in the body or out of the body—worthy of the name of life ?

Answered shortly, and in Christian phraseology, that kind of existence consists in knowledge of God and of Jesus Christ.

There are many who, on scientific grounds, deny that there is any Being higher than man, who also maintain that man, the highest being of whom they have any knowledge, is himself but an automaton, an expression of energy working through cells, his so-called consciousness only one form of the outcome of molecular change. To such minds there can be no moral right or wrong—no ideal to which we may aspire, or from which we may fall—no possibility of learning from past success or failure—no future, in the sense of opportunity for spiritual growth—nothing, in short, but an ever-changing mechanical present, over which we can exercise no control, which shifts continually through a few short years, and ends for ever with the body's death.

With those who think on this wise it is almost impossible to argue. Your very arguments, they would say, no less than the spiritual phenomena which you allege, are but so many instances of our position. These are themselves the outcome of the forces, the working of which you call yourself.

It is refreshing therefore to find that by many a less dogmatic and more rational position is being gradually taken: that, namely, which, while welcoming every discovery of physical science, admits that there are ranges of experience, not less real than are her facts, which she is powerless to explain. To such minds Theism is at least not an absurdity, nor a future existence an impossibility. To such minds spiritual knowledge of a spiritual Being—and, much more, spiritual sympathy with a historical Being,—are not without the range of possible experience. To them, knowledge of God and of Christ is at least a perhaps.

But experience is one thing; its explanation is another. It may be possible, or it may be impossible, to explain it. Still, accounted for or unaccountable, the experience remains. Now it may be safely said that the possession of a spiritual faculty is as true an experience to such as have felt it as can be any other fact of their existence. And millions of the human family have had, and millions still have, that experience. They know that they know God, imperfectly it is true, but still really. They know that they know Christ, at a distance it is true, but still in actual sympathy. It is to them as much a fact that they can hold spiritual intercourse with One higher than themselves as that they can hold every-day intercourse with their fellow-men. That they cannot explain every inner fact, any more than they can explain every outside fact, is to them only what might be expected. The facts however remain, in their inner as in their outer life. These are the "seers," the "prophets" of humanity. They have existed in all ages. They still exist, and in their presence it is impossible to deny—name it how men may, explain it how they can or cannot—that there is such a thing as the "kingdom of God."

Thinking of these three classes of minds, what are we to say about the motto of this sermon? It affirms two things—that there is a state of soul which is eternal life, and that that state is knowledge of God and of Jesus Christ.

For the last-mentioned class it is unnecessary to say more. They know in their inner personal experience, better far than any words can embody it, the meaning of the text.

To the second-mentioned class of minds—those to whom spiritual experience and a spiritual education, here and hereafter, are possibilities,—and to the first class—those to whose theory of the universe they are not so,—we grant that no such consciousness as belongs to the third class can be to them transferred, or by them accepted, by any arbitrary act. We can only appeal to the light that shines from such words as those of the text, and say that, as another matter of experience, that light has broken in upon souls which for years have been unable to see it; and that, by all such, it has been welcomed, when seen, as a spiritual reality. This being so, the words are at least worthy of regard, and their meaning may claim the most earnest consideration on the part of those to whom, as yet, that meaning has not come as defining their own inner life.

The words mean that Jesus of Nazareth manifested forth the character of God, and that—what that character is—is life for the soul of man. They mean that the kind of existence that is worth having is the kind of existence which God has, and that, if we would know what kind of existence that is upon its spiritual side, we will find the fullest and highest revelation of it in the picture which the Christian Scriptures present to us of the mind that was in Christ. They mean that personal and experimental knowledge of God—that is, the degree in which any one has in him the Divine Spirit—is, at any point of existence, the measure of his spiritual life.

If this be granted, it matters little what phrase is used to express the meaning. Say that God knows—then knowledge is life, and ignorance is death for man. Say that God loves—then love is life, and hatred is death for man. Say that God is holy—then holiness is life, and sin is death for man. Say that "in him there is no darkness at all"—then light is life, and its absence is death for man. Go through the dictionary if you will. Pick out any adjective which describes a feature in the character of God. Then the degree in which that adjective describes my character is the degree in which my spirit lives. Take its opposite. Then the degree in which it is applicable to me is the measure of the remainder of that " body of death " from which I am yet undelivered; and from which, till I am delivered, my spirit simply refuses to be satisfied. "Gates of pearl and streets of gold!"—"Fire and brimstone!" He who once realises the nature of the gulf which separates spiritual life from spiritual death would refuse the first were they to risk his likeness to God; and he would welcome the second could they only insure it. What else than this lies at the root of such eccentricities as monkish asceticism and the dogma of purgatory? So profound is the belief of humanity that whatever else heaven and hell may be, and wherever else they may be found, they are cognisable from time to time, in strange alternation, in the experience of the individual soul, as, on the one hand, it suffers itself to be degraded; or, on the other, to be raised in sympathy with what is noble and loving. In the former case it is the victim of a mysterious unrest, in the latter it permits that peace to enter in, which, however much it may surpass the understanding, comforts and strengthens the spirit as naught else can, amid daily struggle and sorrow, and paves the way for a quiet entrance into rest.

The chief points in Christ's teaching on the subject of the nature of Eternal Life may be more fully specified as follows. He taught—

1. The nature of the Fatherhood of God.
2. The nature of spiritual Sonship.
3. The nature of Brotherhood.
4. The nature of Sacrifice.

Not one of these names was new to the world when Christ appeared. Yet He made their meaning virtually new, so much did He purify and exalt men's thoughts about them.

That the infinite Author and Sustainer of the universe cares for every creature of his hand; that man owes to him more than existence, and such powers as are necessary for its maintenance; that his reason is an offshoot of the Divine intelligence, and that his soul is capable of understanding and of appropriating the character of its Source; that this Heavenly Father desires, working within the laws of nature, mind, and spirit, to educate up to his likeness; that He is tender to that wherein we err, and just in all his ways; —that his nature is such as to win our trust, and his leading such as to reward our following; that whether He giveth, withholdeth, or taketh away, it is to our "profit," that we may be "partakers of his holiness;" —to know that we have such a Father is life for the soul.

To accept his daily gifts with joy and thankfulness; to feel that reason is trustworthy in patient and humble exercise; to find our spirits rising to their Source, led upward along the lines of God's own thoughts; to take our daily office from his hand, as that which love has given us to do; to solve its perplexities by his guidance, to vanquish its difficulties by his strength, to meet its seeming impossibilities in the might of "Not my will, but thine be done;" to be unintoxicated by life's gladness, and unconquered by its darkness, mystery, and sorrow; and finally, amid the failing of all outward props and stays to say,

"Father, into thy hands I commend my spirit;"—to experience such sonship is life for the soul.

While feeling, in their full force, the sympathies that are born of natural relationship, of similar education, and of circumstance, to let our affections travel out beyond these smaller circles; to love our fellow-men as men, as children of a common Father, and sharers of the humanity which Christ has glorified; on a small or on a large scale, as power and opportunity are given, to do good to others; to allow for weakness, temptation, and the force of circumstance in others; to be kind to the evil and the unthankful; to forgive those who offend against us; to "love" our "enemies," to "bless them that curse" us, to "do good to them that hate" us:—this is to understand the greatness which consists in ministry, and therein to know that brotherhood which, in proportion as we feel and practise it, is recognised as life for the soul.

To have penetrated below the surface and the type to the central reality of sacrifice—to the truths that sin is put away by the sacrifice of self, and that evil is overcome of good; to know what it is to find life in losing it, and to get in giving away:—this is to feel that the Divine nature, in its most glorious aspect, is being gradually implanted in us. Self-denial is often praised as the loftiest virtue; and to many the cross itself is nothing higher than its fullest example. Noble it is, unquestionably, "not to please ourselves." But this merges into moral commonplace in the full light of the life and death of Jesus. For him, not to have given would have been self-denial. It would have been worse. It would have been denial of himself. Of all that He was, and all that He was able to do, and all that He was able to suffer, He gave—not that He might therein deny any lower desire, but that He might simply therein satisfy the craving of his nature. He gave, simply because He could not help it. To his Father He gave that inner trust and following in which sonship consists. To all around him He gave that many-sided sympathy, and that help in all its manifold simplicities wherein brotherhood consists. And before the world, thus in living and thus in dying, He placed the embodiment of sacrifice, and the definition of that state of soul which is eternally a state of Life.

Be it ours to seek to repeat the story. It is as we succeed in doing so that we will come to feel more surely that Life Eternal is already pulsing within us, however imperfectly; and to trust more deeply that, not for our worthiness, but of God's great mercy, that Life will be imparted to us, on and on throughout the long-drawn future, more and more abundantly.

XXII.

CHRIST'S AUTHORITY.

BY THE REV. R. H. STORY, D.D., ROSNEATH.

Tell us, by what authority doest thou these things? or who is he that gave thee this authority?—LUKE XX. 2.

THIS was a fair enough question on the part of the chief priests and elders of the people. They were expected to keep watch over what was taught, and to inquire into the character and claims of any new teacher to whom the people seemed disposed to listen. The chief priests, in fact, could, if they chose, prevent any one preaching in the Temple, so that their question in itself was natural and just enough. They were not stepping beyond their own province and own right in asking it. But yet, in a very real sense, the question was an unjust one. It was not Christ's part to assert any direct authority given to him to teach the people and preach the gospel. It was their part to judge of his authority for themselves. It was their part to examine into what He taught, in order to see if it had the proof of its own authority in itself. No authority given to him by another would have made his teaching tolerable, if it was in itself unsound and unedifying. No absence of external authority could justify their silencing him, and turning him out of the

Temple, if the words which He spoke were wise and true, if they brought light and help to his hearers. So that in reality the question, "By what authority doest thou these things? or who is he that gave thee this authority?" was quite beside the mark. It had nothing to do with the point whether Christ should be allowed to teach in the Temple or not. No authority could settle that point, except the authority that dwelt in him, in his words and works themselves.

Now, brethren, this same question is still—is always—the question asked by those whose religious life is formal and unspiritual, whenever they are brought face to face with any new light and truth. Wherever you find new light and truth, there you find the work of Christ going on, for you. From whatever quarter these come to you, living light and truth, in virtue of which you feel your spirit live more freely, you know that from that quarter the Spirit of God, which "bloweth where it listeth," is blowing upon you. The light may come to you from a written book, or a spoken word, or from your own thoughts in earnest and patient reflection on the word or works of God; but howsoever it comes, it is to you a revelation from God, an unveiling of what before was hidden, the discovery, as it were, of another letter in the great name of God, which only the pure eye can read.

But still, as in the days of him who "spake as never man spake," there are those who, when brought into contact with new thought, with new teaching, with what professes at least to be clearer light and wider truth than men before possessed, rather than look at the thing itself, will demand—"Whence comes it?

What authority has it? Who gave it its authority?"—will not search into its character to see whether that does or does not bear the mark of the spirit of Christ, but merely seek to know whether any opinion has been pronounced in its favour—what system it agrees with, what usage is on its side. But that is not the point to settle. Any one who believes in Christ's work as a living work, who believes that He still teaches his people, and leads them by his Spirit into clearer and clearer light, is ready, from the very fact of his belief, to receive illumination whencesoever it may come; and is ready also, from the very fact of his belief, to apply to it the test, not "What authority has it?" but "What character has it?"—not "What external claim has it to be received with respect?" but "What inner claim speaking from it tells me that it is of Christ, convinces me that it comes from him?" The external authority is but the stamp upon the coin. The stamp may be a forgery. The internal evidence is the fine gold of which the true coin is made, and which, stamped or unstamped, is of the same intrinsic and unalterable value.

A man may come, invested with all possible authority, and he may teach you what is in part true and in part false, what is in part of Christ, and what is in part of the world; and if you regard his authority only, you will feel bound to receive each part alike and with the same deference, while perhaps your instinctive discernment between truth and falsehood, between right and wrong, will be perplexed and bewildered by finding the same authority thrusting on it that which it recognises as true and right, and that which it is impelled to acknowledge to be false and wrong; and so a conflict between the rights of your own judgment and the claims of the authority you have been bidden to bow down to arises, which, ere it is ended, may shake and shatter all the foundations of your belief and faith.

And in the same way,—to take an example from what we may have been taught ourselves,—when truths of spiritual meaning and matters of mere speculative interest are mixed up together as parts of one great system, and you are required to receive the whole as true, while the progress of your knowledge tells you that part is false, great is the evil that is done. Thus, for instance, when we are bidden by the same authority to believe that Jesus Christ died for our sins, and rose again the third day—most blessed and glorious belief; and that God made the world in six days' time of twenty-four hours each, which it does not concern our religious life to believe or to disbelieve, and which science contradicts, and Scripture does not assert; the injury done to the earnestly inquiring mind, early trained to accept a truth upon authority, is often lasting in its effect, begetting a spirit of almost angry doubt as to every truth which others commonly receive. Through demanding that too much be believed, one may induce repugnance to fixed belief altogether.

But no such injury can be done, and no destructive conflict can arise, if you learn to act on this principle, that authority has no power over you, except in so far as it has its witness in itself; except in so far as your conscience (after earnest trial) acknowledges it as just and right and true; that every thing, every truth, every teacher, is to be judged, not by what is external—authority, or name, or position; but by what is internal—by character. "By their fruits ye shall know them" is a universal rule. Every religious truth that men can believe, every creed, however venerable, had a moral and spiritual meaning of its own before it had any external authority. The authority, that encircles the most ancient truth grew round it gradually, only because that Divine character that was in it appealed to the consciences of men, and was recognised by all; and the common belief and reverence of all raised it to its commanding place. But it can only maintain that place by the same appeal continuing to meet with the same recognition; not by men being constrained to do it honour out of regard to the external authority that has come to surround it. That is worth nothing if the deeper faith in it dies out. Suppose, for instance, that out of men's hearts and minds had died all living belief in those first words of the Church's creed, "I believe in God, the Father Almighty, maker of heaven and earth,"—suppose that, in the course of time, all faith in a Divine Father, the "God of our life," the personal protector and friend of every man, had vanished away, and men had come to believe in nothing but the laws and forces of "nature," and had lost the idea of a "living God," and of a spiritual life nourished by a daily communion with him, and developed towards its highest perfectness through a loving obedience to his will,—suppose all this were gone, had died out of the common heart and mind, and that still, although all actual belief in the words had ceased, the Church kept repeating the ancient creed and authoritatively rehearsed the letter of an extinct gospel, would her authority have any power? Would there be in *it* anything to revive the departed spirit, and to breathe a Divine breath into the hardened and contracted life of the unbelieving? Never! It would be but a monument of the dead, but the cast-off vesture of the faith which it had outlived. Nor would that faith ever be revived by men having its former authority quoted to them, but by having the burning flame of the truth, round which the authority had gathered, again so made to shine as to cause them in its light to "see light."

Every truth, every system, every teacher must be judged according to what it, or what he, produces, and is,—according to the fruits, according to the character. This is the judgment by which Christ wished to be judged. It matters little what a man calls himself— a " prophet," or an " apostle," or a " descendant of the apostles"—the question is, What can he do? What can he teach? What is he in himself? It matters little what men say against or for a new form, or a new truth, or a new system :—that it is not Scriptural; that it is not according to the Fathers of the Church; that it is not according to the common custom; or, that it *is* in accordance with Scripture, and tradition, and the usage and order of the Universal Church. The question is, "Is it true? Is it better than what we have hitherto believed or practised? Does it approve itself to our reason and conscience as a thing reasonable, beneficial, as far as we can see, according to God's will?" If so, then it is no matter what custom or tradition is for it or against it. God has not given us our faculties that we should obey custom and tradition, but that, in the growing light and liberty of our knowledge and faith, we should serve him and learn the most we can of his truth, and do the best we can for his service; not with a grudging terror at every step of going wrong, but with a large and liberal trust in his fatherly guidance of us, as long as our hearts are right with him.

We are not, of course, to run off with the notion, which is very acceptable to those who in all ages (as at the first) cannot, or will not, distinguish between Christian liberty and mere lawlessness or licence, that no regard whatsoever is due to authority,—to the authority of a church, for instance, or of a great system of truth, such as a church's creed or confession. What we have to remember is that we must never let authority override our own judgment and conscience, or lead us to evade the responsibility of proving all things, to the end that we may "hold fast" that only which is good. But, at the same time, we must remember that authority almost always demands respect, because almost always representing a certain weight of right and truth; because representing what the common judgment and conscience of many men (probably in divers ways wiser and better than ourselves) has decided to be worthy of acceptance. And just as a strict rule is necessary for the child at school, and he must be controlled by another when he is too young to control or govern himself, to the end that he may learn self-control and self-government as he grows up; so God often uses authority as a useful and necessary teacher and trainer for his children; but ever for the like end, not that they should always be bound by it; but, led by it till their steps are firm, should then be able to walk alone; ruled by it in their years of ignorance, should, when their faculties are riper, be able to judge conscientiously for themselves; should be able, when they have reached the full knowledge of good and evil, to separate between the two, to "discern" the spirits of good and of evil.

Now, brethren, such a point as this which is suggested by my text, may perhaps appear to be suitable enough for a theological discussion, but to lie a good way apart from the domain of our ordinary life and its concerns. We do not need, you may think, to occupy ourselves with these matters at all. We may leave them to wiser people, and believe what we are taught to believe, and what our fathers believed before us, and no harm is done. But the fact is, that whatever we believe or whatever we are taught, great harm—it may be lasting and immeasurable harm—is done to our spiritual life, if we have no clear idea as to our own duty and responsibility in regard to all that we are taught or called on to believe, or that appeals to our judgment and our conscience, and asks us to decide upon its claim to be received. You cannot evade that claim, and live a healthful and growing life. You cannot let light and truth pass you by, without any effort to see for yourself what they are; or accept just so much as others accept, and as you are told is safe and right; or content yourself with asking the chief Priest's question, and taking what answer you can get, and yet hope to be spiritually nourished and to grow in grace or knowledge afterwards. For religious truth or knowledge is not one set lesson, or one measured quantity, which you can receive and lay by, as you might lay by a store of provisions for the winter's use. It is rather like that "spiritual rock" which St. Paul tells us followed the Israelites in the desert, and of which each drank as he thirsted. It is the fulness of a deep fountain, from which we must draw according to our need and our capacity; and unless we are drawing from it day by day, every seed of Divine life must wither and die within us. It is the exuberant crop of a rich field bringing forth herbs and fruits of which, as we go on our way, we must gather; taking due heed that what we gather is good fruit and wholesome herb; learning to discern between that which would nourish and that which would poison, between that which our experience teaches us would quicken and strengthen the spirit's life, and that which would weaken and corrupt it.

And it is to this knowledge, to this discernment, brethren, that the Spirit of God leads us.

When Christ was about to go away from his disciples, He explained to them that though He went He did not leave them alone, for his Spirit would come to them and abide with them. He called that Spirit emphatically "the Spirit of truth." He said He would guide them "into all truth." They could no more hear their Master's word, behold his works, lean upon his authority, rejoice in his presence. They, like all who would follow him and press toward the mark of the heavenly prize, must do so alone, by themselves, bearing their own burden, fighting their own fight; and yet not alone, because this Spirit should be with them, teaching them all things, bringing to their remembrance all the words of Christ, throwing upon all their future life the light of his teaching, the illumination of the truth that they had learned from him; and so suffering not that truth to remain, as it were, dead and unfruitful in their hearts, but ever adding to it more and more, filling them "with all the fulness of God." And as for them, so for us. We too have this promise of the Spirit; we live under his dispensation. His work in us and for us, as for them, is to lead us "into all truth;" to help us to seek it and to find it, to discern between it and falsehood, between the mere doctrine of man and the revelation of God to our souls, between the wisdom of the flesh, which is as grass that withers and whose flower fades, and the word of the Lord, which "liveth and abideth for ever." That Spirit, brethren, is our great authority; nothing else is; He only leads us to the truth, and, witnessing with our spirits, helps us to discern it.

He who, in the faith of a Divine enlightenment, of a spiritual guidance, earnestly seeks to know all that God would teach him, is never disappointed. The light of the inward witness does not fail. The promise of what the "Spirit of truth" will do holds good. Not more sure is the promise that in the outer world, day and night, seed-time and harvest, summer and winter, shall not cease, than that in the world within, the patient, humble, earnest spirit, shall find an ever clearer light encircling it, an ever higher knowledge filling it with strength and peace.

What then, brethren, in view of this, should be our position, what the character of our search after truth? It should not be, as is too common, a restless gadding to and fro after every new thing. It should not be a hasty dipping into every new subject, and running to look at every new speculation. There are many subjects, and many ways of teaching and trying to influence men, from which a pure and candid mind will feel itself at once repelled, its own moral instinct telling it that it will get no good from them. It is not necessary, in order to find truth, that you should search for it wherever the world may tell you, or the example of others may suggest. It is needful rather to seek where the Spirit seems to lead. It will always guide you rightly; it will discover with a finer tact than yours where truth lies,—where it lies even amidst error and shining out of darkness.

There is a reality, brethren, in that spiritual guidance. Those that say they know it not do not prove that it does not exist; they only prove that they possess it not, because they have not sought it with a pure heart and earnest mind.

And our life, in its relation to God's truth, should be a daily seeking to be led by that Spirit into wider and clearer knowledge; just as our life, in its relation to our brethren, should be a daily seeking to be filled more and more by that same Spirit, with that peaceful and kindly and winning charity, which is the "bond of perfectness" and the "fulfilling of the law."

And as we seek that guidance and strive to follow it, "calling no man master on earth," not suffering any one to step in between us and the Father of our spirits to usurp his authority or to intercept his light, we may perhaps find that we shall be led onwards whither we did not at first expect; we may come to see that many of those things, which we before believed, were wrong; that many were but partial truths apprehended "in part" or seen "through a glass darkly;" that much that we had thought was intended to be permanent must be suffered to pass away, and give place to what is better and truer and more enduring. We may find ourselves led gradually into new paths, until we almost lose sight of the old way and of the "ancient landmarks." But however far we may be led from them, we shall be led only nearer God; our steps, if we follow that guidance, shall not stumble; and though, for a time, we may have to tread the lonely wilderness, we yet shall see the Promised Land, and shall stand within the gates of the city which cannot be shaken, whose everlasting foundations God has laid.

It is only thus, brethren, that our faith can become to us a reality, a source of joy and strength. The life that has not faith, large trust in God, is barren and weak. Where there is no knowledge, there can be no faith. To trust God you must know him. To know him, you must not be content to take for granted what you may be told about him; you must try to learn what He is from himself, to learn more and more of his will, of his character, of his goodness, of his love. And this knowledge comes not at second hand: they who would gain it must seek it for themselves.

Remember how, in the Book of the Acts, the Jews at Berea are commended, and get an honourable name because hearing the preaching of the apostles they would not blindly accept what they told them, but searched the Scriptures daily, to find whether what they taught them agreed with those Scriptures, which were the highest revelation of God's truth which they knew, or could refer to. The same is our duty: to test all truth by the standard of the clearest light which God has given us; and to hold fast that to which his Spirit seems to witness. We may not think much of this duty. Almost any other may appear more important in our eyes. We may go through our life and its routine of religious forms without a thought of this. But if so, what becomes of our spirit's life, that life which the word of God, the truth of God, alone can nourish? Our outward life may prosper; even our intelligence as to worldly knowledge and affairs may grow and ripen, but our "spiritual understanding" remains at the childish stage. We do not and cannot attain to "the measure of the stature of perfect men in Christ."

Snares and temptations, in the region of our Christian knowledge and belief, come to us, brethren, in very different forms, according to our different positions and capacities; but in no more common and frequent form than this which the question of the text specially suggests to us: to be lazily or self-righteously content with what we and our fathers have known and have attained to, counting ourselves as though we had already attained and were already perfect, elevating our own judgment to a place of supreme authority, and challenging the world of truth to produce a higher; and, instead of humbly and thankfully recognising the presence of God's Spirit in his Church, ever teaching us more and leading us onward and upward if only we will move, practically denying his working and setting up some limit of our own, standing by which we say to the advancing wave of Divine light, "Hitherto hast thou come, but no further."

Let us beware of this spirit, made up of selfish indifference and dull self-righteousness; and, acknowledging how little we know, believing how much there is to learn, desiring to be led into all truth that we may not only "know him that is true," but may abide in him, let our language to our Father ever be that of his servant of old: "Lead me in thy truth, and teach me: for Thou art the God of my salvation; on Thee do I wait all the day."

And now to God the Father Almighty, with the Son and the Holy Ghost, be all glory in the church, world without end.   Amen.

XXIII.

CHRISTIAN RIGHTEOUSNESS.

BY THE REV. R. H. STORY, D.D., ROSNEATH.

What shall we say then? That the Gentiles, which followed not after righteousness, have attained to righteousness, even the righteousness which is of faith.—ROMANS IX. 30.

WHAT is that "righteousness," of which we read so much in the Bible, and yet possibly know so little? Have we any clear idea of what we mean when we speak of it, and in speaking perhaps condemn, as we have been taught to do, our own righteousness, and exalt that of Christ? Very probably we have not; but here, as in relation to many other points, use religious language without clear understanding of the fact that it either expresses or conceals (for language must do one or the other). If you use it knowingly, it helps others to know what *you* know. If you use it, not understanding its meaning, it but helps to deepen the ignorance of yourself and others as to what is really meant.

Now, as to this and other words in the Bible which are used both in the Old and the New Testament, it is well to try and see first of all what those who employed the word earliest meant by it—the Jews of the Old Testament; and their idea of what they called "righteousness" seems to have been the fulfilling of the Commandments. He who kept these—who walked in all the precepts of the Lord blameless, such as Daniel in the Old Testament, or Nathanael in the New—was righteous, according to the Jewish idea. It was a very comprehensive idea—comprehensive rather than deep. It included a great deal. It included not only all moral conduct, but even matters of religious observance and ceremonial,—small details, such as tithing the smallest herbs and not eating with unwashen hands, as well as the greatest duties, abstaining from idolatry and theft, and false witness and murder. It was a wide and comprehensive idea of what righteousness should be. But it was not so deep as it was wide—at least it was not so as people generally held it. For most men of any delicacy of conscience have a stronger instinct than that merely of doing the thing which is right, and preserving a fair outward conduct. There is in them the instinct or desire not only of moral rectitude, but of spiritual perfectness. There is a voice which, when every visible obligation has been carefully discharged, calls out within, "All these cannot make the doers thereof perfect." When every external obligation has been fulfilled, the internal begins. Action is not enough. Thought and intention and desire and will must be ruled too; and in as far as the Jewish idea of righteousness did not realise this, it was, though wide enough, not deep enough. It did not realise that the law must not rest in being a written commandment, but must become a living spirit, a fountain of moral life and strength within. Now, as the Jewish idea of righteousness fell short of this, so does the Christian idea of it—the idea which we gather from the New Testament, and specially from St. Paul—seem even to go, to a certain extent, beyond this. To St. Paul, in the light of Divine righteousness, the law did not so much seem to be transfigured, "magnified and made honourable," as to be actually absorbed and lost sight of. What he felt God required of men was not a legal obedience. It was a "new creature"—a new creation. It was a return to God and to the pure nature God had given, to that state in which law, by which "is the knowledge of sin," should not be needed. The kind of thing, of which St. Paul thought when he spoke of righteousness, was not so much a pure outward conduct springing from a pure and dutiful respect to the law in the heart, and a careful obedience to every whisper of conscience there, as a spirit which raised him who possessed it above the burden of ordinances and the sense of an effort to learn and to fulfil a prescribed commandment, and brought him into living and personal communion with his God. It was a righteousness not of law but of faith—a righteousness which expressed in the earthly the principles and spirit of the heavenly or Divine life; as different from the legal righteousness which attended to outward detail, or which thought its best aim was to have the law so written on the heart as to be unable to miss one of its requirements or break one of its rules, as the free and expressive language of a native of a country is different from the formal attempt of a foreigner to speak the tongue correctly. The foreigner may learn the language. He may know every rule of its grammar and be at home in its idioms, and through his knowledge, painfully acquired, come at last to speak, as we say, "like a native;" but the highest praise that you can give him, after all, is that he does it *like* the other,—that through laborious practice he does what the other does better naturally; and even then the easy phrase, the perfect idiom, the homely familiarity with the power of the language, which mark the native's speech, seldom if ever grace his. So is the righteousness, which cherishes the idea of a fulfilled law as its highest, compared with that which rises, like its proper flower and fruit, out of the new creature—the new spirit, which is at home with God and delighting itself in him.

Now, it is this higher, deeper, inward righteousness which St. Paul thinks of when he speaks of "the righteousness of faith." It is righteousness of character, which is deeper and greater than any righteousness of conduct.

Now, what is the special connection between this righteousness and faith? Why does St. Paul call it, as he does here, the "righteousness of faith"?

Because he felt that the true root of this righteousness was Christ; and faith, he felt also, was that which takes us out of ourselves and joins us to Christ, so that, as living branches springing from the vine, we may bear much fruit. The power of laying hold of Christ is the root of the deeper righteousness. St. Paul felt that it had been so in his own case. The vision he had seen, the voice he had heard on his road to Damascus, had opened his eyes and ears to that world unseen, which till then he had not realised,—had revealed to him One who watched his way, who was wounded by his hostility, who was striving to lead and influence him in spite of all his self-confidence and self-will, whose plan for his future life was something quite different from his own. It was through this revelation, he felt, that God had led him to a deeper righteousness. It was the faith that it *was* God who had so led him that was the root and strength of his new and better life. The way by which God had led him he felt sure was, in reality, none other than the way by which He was leading, and would lead, all men. So that when he preached the necessity of a deeper than legal righteousness, and called it "the righteousness of faith," his conscience bore him witness that it was through this faith he had himself passed from darkness to light, from the burden of law and ordinance to the power and freedom of an endless life;—by which same way he felt assured all men must pass.

The deeper righteousness then, as it appears to St. Paul, we may say, comprehensively, is the *Christian Life*. The root of it is Christ, and it is called the "righteousness of *faith*" because by faith we lay hold of him.

This is a simple matter if you look at it candidly. But it has been much confused by too great a mixture of human dogma and definition with the simplicity of the truth. A man, we shall say, is living a life of self-will and self-reference, recognising either his own will as his only rule, or, like St. Paul before he reached Damascus, setting before him a certain formal standard of duty, and trying to come up to that; but with no sense of spiritual want about him, sufficient to himself. Suddenly, or gradually, it comes to him that this is not enough, that his life is not what it should be and might be, that in its regions of highest hope and interest it is barren, that, spiritually, it is wellnigh dead. He looks about for help and finds none. He tries to rest in himself, and in his worldly life and work, and cannot rest. At last, through the trouble of his own spirit, or the light of God's Spirit witnessing with his, or through the word of truth, he is brought to think of Christ, and he turns eagerly to him. His old life falls away from him like a worn-out garment of which he is ashamed, as he sees more and more clearly the character of the life Christ would have him and help him to live, as he compares himself with him, as he realises Christ's desire to work out in him a life of a nobler and purer type. His own righteousness, his own standard, such as it was, had been enough for him before. Now it is as "filthy rags," never to be looked at or thought of more. Christ's righteousness, Christ's standard, which rises in its clear beauty before the eye of his faith, shines upon him with such brightness that he cannot bear to look back upon his former self.

This is a natural experience, is it not? A plain and simple road by which to travel from the worldly to the heavenly region, from the life of the world to the life of Christ, from the righteousness of self or of law to the righteousness of faith.

But to suit their systems, men have changed all this; and, in regard to man's righteousness and Christ's, have taught much that it is hard to reconcile with Christian truth, or even with what is morally right and true. They have taught, for instance, that all a man's own works, which are not done through faith in Christ, are necessarily evil,—that even "the good works" of the "unregenerate" are bad works; as if any work could be a good work which was not done with a good intention, and with that unselfish regard to higher than merely worldly or selfish interests, which is called in the Bible "faith," whether the direct object of that faith be Christ, in the full knowledge of him and of God, or not: or as if any work done with that intention, done with a pure motive, with the honest conviction, "This world is not all, and I shall not act as though it and its interests were supreme; this self is not the first object in the universe, and I shall not act as though it were," could be evil and displeasing in the sight of God the Father. And having taught this about the good works of the unregenerate or non-elect, they then teach that nothing that a man who is regenerate can do is of any value in God's sight, and that all that the best of men can effect is to *clothe themselves*, as it is called, with the righteousness of Christ; as though there were in him a vast magazine or deposit of righteousness, from which we might draw what would cover our own nakedness or rags. All which is unhealthy teaching—false in form if not in substance. The righteousness of Christ is not a great fund, so to speak, out of which sums may ever and anon be taken and "imputed" to his people. It is the pure and perfect character and life which we by knowledge of him see, which we by faith in him set before us as our only aim, as our only example, as our only stimulus and help to overcome self and the devil and the world: and that righteousness, imperfect in its measure, yet in kind like his, inspired by his Spirit, upheld by his example, which we are able to show forth, is, in the sight of God who sent him forth, that believing we might have life through his name, of great, even of inestimable price; for it is not our own but the righteousness of Christ living in us, not a righteousness outside of us and put upon us as a cloak to hide our sins from God, not "imputed" to us as ours when it is really another's, but the fresh and healthy outcome of our own heart and conscience and energy, quickened, transfigured, sanctified, by the indwelling spirit of the "Lord our Righteousness."

Now, it is of great importance that we should think rightly of this matter. I think any one with a healthy conscience must see that, as Scripture tells us, only that which is righteous, right, true, honest, is acceptable in the sight of God; that only those who are righteous can stand before him. To deny this is to overthrow all ideas of righteousness and truth, and to obscure all lines dividing right from wrong. And those who can so stand before God must be able to do so in virtue of that which is in themselves, not of something which is not in them but is "*imputed*" to them; in virtue of Christ's righteousness shared by them and growing within them, not of Christ's righteousness reckoned as belonging to them, by a mere exercise of God's will and pleasure. In the last resort, in the court of highest appeal, at the very throne of God, that which we wish to find is a perfect *reality* of dealing; no fiction, no assumption of fact where there is no fact; no imputation of character where there is no character. What we wish to be assured of *there* is, that God will deal with us as we are in ourselves; that if there is evil in us He will not cloak it and so leave it in us, but will spare no pains to work it out of us and take it away; that He will not, because He has made a decree in our favour, take Christ's righteousness and clothe us with it, and say, "Now you are in him, you are sanctified, you are justified;" but that He will, because He loves us, try to bring out in us the character and image of the Son of his love, so that of us as of him He may be able to say, "These are my beloved sons, in whom I am well pleased."

And desiring this perfect reality and truth in God's dealings with me, I cannot be satisfied with any doctrine of "imputation," or any talk about being "clothed with Christ's righteousness," and, as it were, under cover of this passed into the secret place of God's favour. What I want, if I am honest in the matter, is not to be accounted as righteous, but to be made righteous; not to be called righteous, but to *be* righteous. Why, in the region of my eternal interests, should that satisfy me, which never could in the lower region of my temporal interests? If I am wrongfully accused and brought to the bar of the law, I do not wish to get off with a verdict of "Not proven." I wish to be discharged on full evidence that I am not guilty. Or if I am guilty, and have any real consciousness of guilt, and am touched with any true sorrow for it, I am willing to suffer whatever be the just and proper punishment. It is only the dishonest and impenitent law-breaker who would wish to escape because he has friends in the jury, or trusts to some one who will win over the judge. So, in the same way, if I am honest in my desire to live the life of Christ, it is nothing to me to be told his righteousness shall be imputed to me. Nay, were it so imputed, it would be a hindrance in my way. I should be inclined to say, "Do not reckon that mine which is not mine. Do not call me righteous who am still unrighteous. Do not tempt me to think I have learnt, or done, or suffered, enough. I would 'go on unto perfection.' I would know Christ, and know nothing of his righteousness except as I see it in him, and try day by day to work it out in my own self till He is formed in me, —the hope of glory."

"After all, then," some will probably be inclined to say, "you are trusting to your own righteousness. You are resting on yourself. It is yourself you trust to in the end."

Now, here we are very apt to confuse points that should be kept separate. All my confidence for anything beyond what I see and handle, for any spiritual truth, for any hope of the future, is and must be in God, and in God as Christ revealed him. It is because I believe God to be the God whom Christ revealed, that I have any hope or trust in him. My only foothold for the future is on my consciousness of his fatherly character and relation to me. And this consciousness is so rooted and grounded in Christ, that it is best described as trust in Christ. Our trust is in him. But I am never told that I am to trust in the *righteousness* of Christ, in any sense which excludes the idea of my being required to have a righteousness of my own. *I* must be righteous, as St. John tells me, "even as He is righteous." And the consciousness of that righteousness must take its place, beside my trust in God, as a true and necessary ground of confidence; the consciousness that here, amid whatever frailty and imperfection, I have yet honestly striven after a righteousness that was Divine.

The life of the future, brethren, is but the full development of the life of the present. It is not a new life suddenly discovered. It is an old life renewed under different conditions, but with the unbroken thread of one identity binding it to that which has gone before. Whatever else it may be, it must be this, if the hope of it is to shine for us with any brightness at all. And if so, then that which is to mark our character there must have, at least, begun to mark it here. If there my life is to be bound up in near unity with Christ's, the root of that unity must be planted now. If I am to find myself in his presence when I go hence, I must carry with me, as I pass into the silent worlds, something which will not fail me because of the greatness, and, for aught I know, the terribleness of the way; something which, when I stand before the throne, "the Lord, the righteous Judge," shall recognise as having affiance with himself, as having in it ever so feeble a breath of the spirit of his own eternal life, of that life which is not of the world but of God, whose fountain is not from beneath but from above. Without this there can be no sound and safe trust in Christ. There may be no more growth of righteousness in the character, than that most elementary movement of self-reproach and acknowledgment of sin, which opened the lips of the penitent thief upon the cross, and won for him the promise of Paradise, but there must at least be this, ere there can be any honesty in confidence towards God. The confidence of the unawakened and unrighteous, the confidence with which you will hear sometimes those that have grown old in worldliness, say, when lying on their deathbeds, that they look to Christ, while they have never once tried, or even desired to try, to love him, and to live his life, and to copy his example, is not faith, but self-deception. The boast of leaving everything to Christ, of rejoicing to know that you can do nothing, and need do nothing, for your own salvation; that all your own righteousness is as "filthy rags," and that you are yourself a worm, and vile and incapable of good; which you often hear (and often hear from persons who are yet in spirit very self-righteous, and the reverse of humble and meek), is a boast, which from any lips is foolish, which from some lips is a mere falsehood—to be avoided by all who would truly follow Christ and be saved by him; by all who really understand that their own righteousness, their own projects and efforts for good which have no reference to God's will, and do not proceed on an honest faith in One who is true and righteous, and who loves truth and righteousness, are of no worth at all; but that their own righteousness, when it is "of faith," when it is the fruit of that faith in Christ without which a spiritual life must grow feeble and decay, *is* of real value, and precious in the sight of God—of God, who regards what we *are* rather than what we *do*—and who, in some that do a great deal that seems good, may yet see nothing of that spirit without which it has no inner virtue; who, in some that are perhaps able to do very little, who can but suffer, or can but "stand and wait," perceives the savour and the beauty of that "unction from the Holy One" which we receive of Christ.

We must be "in Christ," united to him who is our life, in faith and love; and out of the strength of that union we must bring forth the fruits of his Spirit, we must show in ourselves, not a righteousness of our own, but that which is the result of Christ's Spirit living and working in us, the righteousness of faith, of "the new creature" walking not after the flesh but after the Spirit.

Consider for a moment, ere we close, brethren, the ascending scale by which we rise to this.

We begin from the lowest type of human life which has known any Christian influence at all,—the life which is either sunk in carnality, or in worldliness, which has no aim beyond personal pleasure or personal profit, without generosity, without the capacity of self-sacrifice, without the sense of its own meanness and unworthiness. That is the life of many, and goes on in many, only deepening in its worst features to the close. A step higher you have the kind of life which, in the common language of the ancient Jew, or of the modern Pharisee, would be called righteous,—the life of respectable deference to law and religious opinion, and of consistent desire to do the prescribed duty properly, whatever the demands of duty may be. This, too, is the life of many, a life in its outward aspect, at least, and often also in its inner character, morally fair and just. Above it stands the life of yet higher cast, in which the law of God is understood to be a living law, searching into even the thoughts and intents of the heart, requiring truth in the inward parts, a life which sees that "the law" is not all, but hears in it the voice of the Lawgiver, and has some understanding, more or less clear, of his character, and desires not only to obey, but to please him in obeying. This is a life of yet purer and more exalted principle and motive; but still above it stands that highest of all, the life of faith, the spiritual life, in which the unseen is realised, in which God's presence is acknowledged as the great reality, and his will as the one guide, and his friendship as the highest blessing; in which the commandment is kept out of love, and the law is observed, because the child recognises in it the voice of the Father. This life of divine communion, of exalted fellowship with God, of "righteousness by faith," is the highest and the best. It is that to which we are called in Christ.

Have we in any wise attained to it? Are some of us still mere servants in the house—not children? servants to whom obedience is difficult and work hard? Are some not even at this stage, but still sunk in selfish indulgence, or in utter worldliness of spirit and of aim? If so, let us remember that for all " the time is short," and we have far to go, ere we can attain to the measure of the perfect man in Christ. Let us not stay so far away from him that we shall never be able to reach him at all; whom to know is eternal life, whom to serve is perfect freedom: and to whom be all glory in the church, world without end: Amen.

www.ingramcontent.com/pod-product-compliance
Lightning Source LLC
Chambersburg PA
CBHW022121290426
44112CB00008B/759